Citizenship, Gender and Diversity

Series Editors
Beatrice Halsaa
Centre for Gender Research
University of Oslo
Oslo, Norway

Sasha Roseneil
Department of Psychosocial Studies
Birkbeck College - University of London
London, United Kingdom

Sevil Sümer
UNI Rokkansenteret
University of Bergen
Bergen, Norway

Aims of the Series
Developed out of FEMCIT, a research project funded under the Sixth Framework of the European Commission examining gendered citizenship, multiculturalism and the impact of contemporary women's movements in Europe, the series also welcomes submissions from scholars around the globe working in this area on projects with either a European or international focus.

More information about this series at
http://www.springer.com/series/14900

Hilde Danielsen • Kari Jegerstedt • Ragnhild L. Muriaas
Brita Ytre-Arne
Editors

Gendered Citizenship and the Politics of Representation

palgrave
macmillan

Editors
Hilde Danielsen
Uni Research Rokkan Centre
Bergen, Norway

Ragnhild L. Muriaas
Department of Comparative Politics
University of Bergen
Bergen, Norway

Kari Jegerstedt
Centre for Women's and Gender Research
University of Bergen
Bergen, Norway

Brita Ytre-Arne
Department of Information Science
and Media Studies
University of Bergen
Bergen, Norway

Citizenship, Gender and Diversity
ISBN 978-1-139-70421-7   ISBN 978-1-137-51765-4 (eBook)
DOI 10.1057/978-1-137-51765-4

Library of Congress Control Number: 2016942645

© The Editor(s) (if applicable) and The Author(s) 2016
Softcover reprint of the hardcover 1st edition 2016 978-1-137-51764-7
The author(s) has/have asserted their right(s) to be identified as the author(s) of this work in accordance with the Copyright, Designs and Patents Act 1988.
This work is subject to copyright. All rights are solely and exclusively licensed by the Publisher, whether the whole or part of the material is concerned, specifically the rights of translation, reprinting, reuse of illustrations, recitation, broadcasting, reproduction on microfilms or in any other physical way, and transmission or information storage and retrieval, electronic adaptation, computer software, or by similar or dissimilar methodology now known or hereafter developed.
The use of general descriptive names, registered names, trademarks, service marks, etc. in this publication does not imply, even in the absence of a specific statement, that such names are exempt from the relevant protective laws and regulations and therefore free for general use.
The publisher, the authors and the editors are safe to assume that the advice and information in this book are believed to be true and accurate at the date of publication. Neither the publisher nor the authors or the editors give a warranty, express or implied, with respect to the material contained herein or for any errors or omissions that may have been made.

Cover illustration: © CHROMORANGE / Heike Bracier / Alamy Stock Photo

Printed on acid-free paper

This Palgrave Macmillan imprint is published by Springer Nature
The registered company is Macmillan Publishers Ltd. London

Acknowledgements

The idea for this book emerged while we were organizing the *Ida Blom Conference—Gendered Citizenship: History, Politics and Democracy* in Bergen, Norway, 14–15 October 2013. The conference was a part of the 100-year celebration of universal suffrage in Norway and gathered scholars from all over the world to discuss new avenues for research on gendered citizenship. The conference was named after the distinguished Norwegian historian Ida Blom, renowned for her work on suffrage and introducing gender as an analytical tool in global history. We thank her for lending her name to the event.

Our goal was to engage in questions of citizenship, democracy and equality within a multi-disciplinary context, with both historical and contemporary perspectives. After the conference, we saw that the lens of representation, in a broad sense of the concept, would be suitable to bring together different questions that were raised during the conference.

The contributors and the editors of the collection come from different disciplines and traditions. Throughout the writing and editing process, discussions and comments have arisen that reflect the multi-intellectual environment in which our debates on representation have taken place. The process has been both fruitful and instructive to the extent that it has clarified what can and what cannot be taken for granted in a multi-disciplinary and international intellectual setting.

We wish to thank the University of Bergen and The Uni Research Rokkan Centre in Bergen, Norway, for providing money and support for the conference in 2013 and for this book.

We are indebted to the anonymous reviewers who gave valuable feedback on the chapters included in this volume and to Hanna Skartveit, who took on the big job of finalizing the formal side of the manuscripts.

We will also thank our publishers for providing us with very fruitful comments regarding the organization of the book and for the smooth process towards publication.

Hilde Danielsen
Kari Jegerstedt
Ragnhild L. Muriaas
Brita Ytre-Arne

Contents

1 Gendered Citizenship: The Politics of Representation 1
   Hilde Danielsen, Kari Jegerstedt, Ragnhild L. Muriaas, and Brita Ytre-Arne

Part I Becoming a Citizen–Interrogating the Constitution of Political Subjects 15

2 What Is It to Vote? 17
   Gayatri Chakravorty Spivak

3 Troubled and Secure Gender Identities in a Changing Society: Norway at the End of the Long Nineteenth Century 37
   Ida Blom

4 Representations of Equality: Processes of Depoliticization of the Citizen-Subject 61
   Sara Edenheim and Malin Rönnblom

Contents

Part II	Gendered Participation in Representative Democracies–Working from Below and/or Above?	85

5 The Costs and Benefits of Descriptive Representation: Women's Quotas, Variations in State Feminism and the Fact of Reasonable Pluralism   87
Cathrine Holst

6 Substantive Representation: From Timing to Framing of Family Law Reform in Morocco, South Africa and Uganda   111
Ragnhild L. Muriaas, Liv Tønnessen, and Vibeke Wang

7 Constructing Citizenship: Gender and Changing Discourses in Tunisia   137
Mounira M. Charrad and Amina Zarrugh

Part III	Challenging the Public–Private Divide	159

8 Representations of Women Voters in Newspaper Coverage of UK Elections 1918–2010   161
Emily Harmer and Liesbet van Zoonen

9 The Pedagogy and Practice of En-Gendering Civic Engagement: Reflections on Serial-Viewing Among Middle-class Women in Urban India   185
Mahalakshmi Mahadevan

10 Vietnam Women's Union and the Politics of Representation: Hegemonic Solidarity and a Heterosexual Family Regime   209
Helle Rydström

Part IV Can Exclusions Speak? 235

11 Can the Irregular Migrant Woman Speak? 237
    Synnøve Bendixsen

12 Pin Ups and Political Passions: Citizenship Address
    in Post-War Men's Magazines 261
    Laura Saarenmaa

13 "The Venus Hottentot Is Unavailable for Comment":
    Questioning the Politics of Representation Through
    Aesthetic Practices 281
    Jorunn Gjerden, Kari Jegerstedt, and Željka Švrljuga

Index 305

Notes on Contributors

Synnøve Bendixsen is a postdoctoral research fellow in the Department of Social Anthropology, University of Bergen, Norway. Her research interests include irregular migration, political mobilization, Islam and Muslims in Europe, the study of inclusion and exclusion, and processes of marginalization. She has written a number of articles and book chapters, and one monograph: *The Religious Identity of Young Muslim Women in Berlin* (2013). Bendixsen has also been a visiting scholar at COMPAS, Oxford University, and New York University. Since 2013 she has been the co-editor of the *Nordic Journal of Migration Research*.

Ida Blom is a professor emerita in the Department of Archaeology, History, Cultural Studies and Religion, University of Bergen, Norway. Her extensive research career reflects an interest in everyday life, and the history of women and gender. Among other subjects, she has studied the politics of birth control, gender perspectives on health history and the gendering of central aspects of national politics. Starting from a Norwegian perspective, her research has gradually widened to include transnational comparisons. Blom has published a great number of articles as well as authored six books and co-authored and edited/co-edited another six. Her latest book is *Medicine, Morality and Political Culture. Legislation on Venereal Disease in five Northern European countries, c. 1870–c. 1995* (2012). She was among the founders and the first president of the International Federation for Research in Women's History, 1887–1995, and has received a number of rewards. In 2001 she was appointed Commander of the Royal Norwegian Order of St. Olav and in 2006 she became honorary foreign member of the American Historical Association.

Notes on Contributors

Mounira M. Charrad is Associate Professor of Sociology at the University of Texas in Austin; and non-resident fellow at the Baker Institute, Rice University. Her book, *States and Women's Rights: The Making of Postcolonial Tunisia, Algeria and Morocco*, won several national awards, including the Distinguished Book Award from the American Sociological Association and the Best Book on Politics and History Greenstone Award from the American Political Science Association. Her articles on state formation, law, citizenship, kinship and gender have appeared in major scholarly journals. She has edited/co-edited *Patrimonial Power in the Modern World*; *Patrimonial Capitalism and Empire*; *Women's Agency: Silences and Voices*; and *Femmes, Culture et Societe au Maghreb*. Funded by grants from the National Endowment for the Humanities, the Mellon Foundation, and the American Association of University Women, her research focuses on how struggles over state power shape women's rights historically and today. She received her undergraduate education from the Sorbonne in Paris and her Ph.D. from Harvard University.

Hilde Danielsen is Research Professor in Cultural Studies at the Uni Research Rokkan Centre in Bergen, Norway. She is working with issues of gender and equality, family life, place, inclusion and exclusion with historical and contemporary perspectives.

Sara Edenheim is Associate Professor/Reader of History and Senior Lecturer in Gender Studies at Umeå University, Sweden, and a visiting researcher at the Institute for Advanced Study, Princeton. Recent publications in English include "Lost and never found—The Queer Archive-of-Feelings and its Historical Propriety" (2013) *Differences—a Journal of Feminist Cultural Studies* 24(3), and "Politics Out of Time—Historical Expertise and Temporal Claims in Swedish Governmental Reports", in Lundqvist Å and Petersen K, (2010) (eds) *Experts We Trust—Science and Politics in Nordic Welfare States*, Syddansk Universitetsforlag.

Jorunn S. Gjerden is Postdoctoral Fellow in French Literature in the Department of Foreign Languages, University of Bergen, with a research project on literary and cinematic fictive representations in French of Sara Baartman, the Hottentot Venus. Her research and teaching focus on ethics and aesthetics, performativity, literary modernism, and postcoloniality. Recent publications include "Emotion, knowledge, alterity: Aesthetic experience in Proust", in L. Sætre, P. Lombardo, J. Zanetta (eds) *Exploring Text and Emotions* (2014), "Éthique et perspectives postcoloniales: sujet, altérité, langage. Emmanuel Lévinas, Aimé Césaire et Édouard Glissant" (2012), "The reader address as performativity in Nathalie Sarraute's *L'Usage de la parole*", in L. Sætre,

P. Lombardo, A. Gullestad (eds) *Exploring Textual Action* (2010), and *Éthique et esthétique dans l'œuvre de Nathalie Sarraute. Le paradoxe du sujet* (2007).

Emily Harmer is a postdoctoral researcher in the Department of Social Sciences at Loughborough University. Her research brings together the relationship between media and gender, political communication and media history.

Cathrine Holst is a research professor at ARENA—Center for European Studies, University of Oslo, where she coordinates a project on the expertization of Nordic public inquiry commissions. She is also connected to Centre for Research on Gender Equality (CORE), Norwegian Institute for Social Research (ISF), and professor at the Department of Sociology, University of Oslo, from fall 2016. Holst's most recent publications are "The Expert-Executive Nexus in the EU" (with Åse Gornitzka), *Politics and Governance*, vol. 3, no. 1, 2015, "Jürgen Habermas on public reason and religion: Do religious citizens suffer an asymmetrical cognitive burden, and should they be compensated?" (with Anders Molander), *Critical Review of International Social and Political Philosophy*, vol. 18, no. 5, 2015, "Institutional Váriation and Normative Theory: Lessons from a Local Equal Pay Controversy", in *Cooperation and Conflict the Nordic Way* (De Gruyter, 2015), and "Equality Europeanized? Mainstreaming and judicialisation in Norwegian gender+ equality debate" (with Hege Skjeie and Mari Teigen), in *Towards Gendering Institutionalism* (Rowman & Littlefield, 2016).

Kari Jegerstedt is Dr. Art in comparative literature and Associate Professor of Gender Studies in the Humanities at the University of Bergen. She has published on British, South-African and Scandinavian literature, as well as on gender and feminist theory.

Mahalakshmi Mahadevan has inter-disciplinary expertise and research interests in South Asian mediated culture, gendered citizenship, comparative media research and, more recently, the global sustainable development agenda, particularly through the lens of energy and climate issues. Her professional interests straddle journalism, non-profit communications and academia. She has been a practicing journalist since 2001; from 2006 to 2010, she was a research scholar and visiting lecturer at the Communication and Media Research Institute, University of Westminster. In her most recent role, she supported communications and advocacy for the United Nations Sustainable Energy For All initiative. Her doctoral thesis from the University of Westminster explored how patriarchal narratives of gender and family are implicated in shaping civic discourse and practice among middle class women in urban India. She is an independent researcher based in Washington D.C.

Ragnhild L. Muriaas is an Associate Professor of Comparative Politics at the University of Bergen. She has published research on women's representation, gendered electoral financing, traditional institutions, subnational elections and political parties in Africa in several international journals like *Democratization, Women's Studies International Forum, Representation, Journal of Modern African Studies* and *Government and Opposition*. She has extensive teaching experience in comparative politics and methods, and conducted several fieldwork in Malawi, South Africa, Zambia and Uganda. She is currently (2014–2016) the editor of Norsk statsvitenskapelig tidsskrift (*The Norwegian Journal of Political Science*).

Malin Rönnblom is Associate Professor in Political Science, Karlstad University, and Senior Lecturer in Gender Studies, Umeå University. Her research interests are critical policy studies, poststructural approaches to comparative studies, and feminist theory with a special focus on power and politics. Recent publications in English are *Debates in Nordic Gender Studies: Differences Within* (2015), with Cecilia Åsberg, and "Contesting feminist discursive institutionalism—a poststructural alternative", in *NORA* no. 3 (2014) with Carol Bacchi.

Helle Rydström is a professor in the Department of Gender Studies at Lund University. Her research focuses on the anthropology of gender in Asia and she has been in charge of a large number of funded research projects on Vietnam, and on Vietnam in comparison with countries such as India and the Philippines. Helle Rydström has conducted long-term ethnographic fieldwork in Vietnam to study violence, masculinity, sexuality, gender socialization, and education about which she has published extensively. Some of her recent publications include "Politics of Colonial Violence: Gendered Atrocities in French Occupied Vietnam", *European Journal of Women's Studies*, vol. 2(22): 191–207, 2015; "Nordic Gender Studies Conferences: Windows to a Global and Postcolonial World?", *NORA*, vol. 22(2): 147–154, 2014; "Gendered Corporeality and Bare Lives: Sacrifices and Sufferings during the Vietnam War", *Signs*, vol. 37(2): 275–301, 2012; and with Paul Horton, "Heterosexual Masculinity in Contemporary Vietnam: Privileges, Pleasures, and Protests", *Men and Masculinities*, vol. 14(5): 542–564, 2011.

Laura Saarenmaa is currently working as a postdoctoral researcher funded by the Academy of Finland. Her research interests include print media history and sex and politics in the popular public sphere. Her research project "Addressing Male

Citizens" approaches post-war Finnish men's magazines from the perspective of gendered citizenship. Saarenmaa is co-editor of *Pornification: Sex and Sexuality in Media Culture* (2007). Her other publications include work on Finnish female top politicians and their interdependence with women's magazines.

Gayatri Chakravorty Spivak is University Professor and Founder of the Institute for Comparative Literature and Society at Columbia University. Her most recent book is *Readings* (2014). Her essay "Can the Subaltern Speak?" is recognized as a major feminist intervention. She holds honorary degrees from the Universities of Toronto, London, Rovira I Virgili, Rabindra Bharati, San Martín, St. Andrews, Vincennes à Saint-Denis, Yale, Ghana-Legon, Presidency University, and Oberlin College. She is involved in international women's movements and issues surrounding ecological agriculture. She has been engaged in rural education in West Bengal for nearly three decades.

Željka Švrljuga is Associate Professor of American Literature at the University of Bergen, Norway. She is currently working on a book project *The Neo-Slave Narrative and the Parodic Turn*. She is the co-editor of *Performances in American Literature and Culture* (1995) and the author of *Hysteria and Melancholy as Literary Style* (2011), as well as a series of articles on the rhetoric of pain in literature and the arts, the Holocaust, and the neo-slave narrative genre. Current publications focus on postmodernist tendencies in the slave-narrative novel in the US, Canada and Anglophone-Caribbean literature; the Black Atlantic and cultural hybridity; writing black bodies/writing difference; and the fantastic in fin-de-siècle literature.

Liv Tønnessen is a senior researcher at Chr. Michelsen Institute (CMI). With a research focus on the intersection between gender, politics and religion, her work spans: Islamic law reform with a particular focus on family law and criminal law, women's movements including women's participation in Islamist and Salafist movements, women's representation, resolution 1325, and violence against women. She has a track record in the Middle East and Northern Africa with long-term stays in Sudan, Lebanon and Syria. She has conducted extensive fieldwork in Sudan during the last ten years, including teaching at Ahfad University for Women. Tønnessen has published international peer-reviewed articles with several publishers.

Liesbet van Zoonen is Professor of Popular Culture at Erasmus University Rotterdam and Dean of its Graduate School of Social Sciences and Humanities. She has published widely about politics, popular culture and gender, and is currently leading a research project about the articulation of youth, ethnicity and sexuality.

Vibeke Wang holds a Ph.D. in comparative politics and is a Postdoctoral Researcher at CMI with a long track record of research on Sub-Saharan Africa. Wang is the coordinator of the gender politics cluster at CMI and the author of several peer-reviewed articles in international journals. Her work focuses on the study of politics and gender, including representation, electoral gender quotas, and legislative institutions. In her recent work she explores the effects of aid to women's political representation in Uganda, Malawi and Zambia.

Brita Ytre-Arne is a postdoctoral scholar at the Department of Information Science and Media Studies at the University of Bergen. From fall 2016 she will be Associate Professor of Media studies, also at the University of Bergen. Her research has focused on media use, social media, qualitative methods, the public sphere, magazines, gender and media, and popular journalism. She is co-director of CEDAR–Consortium on Emerging Directions in Audience Research, an international network of early career audience researchers.

Amina Zarrugh is a an Assistant Professor in the Department of Sociology and Anthropology at Texas Christian University. She has co-authored "Equal or Complementary? Women in the New Tunisian Constitution After the Arab Spring", with M.M. Charrad, in the *Journal of North African Studies* (2014) and "Gender, Religion, and State in the Middle East", with M.M. Charrad in *Emerging Trends in the Social and Behavioral Sciences: Interdisciplinary Directions* edited by R.A. Scott and S.M. Kosslyn (2015). Her research interests include gender, violence, race and ethnicity, and religion, especially in North Africa and the Middle East. Her dissertation focuses on a social movement composed of families that developed in response to a contested prison killing at Abu Salim Prison in Tripoli in 1996. She received her B.A. in sociology and government as well as her M.A. in sociology from the University of Texas at Austin.

List of Figures

Fig. 2.1　List of countries by GNI, "Gross National Income"　　27
Fig. 2.2　UNDP *Human Development Report 2013*　　29

1

Gendered Citizenship: The Politics of Representation

Hilde Danielsen, Kari Jegerstedt, Ragnhild L. Muriaas, and Brita Ytre-Arne

---

H. Danielsen (✉)
Uni Research Rokkan Centre, Bergen, Norway

K. Jegerstedt (✉)
Centre for Women's and Gender Research, University of Bergen, Bergen, Norway

R.L. Muriaas (✉)
Department of Comparative Politics, University of Bergen, Christiesgt 15, 5007 Bergen, Norway

B. Ytre-Arne (✉)
Department of Information Science and Media Studies, University of Bergen, 5020 Bergen, Norway

© The Author(s) 2016
H. Danielsen et al. (eds.), *Gendered Citizenship and the Politics of Representation*, DOI 10.1057/978-1-137-51765-4_1

Introduction

As we entered the new millennium, suffrage, the founding gesture of all representational democracies, is almost taken for granted. Yet the rights, privileges and duties of citizens, as well as the possibilities to be seen and heard as part of a democracy in other ways than through voting or engagement in formal political forums, are not equally distributed—neither within nation states nor across the globe. These differences are gendered, as well as economic, racial and sexual, and form an ingrained part of everyone's situatedness in a globalized world where capital and new technologies reign. Who counts as a citizen and in what ways is part of an ongoing global struggle for hegemony. What are the relationships between representation and equality? And how can they be analysed and conceptualized in present times?

This book presents new avenues for research on gendered citizenship precisely through the prism of representation, bringing together scholars who discuss what are the possibilities and pitfalls of being represented and of representing someone, highlighting in particular the gendered aspects of representation. The present interrogation of the gendered processes in which humans become political citizens has moved beyond traditional understandings of representation to open for a more thorough questioning of the very concepts of citizenship, democracy and gender. Not only does the concept of gendered citizenship allow for a reflection on rights, participation, entitlements and voice, as well as political, economic and cultural processes of inclusion and exclusion, it also evokes questions of belonging, language, identity and the body, calling for a more thorough rethinking of what it means to be a human being and a member of society.

In order to address these questions, we believe that it is necessary to retain and further develop the duality of the very term "representation": representation points both to the endeavour of "standing (in) for/acting for"—as in representational democracy—and to the act of "re-presenting"—as in presenting something/somebody in language, discourse, texts, images and so forth. This duality has been noted repetitively in feminist scholarship and has found several forceful examinations, most notably following

Gayatri Spivak's seminal essay "Can the Subaltern Speak?" (Spivak 1988), where she points out that the relationship between these two meanings are that between "proxy" and "portrait"—a distinction she rehearses in her contribution to this volume. The distinction between the two needs to be kept alive, Spivak argues. To confuse them—that is, to believe that you represent someone without also re-presenting them or, indeed, to believe that you represent someone by re-presenting them—amounts to nothing short of a fundamentalist shortcut: the belief that there is a stable, unitary "woman", "class" or other "identity" behind representation, that speak, act and know for themselves.

Spivak's aim is to call into question the power implicit in representation: Representation—in both meanings—is steeped in power relations, involving not only inclusion and exclusion, but "othering" and "worlding"—the imperialistic processes through which the "other" comes to know its "self"—as well as the international division of labour (Spivak 1988). This vexed problematic also concerns attempts at feminist subject constructions. As Judith Butler reminds us in the introduction to *Gender Trouble*: "The suggestion that feminism can seek wider representation for a subject that it itself constructs has the ironic consequence that feminist goals risk failure by refusing to take account of the constitutive powers of their own representational claims" (Butler 1990: 6). In other words: goals of inclusive representation need to take heed of the processes of re-presentation, whether feminist or not: What are the wider (political, economic and ideological) structures and discourses through which and in which a feminist subject can assert itself? Is it enough to be asserted within these, or does that simply mean new forms of subordination? This problematic is not any the less relevant in a postcolonial, globalized world where, as Barry Hindess, amongst others, has pointed out, the granting of citizenship to populations formerly denied citizenship has become the aim of a new transnational governance subjecting populations to the demands of a common, globalized marked (Hindess 2002). Thus, if we are to continue to work for wider and more inclusionary citizenship, we need to simultaneously and continuously ask: What does it mean to have access to representation? Which power structures regulate and produce this accessibility, and on whose and what premises is representation possible? What is necessarily excluded by and in the act of representation? Is it possible to represent someone or be represented if you do not have access to citizenship? Is it possible to act out citizenship if you do not have access to representation?

As will be shown throughout this book, which is the seventh volume in the series *Citizenship, Gender and Diversity*, the concepts of citizenship and of representation share many dilemmas and are deeply connected to each other. T.H. Marshall's original concept of citizenship (Marshall 1950) is based on an understanding of representative democracy tied to legal and social rights, while feminists have developed a wide range of concepts pointing to other aspects of citizenship. Other books in this series explore intimate, bodily and cultural citizenship. Like representation, citizenship is a troubling proposition for feminism, as noted by the sociologist Sasha Roseneil, one of the series' editors: "Intensely luring in its expansive, inclusionary promise, yet inherently rejecting in its restrictive, exclusionary reality, it is an ambivalent object for those of us committed to radical projects of social transformation" (Roseneil 2013: 1). Citizenship speaks of inclusion and points to exclusion; it is always constituted in relation to its outside, its opposition. This paradox in the understanding of citizenship is also inherent in the concept of representation. When addressing representation we also need to point to the lack of representation or challenges regarding representation.

The Dual Meanings of Representation

Our book embraces an interdisciplinary and broadly framed approach to historical and contemporary questions concerning representations, gender equality and democracy, both in the political and in the cultural sphere. Thus, we hope to renew the debate on the dual meaning of representation and its relation to citizenship, placing it firmly within contemporary, global challenges to thinking gendered citizenship on a large scale, creating a meeting point for research both from the social sciences and from the humanities addressing the problematic of representation from diverse perspectives. This book covers empirical examples from

Europe, Africa and Asia, and contains chapters that problematize gendered citizenship and representation in a transnational perspective. In the following sections, we briefly present some different conceptualizations of representation and how these have resulted in multifaceted streams of research within the humanities and the social sciences.

Representation as Standing/Acting for

Broad sections within the literature on representation base their understanding on the distinction of representation as standing for and acting for women, a distinction coined in Hanna Pitkin's seminal work, *The Concept of Representation* (Pitkin 1967). In Pitkin's conceptualization of political representation, she develops three dimensions of representation that exceeds that of formal representation. Two of these dimensions understand representation in terms of a representative that stands for those represented. *Descriptive representation* refers to the compositional similarity between representatives and the represented. *Symbolic representation* (*role modelling*) refers to the feelings of the represented of being fairly and effectively represented. The last dimension understands representation in the sense of a representative acting in the interest of the represented, in a manner responsive to them (Pitkin 1967: 209). This dimension is *substantive representation*, which then refers to the congruence between the actions of the representatives and the interests of the represented.

Although several works study only one of these notions of representation, a significant stream of research involves the connection between descriptive and substantive representation, studying how the composition of legislatures affects policy outcomes. The key assumption is that if more women are elected into political office, the outcome will be more pro-women legislation. The inspiration for these studies is, amongst others, Drude Dahlerup's notion of gender balance and critical mass theory (Dahlerup 1988) and Anne Phillips' notion of gender parity (Phillips 1995). Critical mass theory postulates that legislatures should be composed of "more than 30 per cent female politicians" as only then would they become "strong enough to begin to influence the culture of the group". Gender parity theory demands a composition of 50/50, based on *the justice argument*—women shall have half of the seats because women are half the population—and *the experience argument*—a conflict of interests exists between men and women on a number of issues, which implies that men cannot represent women (see also Threlfall et al. 2012: 145).

The assumed link between descriptive and substantive representation faced stark criticism amongst scholars in political science (Childs and Krook 2006), yet the idea has gained recurrence amongst politicians across the world and contributed to the global spread of various kinds of gender quotas. The key criticism against the focus on descriptive representation and its effects highlight that identities are not only gendered but also formed by the intersections of class, ethnicity/race, age, physical ability, sexual preference and so on (Celis 2013: 179). For example, women hold contradicting and conflicting views on what their interest is, and since conflict is the essence of politics, one should not expect that women agree on how their interests are best served (Celis 2013: 184). What would actually be the purpose of an increased presence of women in elected offices across the world? Should we assume that women should only stand for women or should they also act for women? Such approaches also include questions regarding whether it is really possible to represent those that are excluded from having a citizenship that makes them entitled to hold certain positions and articulate their claims. It is difficult to talk about responsiveness to the represented if there are clear restrictions on the legal status of a person, a person's right to act as a participant in political institutions and a person's membership in a political community (Threlfall et al. 2012: 141).

Representation as Re-presenting

In scholarship on media, arts and culture, both understandings of representation have played a role while the main emphasis has been on issues of representation as re-presenting. The idea that women deserve equal representation as men within the media, for example, has echoed notions of descriptive representation. Similarly, there have been attempts to include female writers and artists in the traditional canons and historians have written the histories of different marginalized groups. Yet, analysis of gendered representation in media, arts and culture is not merely a question of counting, but rather of analysing how gendered re-presentations are constructed, expressed and interpreted within shifting social, cultural and political contexts, and how they are bound up in a network of intersectional power structures (van Zoonen 1994; Carter and Steiner 2003; McRobbie 2009). In the words of cultural theorist Stuart Hall, representation is "one of the central practices which produce culture" (Hall 1997: 1).

While feminist critiques of gendered representations in media and culture abound (McRobbie 1991; Brunsdon and Spiegel 2007; Thornham 2007), several strands of research have also taken self-reflexive and self-critical turns and questioned the perspectives and power positions of researchers as critics (Hermes 1995; Gill 2007; McRobbie 2009). Even more fundamentally, the focus has been on the enabling constraints and laws governing the systems of representation as such, whether phallogocentrism in language and Western philosophical thinking (Derrida 1978; Irigaray 1985), the privileging of the male, objectifying gaze (Mulvey 1975; Irigaray 1985), heteronormativity and the heterosexual matrix (Butler 1990) or orientalism and the othering of the colonial subject (Said 1978; Spivak 1981). These investigations speak to the need of destabilizing hegemonic, binary oppositions in order to radicalize difference and open spaces for alterity. For example, the "French feminists"—notably Irigaray, Kristeva and Cixous—countered empirical attempts at recovering female voices, arguing that the governing structural law of language did not allow for the expression of femininity as radical difference, claiming what was needed was work on language as such. Later, Butler has proposed similar arguments concerning how hegemonic discourses (including feminism) produce certain desires and sexualities as "non-understandable". Spivak has in turn argued that the subaltern—the position excluded from all channels of social mobility—cannot speak, because these voices, often expressed through other means, are not heard and listened to but radically exceed the circuit of hegemonic exchange. These attempts also speak to important trends within political philosophy, asking not only what is possible within society, but how is society possible; in other words, what is the possibility of possibilities (Laclau 1990; Mouffe 2013).

The Chapters of the Book

The above-mentioned perspectives on representation, evolving not only from different disciplines but also from different empirical and theoretical questions, inform the majority of the chapters in this book, allowing them to address a whole range of thematic concerns relevant to our times. The interdisciplinary orientation is reflected in the book's structure, where we have divided the contributions into four different sections based on the overarching problematic they speak to. Halsaa, Roseneil and Sümer state in their introduction to the book *Remaking Citizenship in Multicultural Europe* (the second volume in the series) that they address both the promise of citizenship and its instantiations (2012: 3). Following their argumentation, our volume in the series will address the promise of representation and the obstacles challenging representation. What can it be, how can it be and what are its inherent dilemmas?

Part 1: "Becoming a Citizen—Interrogating the Constitution of Political Subjects" comprises the starting point for the collection's interrogation of gendered citizenship. "What Is It to Vote?" by the literary critic and feminist philosopher Gayatri Spivak is based on a keynote held at the *Ida Blom Conference, Gendered Citizenship: History, Politics and Democracy* in Bergen, Norway (2013). In her contribution she reminds us that gendered citizenship must always be crosshatched by classed citizenship and racialized citizenship, even "global citizenship". To vote cannot simply be the casting of a ballot; in order to achieve true development and equal participation and as such fulfil the promise of democracy as power to the people, there needs to be fostered a "fitness to vote". Starting from the premise that democratic intuition must be trained, Spivak addresses the genderedness of citizenship through such issues as feminist global practice, language training, rote education, Western benevolence and the digital enthusiasm of the Human Development Index, arguing for another form of intuition developing from the formula "other people's children". At the core of her argument is the importance of language and deep language learning when working with the subaltern, to whom the very concept, as well as the practice, of democracy as power to the people is inaccessible except as violence.

In the second chapter, historian Ida Blom critically traces the impact suffrage rights and women's access to academic education have had on notions of gender identity and gendered representation in democratic institutions in the Norwegian context, illustrating the close and constitutive ties between rights and identity formation. Of special interest here are not only the concepts of difference femininity versus equal rights femininity but, first and foremost, class and masculinity. Blom's chapter is important in calling attention to how women's rights had massive influence on how new confident masculine gender identities developed.

Then, the political scientists Sara Edenheim and Malin Rönnblom critically analyse the demand for inclusion, also within feminist movements, in lieu of the present economic logic of new liberalism. As an effect of recent economic and managerial changes, they argue, the citizen-subject claiming equality within a regime of individual rights is turned into a self-regulating subject managing its own success or failure. Discussing recent feminist politics and debates in Sweden—where the feminist party "Feministisk Initiativ" is one of their main empirical examples—Edenheim and Rönnblom show how contemporary forms of governing have led to a depoliticization both of the political subject and of the movement itself. Taken together, the three contributions in the first part examine different aspects of the Constitution of political subjects, dealing with overarching and conceptual concerns of fundamental relevance to discussions on gendered citizenship.

Part 2: "Gendered Participation in Representative Democracies—Working From Below and/or Above?" discusses gendered representation in the political systems of representational democracies, focusing on various discursive and institutional strategies. In the first chapter in this section, the sociologist Cathrine Holst revisits the debate on descriptive representation, assessing the costs and benefits of descriptive representation under state feminism in light of institutional variations—schematized along the axis of a democratized, intersectional state feminist regime and a woman-centred technocratic one. The crux of the argument is however normative and philosophical, upholding that future exchanges on descriptive representations should have a firmer and more explicit focus on fundamental normative discussions.

In the next chapter, political scientists Ragnhild L. Muriaas, Liv Tønnesen and Vibeke Wang ask what kind of strategies works best to promote women's interests where the ideal of female representation is strong but where equal rights are lacking, comparing data from Morocco, South Africa and Uganda. Muriaas, Tønnessen and Wang show that legislation on family law shapes the possibilities for women to act as full citizens, and by that, how women's political citizenship is also constrained. Their contribution centres on the process in which the framing of new family laws were enacted, giving prominence to how pro-women actors, at different sites, had to negotiate their strategies when faced with the counter-claims of traditional, religious and cultural leaders.

Finally, the sociologists Mounira Charrad and Amina Zarrugh explore how different dimensions of "being a citizen" come to the fore in national politics in different political contexts, drawing from empirical data from Tunisia. The point of their chapter is to demonstrate the genderedness of citizenship discourses, whether from "above" or from "below". By tracking the history of the construction of citizenship in Tunisia, this study shows that even if Constitutions may include propositions that men and women should be equals, there is a constant pressure for more conservative family laws that convert women to minors under the guardianship of her husband or father.

Part 3: "Challenging the Public–Private Divide" revisits the debate on the public–private divide from the perspective of representation. Here, the contribution from media scholars Emily Harmer and Liesbet van Zoonen brings new empirical insights to how the media represents political processes within representational democracies. Rather than focusing on the previously studied question of how women politicians are represented in the media (e.g. Garcia-Blanco and Wahl-Jorgensen 2012), their study investigates media representations of female voters. This gives a fresh perspective on how women are represented as political citizens, highlighting the more accessible role of the voter to the more elitist position of the politician. Their main argument is that the traditional public–private divide continues to structure public constructions of politics from 1918 to 2010, upholding a simplistic view both of women and of political identities. Next, the media scholar Mahalakshmi Mahadevan examines gendered media use practices in familial, cultural and societal contexts through an ethnographic analysis of television viewing amongst middle-class Indian women. Through theoretical and empirically situated emphasis on the complexities of gendered audience encounters, Mahadevan connects questions of everyday practices to gendered citizenship. She discusses how representational practices influence the gendered permeability between familial and civic spaces, particularly highlighting the notion of "invisible pedagogy" through media and popular culture. In the third chapter, the social anthropologist Helle Rydström takes international research on political organizations to bear on an analysis of the Vietnam Women's Union, interrogating how the representation of women and the construction of the family become a locus of both intervention and transformation. In this chapter she shows how the Union has become the voice of a hegemonic solidarity with heterosexual women and their families. This characteristic of the Union's politics is epitomized by current contestations in Vietnam over the legal recognition of same-sex marriage. All three chapters in this section work within a long-standing feminist tradition of questioning the public–private divide and, at the same time, broadening its scope, both theoretically and empirically.

Part 4: "Can Exclusions Speak?" addresses representational democracy from the perspective of its antagonisms and exclusions, asking not only who and what are excluded or marginalized but also in which ways the excluded might speak back and be an agent of change. Interrogating irregular migrants' struggle for recognition in Norway, the social anthropologist Synnøve Bendixsen asks whether and how these collective practices from below contest existing conceptions of citizenship and assert new modes of political belonging. Are right claims at all possible when you do not have access to legal citizenship in a nation state? How are irregular women constructed through the process of representation? The chapter draws attention to political acts and engagement as dynamic processes situated within nation state power relations. Next, the media scholar Laura Saarenmaa analyses Finnish men's magazines of the 1940s and 1950s as examples of counter-publics articulating antagonisms and exclusions, taking up controversial social issues and voicing oppositional stances. Research on cultural citizenship (Hermes 2005; van Zoonen 2005; Stevenson 2003) has emphasized how diverse expressions of media, arts and culture contribute to create feelings of inclusion and exclusions in social and cultural communities. Saarenmaa intervenes in this debate by highlighting the potential relevance of men's magazines as counter-publics in particular historical contexts, connecting questions of representations to potential political effects in terms of visibility and mobilization in the public sphere. Finally, the literary scholars Jorunn Gjerden, Kari Jegerstedt and Željka Švrljuga employ various aesthetical representations of the Hottentot Venus to ask whether aesthetic practices open up the possibility of signifying otherwise. Their main argument is that aesthetics can supplement, rather than complement, politics by challenging representation as such, taking us firmly beyond representation to interrogate how the radically un-representable may speak and act as agents of change—beyond neo-imperialistic, nationalistic and identity politics discourse.

References

Brunsdon, C., & Spiegel, L. (Eds.). (2007). *Feminist television criticism*. Maidenhead: Open University Press.
Butler, J. (1990). *Gender trouble. Feminism and the subversion of identity*. London: Routledge.
Carter, C., & Steiner, L. (Eds.). (2003). *Critical readings: Media and gender*. Maidenhead: Open University Press.
Celis, K. (2013). Representativity in times of diversity: The political representation of women. *Women's Studies International Forum, 41*(Part 3), 179–186.
Childs, S., & Krook, M. L. (2006). Should feminists give up on critical mass? A contingent yes. *Politics and Gender, 2*(4), 522–530.
Dahlerup, D. (1988). From a small to a large minority: Women in scandinavian politics. *Scandinavian Political Studies, 11*(4), 275–298.
Derrida, J. (1978). *Writing and difference* (A. Bass, Trans.). Chicago: University of Chicago Press.
Garcia-Blanco, I., & Wahl-Jorgensen, K. (2012). The discursive construction of women politicians in the European Press. *Feminist Media Studies, 12*(3), 422–441.
Gill, R. (2007). *Gender and the media*. Cambridge: Polity.
Hermes, J. (1995). *Reading women's magazines*. Cambridge: Polity.
Hermes, J. (2005). *Re-reading popular culture*. Malden: Blackwell.
Hall, S. (Ed.). (1997). *Representation: Cultural representations and signifying practices*. London: Sage.

Halsaa, B., Roseneil, S., & Sümer, S. (Eds.). (2012). *Remaking citizenship in multicultural Europe: Women's movements, gender and diversity.* Basingstoke: Palgrave Macmillan.
Hindess, B. (2002). Neo-liberal citizenship. *Citizenship Studies, 6*(2), 127–132.
Irigaray, L. (1985). *This sex which is not one* (C. Porter, & C. Carolyn Burke, Trans.). Ithaca, NY: Cornell University Press.
Laclau, E. (1990). *New reflections on the revolution of our time.* London: Verso.
Marshall, T. H. (1950). *Citizenship and social class and other essays.* Cambridge: Cambridge University Press.
McRobbie, A. (1991). *Feminism and youth culture.* Basingstoke: Macmillan.
McRobbie, A. (2009). *The aftermath of feminism. Gender, culture and social change.* London: Sage.
Mouffe, C. (2013). *Agonistics: Thinking the world politically.* London: Verso.
Mulvey, L. (1975). Visual pleasure and narrative cinema. *Screen, 16*(3), 6–18.
Phillips, A. (1995). *Politics of presence.* Oxford: Oxford University Press.
Pitkin, H. (1967). *The concept of representation.* California: University of California Press.
Roseneil, S. (2013). *Beyond citizenship? Feminism and the transformation of belonging.* London: Palgrave Macmillan.
Said, E. (1978). *Orientalism.* New York: Pantheon Books.
Spivak, G. (1981). French feminism in an international frame. *Yale French Studies, 62,* 154–184.
Spivak, G. (1988). Can the subaltern speak? In C. Nelson & L. Grossberg (Eds.), *Marxism and the interpretation of culture* (pp. 271–313). Basingstoke: Macmillan Education.
Stevenson, N. (2003). *Cultural citizenship. Cosmopolitan questions.* Maidenhead: Open University Press.
Thornham, S. (2007). *Women, feminism and media.* Edinburgh: Edinburgh University Press.
Threlfall, M., Freidenvall, L., Fuszara, M., & Dahlerup, D. (2012). Remaking political citizenship in multicultural Europe: Addressing citizenship deficits in the formal political representation system. In B. Halsaa, S. Roseneil, & S. Sümer (Eds.), *Remaking citizenship in multicultural Europe: Women's movements, gender and diversity.* Basingstoke: Palgrave Macmillan.
van Zoonen, L. (1994). *Feminist media studies.* London: Sage.
van Zoonen, L. (2005). *Entertaining the citizen. When politics and popular culture converge.* Lanham: Rowman & Littlefield.

Part I

Becoming a Citizen–Interrogating the Constitution of Political Subjects

2

What Is It to Vote?

Gayatri Chakravorty Spivak

I was deeply honored to have been asked to participate in honoring in turn a forerunner, Professor Ida Blom. On October 5, we celebrated the centenary of my mother, Sivani Chakravorty, who was also a forerunner. An activist intellectual, a member of the All India Women's Congress before Indian Independence, a tireless and innovative social worker, and a lasting inspiration for my intellectual and ethical life. She did "foster a generation to which she [had] given values for life and which [knew] when to act; and she [had] herself actively contribute[d] to forming a society that [made] life worthwhile for everyone", to quote a passage quoted by Ida Blom in "Women, Men, and Socialism in Norway" (Blom 1998:

This chapter would not have been possible without my research assistants, Yohann Ripert and Pieter Vanhove. I also want to thank Kari Jegerstedt for walking me through this intellectual task.

G.C. Spivak (✉)
University Professor's Office, MC4927, Columbia University, 1150 Amsterdam Ave, 602 Philosophy Hall, 10027 New York, NY, USA

© The Author(s) 2016
H. Danielsen et al. (eds.), *Gendered Citizenship and the Politics of Representation*, DOI 10.1057/978-1-137-51765-4_2

450). It seemed symbolically important to me that 1913 also marked the year of the establishment of general suffrage in Norway.

In the 1980s, when I was active in Algeria, "What is it to vote?" is the question that I would put to women in the so-called socialist villages established by Ben Bella, the first president of Algeria. The answers I received made it clear to me that there was no understanding that voting had something to do with any sort of conviction that the postcolonial state belongs to its citizens, female and male. I saw no significant contradiction to this, except the usual class contradictions. And then in 1991, after the election of the Islamic Salvation Front by democratic procedure, I also saw the massive involvement, altogether underreported, of working-class women in overturning the elected government. And the rest is history. Since 1986, my involvement with the landless illiterates in the country of my citizenship, and the state of my first language, has made me realize that the presupposition for developing democratic intuitions is that that question—"What is it to vote?"—should indeed be asked. But it is not a test.

In an important passage in *Groundwork for the Metaphysics of Morals*, Immanuel Kant speaks of "passive citizenship". In 1993, Bruce Ackerman, the legal philosopher, published the first volume of an important series called *We the People*, where he suggested that the electorate in the USA remained passive unless a Supreme Court decision or some comparable phenomenon called for their participation (Ackerman 1993). Keeping this in mind, let us read what Kant wrote, in 1797:

> Fitness to vote is the necessary qualification which every citizen must possess. To be fit to vote, a person must have an independent position among the people. He must therefore be not just a part of the common-wealth, but a member of it, i.e. he must by his own free will actively participate in a community of other people. But this latter quality makes it necessary to distinguish between the *active* and the *passive* citizen, although the latter concept seems to contradict the definition of the Concept of a citizen altogether. The following examples may serve to overcome this difficulty. Apprentices to merchants or tradesmen, servants who are not employed by the state, minors (*naturaliter vel civiliter*); all women [*alles Frauenzimmer*] and all those who are obliged to depend for their living (i.e. for food and

protection) on the offices of others (excluding the state)—all of these people have no civil personality, and their existence is, so to speak, purely inherent. (Kant 1991: 139).

In writing that "all women" were lacking in "civil personality", Kant was no more than a symptom of his time. This particular conviction exists in the world today, and not only outside of Europe and the USA. I have no interest in excusing Kant. On the other hand, I am also not interested in accusing him, because, through careful auto-critique, we can come to examine and attempt to correct the ways in which we ourselves are symptomatic of our time. I would rather place myself, with sympathy, in Kant's egregious remark, shared by many great works of literature and arts, and turn it around to mean that this historical situation can also be turned around. The struggle for suffrage is proof of this. Any research into women's history, on the other hand, must also be subject to a critique of historical symptomaticity. Unless you can say "yes" to the enemy with your heart, you cannot make real change, perhaps. This is imaginative activism.

It is with this proviso in mind that we can recall that Mary Wollstonecraft and Kant were contemporaries. Kant died just short of 80, Wollstonecraft at 38, giving birth to the future Mary Shelley. If one thinks of Wollstonecraft's *Vindication of the Rights of Women*, one inevitably thinks, and rightly so, of course, of the French Revolution, of Thomas Paine's *The Rights of Man*, and of the fact that these, with cultural modifications and translations, have come to stand for inalienable human rights or natural law (Wollstonecraft 1995). However, Kant, in a position where he did not have to think about good statements of rights, or worry about childbirth, was able to see, in his own way, not so much in his much lauded political writings, as in his philosophical method, and had the time to do so, that, at the end of the eighteenth century, mere reason had to be resigned in, leading just as much to our world today, where all crisis is managed in the name of rational choice, a version of "mere" reason.

It is with this double bind in mind that we can recognize that the hugely difficult first step of getting suffrage or secular laws is a beginning, not an end. Literacy, or voting, can be counterproductive if there is no effort at producing "fitness to vote".

I want to turn to stories now, at two ends of the Indian spectrum.

I was visited two days ago by a young Indian-American woman wanting to make a film about the rape of Jyoti Singh in Delhi in December 2012, by consulting "experts" like Noam Chomsky, Sudhir Kakar, and Gayatri Spivak. I was not able to rise to her request, because I felt that this was not a productive enterprise. In the process, since she was also using the fact that this came to her through her son's sex education class in the Midwest region of the USA, I tried to tell her about the use made by men on the Left, so-called, of women who believe in the Enlightenment, just exactly as use is made of women who believe in anti-feminist traditions. I told her that the general sympathy for a mother–son discourse, family values (my son's sex education class), and women who still make use of it would be diagnosed by the most relentlessly honest philosopher of the Enlightenment as keeping them enclosed within a natural absence of civil personality. I told her we must learn to disprove this. I told her that among the subaltern, as among the elite, one clue to developing democratic intuitions that might travel is "other people's children".[1]

Who is the subaltern? This nuances the mechanical Marxist focus on the working class or, today, in Europe, on "visible minority" immigrants. Let us first take a glance backward.

I have often argued that gender is our first instrument of abstraction, an instrument of abstractability that is so old that to follow in its tracks is to develop ways of critical intimacy rather different from rational critique. It works before reason, a model which Comparative Literature has in first-language learning. I am certainly not reading, or even attempting to read, the syntagmata of gendering. To be able to enter that multiply located discursivity, I cannot be the privileged speaker of a lecture. The unselfconscious use of gender as an instrument of abstraction begins at the inception of the transaction between the sacred and the profane, the establishment of human nature as distinguished from nature as such

---

[1] At the Ida Blom conference, Jasbir Puar suggested correctly that this might be interpreted as liberal bio-politics. Let us put this down to affirmative sabotage—a practical choice of what would travel to the broadest sector of a thoroughly and long-standingly bio-politicized audience needing rearrangement of desires. For the top end, bio-politics is the very air they breathe; the bottom end is below that radar. For me, a grounding error: a strategy, not a theory, where the lines cannot be kept separate. Theory is a halfway house, a risk outside the famous ivory tower.

2 What Is It to Vote?   21

(ontogeny playing with phylogeny?). The moment of the abstractability of gender is what allows access to abstraction. It is this instrument or weapon that, in the course of the centuries, will enable the encounter with the abstract as such, in the historical moment of the emergence of Capital, in the eighteenth century. It is then—and this remains inaccessible to Kant—that the theme of women's leadership, of equality before the law—as if the encompassing narrative were nothing but an abstraction called "concrete materiality"—with no diversity but that of class begins to emerge. The point here is that gender, unrecognizable as the prime mover, is now introduced as a belated item made possible by the movement of history. From now on, leadership studies—male, female or queer—is the production of a vanguard, however fragmented or particularized. By contrast, I remain interested in just anyone, not merely the vanguard.

Antonio Gramsci attempted to distinguish the subaltern from the proletarian. To bring together the subaltern and the proletarian—both seen as riddled with prejudices—and Gramsci was after all in the thick of things, not just writing books—was the last piece of writing Gramsci was engaged in when he was nabbed by the fascists. This piece is already distinctly different from the kind of positive reinforcements that, as a leader of the Communists, he wisely produced for the Turin proletariat hitherto. Acknowledging that the General Strike of 1920 had not worked, he was now looking at the possibility of making long-term change. Once incarcerated, Gramsci expanded this into the period of self-study leading to a book (that he did not have the time to write) that would take all this into consideration. And in that period, he distinguished the subaltern very carefully as follows: "The subaltern social groups [*gruppi sociali*], by definition, are not unified and cannot unite until they are able to become a 'State'": for the current conjuncture, we must write "create global interference". Yet "their history", as Gramsci wrote in 1934, just 14 years before Bretton Woods, is still "intertwined with that of

> the history of States and groups of States. Hence it is necessary to study: 1. the objective formation of the subaltern social groups, by the developments and transformations occurring in the sphere of economic production; their quantitative diffusion and their origins in pre-existing social groups, whose

mentality, ideology and aims they conserve for a time; 2. their active or passive adherence to the dominant political formations, their attempts to influence the programmes of these formations in order to press claims of their own, and the consequences of these attempts in determining processes of decomposition, renovation or neo-formation; 3. the birth of new parties of the dominant groups, intended to conserve the assent of the subaltern groups and to maintain control over them; 4. the formations which the subaltern groups themselves produce, in order to press claims of a restricted and "partial" character; 5. those new formations which assert the autonomy of the subaltern groups, but within the old framework; 6. those formations which assert the integral autonomy"...etc. (Gramsci 1971: 52)[2]

How Gramsci would have developed these thoughts and the many meditations on the relationship between the intellectual and the subaltern classes can only be surmised. This, however, remains one of his most important themes, precisely because of the fact that the subaltern is not the proletariat. Politics did not permit him to write his books. Many of his notes end in "etc.". But this is the electorate, male and female, with whom we must pose the question today: "What is it to vote?"

Incidentally, I would add here a footnote to Ida Blom's important study of Eurocentric interest in gender in distinguishing between "barbaric" and "civilized" nations. Kathleen Collins has recently found, in accounting for clan/goon politics in some places and not in others, that such politics were determined by the gap between the establishment of the absolutist state and the formal structure, at least, of democracy. Into this argument we can also place the colonial state, without direct access to the agency of power at the top and, of course, the totalitarian state (Collins 2006).

The subaltern, strictly speaking, is not important to Northwestern Europe, but they must become important to European globalist activists.

---

[2] Antonio Gramsci's *Selections From the Prison Writings* (1971) (tr. Hoare Q and Nowell Smith G, translation modified). The translators have disfigured Gramsci's title to his speculative note (not an essay): "Ai margini della storia (Storia dei gruppi sociali subaltern)"—"In the Fringes of History (the History of Subaltern Social Groups)". As indeed they have taken away his insistence on a method/methodology gap here, a moment of necessary auto-critique.

In 1983, before I began my journey to learn from the subaltern how to insert them in the circuit of hegemony in a necessarily restricted focus, I wrote "Can the Subaltern Speak?" where the only access I had to the social group was through women.

In the next 30 years, pushing along, I have learned that "other people's children" is a good way in to the internalized teaching of democratic intuitions in adults, across race and class, all the way from subalternity to access to (even the agency of) liberal bio-politics.

Democracy. The word means roughly "power to the people". What I have learned from my work with the subalterns comes these days to bleed into my metropolitan talk. And it is because it is my conviction that work at what Gramsci called "producing the subaltern intellectual" and I call "supplementing vanguardism" cannot be undertaken with an interpreter. I'm obliged to work at it in the language I know best, my first language, Bengali, one of the major North Indian languages. This also allows me the privilege of working in the "World's Largest Democracy" (courtesy CNN) in deep and sustained focus with the timely part of the largest sector of the electorate.

Here is how I described my efforts among children (other people's children) for the US Internal Revenue Service, in the third person, because I travel on an Indian passport and the schools are run on my salary. I quoted it some years ago to a European feminist contemporary Friga Haugg, whom I respect greatly:

> No grant proposals written to preserve intellectual freedom. Professor Spivak's project relates to the fact that national liberation does not always lead to a good and democratic society. Current research in the area (Fareed Zakaria, Jack Snyder etc.) states that no society below a certain per capita level is "ready for democracy". Zakaria, Snyder and others in the field are social scientists. Professor Spivak's research, relating to the work of such rare thinkers as John Sowarti in Kenya, investigates the reason for this. Typically, a newly liberated country, in the absence of established infrastructure, is obliged to put planning and development in the hands of a vanguard. In the absence of a people educated in the habits of democracy, there are no constraints upon the vanguard and social scientists to declare the place "unready for democracy". The generosity of Human Rights NGOs does not confront this problem but perceives education as a "human right". Typically, such work ends in fundraising, building schools, providing textbooks, and often

part of peacekeeping enforcement. Spivak insists that focus must be placed on the quality of the education. There are three points here. (a) Without deep language learning and long term effort no cultural infrastructure can be accessed. Here Spivak's salaried work (she has been teaching fulltime at US universities for 51 years) as director of the Institute of Comparative Literature & Society, with its insistence on deep language learning ignored in today's speed-oriented globalized world, joins her rural research. (b) The current quantified tests for educational success are unable to assess results here. (c) Because these largest sectors of the electorate have been oppressed sometimes for millennia (as in the case of India or China), their cognitive mechanism has been damaged and educational generalizations such as Dewey's or Montessori's do not apply. Work such as Paulo Freire's early attempts relates to making populations aware of oppression. (Freire's word is "conscientization"). Spivak believes that democratic habits and the intuitions of citizenship are developed in children under such difficult circumstances by changing their intellectual habits rather than developing political movements. In order to bring this about, Spivak is also interested in developing "green" habits in extreme poverty and interacting with state leaders and the rural gentry to see how such educational efforts can be stabilized. Currently, Spivak's research base is 6 hamlets. On each research visit Spivak leads four training sessions per hamlet, two in class and two out of class & meets with educators collectively on the final day to assess progress. Some time is spent in social interaction and monitoring "green" habits. On their own initiative, the participants are now sowing rice with seeds that belonged to this area before the so-called "green revolution" produced genetically engineered high-yield varieties. This immense project is not yet well developed enough to result in direct publication, but incidental publication is all over the place.

Today I am obliged to add: without practice of freedom and as victims of caste-prejudice, their initial projects reproduce an unprecedented grass-roots lattifundism, with themselves as (very small) landowners, turning other "scheduled tribes" into sharecroppers. Rearrangement of desires needed, not just for the teachers but the currently landless sharecroppers.

How might "other people's children" travel to develop democratic intuitions among the elite?[3] The trivial Euro-sequential truism—time

---

[3] In the rest of the chapter, I have integrated material from "What Good Are the Humanities for the Study of Development?" Keynote, Golden Jubilee lecture series, Center for the Study of Developing

moves from the pre-modern to modern through colonialism into globality—spiced up now by "culture" as invented by Anthropology and now bowdlerized by the United Nations Educational, Scientific and Cultural Organization (UNESCO) and the Nara Document of 1994—that runs the world can be revised, giving us the agency of complicity. We will need to think of complicity in its root sense, as being historically and ideologically folded together, even with bio-politics as we plan for our own children, rather than in the colloquial sense of intended conspiracy or collaboration.

Without this sort of general and customized training of the imagination, it is impossible to remember that, although, to measure societies at large, we need nation states, regions, and other categories for quantification, these do not give us a sense of "development" in any rich sense, pun intended. I am sharing with you my conviction that sustainable *under*development is the rule, and the peculiarly intractable notion of "developing", studiable through quantifiable indexes whose items are quantifiably expandable, is not isomorphic with epistemological change. Let us take a look at a paragraph from the 2013 Human Development Report and note how quantification is its only value:

> The education component of the HDI is now measured by mean[s] of years of schooling for adults aged 25 years and expected years of schooling for children of school entering age. Mean years of schooling is estimated based on educational attainment data from censuses and surveys (available in the UNESCO Institute for Statistics database and Barro and Lee (2011) methodology). Expected years of schooling estimates are based on enrolment by age at all levels of education and population of official school age for each level of education. Expected years of schooling is capped at 18 years. The indicators are normalized using a minimum value of zero and maximum values are set to the actual observed maximum value of mean years of schooling from the countries in the time series, 1980–2012, that is 13.3 years estimated for the United States in 2010. Expected years of

---

Societies, New Delhi, August 5, 2013.

schooling is maximized by its cap at 18 years. The education index is the geometric mean of two indices.[4] (McGillivray et al. 2013: 81).

I am not undervaluing the Human Development Index (HDI) or the United Nations Development Program, although of the latter's feudality without feudalism I have had personal experience that is not necessarily conducive of hope; I am not alone in this opinion. The HDI, introducing education, life expectancy, and income into measurement by economic growth alone, was unprecedented, of course. I remember Amartya Sen saying, at Mahbub-ul-Haq's memorial service at the United Nations in 1998, that the HDI had to be as tough as all the other indices in order to change them. I am also aware that the HDI attempts to make its measure more meaningful by disaggregation, by introducing measures for inequality, by questioning the relationship between material growth and human development, ceaselessly. I am just suggesting that, in order to fulfill these goals, its measurement work must be supplemented by the humanities-style work that I am proposing. Its toughness, that Mahbub-ul-Haq correctly recommended, produces a powerful weapon, reflected in new sets of tables (Fig. 2.1).

In order, however, to be supple enough to become "real" rather than merely powerful, it should not be replaced or opposed, but supplemented, by humanities-style reading skills, not remain confined to a charmed circle, circulating in its own circuit, quite apart from R&D and policy, which also circulate, in their own charmed circuit, apart from the readers of the social text. Humanities in my sense is a form of imaginative activism that must permeate qualitative and quantitative welfare and economic disciplinary training as well as human rights training, in order to produce "fitness to vote". Currently, it is human rights training that shares something with the humanities, at least in select elite universities in the USA. In these programs, human rights legalisms trump the slow reading skills of the humanities. In the same way, when a former officer of the National Council for Educational Research and Training in India had worked at making environmentalism, as a form of imaginative activ-

---

[4] From UNDP, *Human Development Report 2013. The Rise of the South: Human Progress in a Diverse World* (New York: United Nations Development Programme, 2013), pp. 33 and 147. The reference to the methodology source is Barro and Lee (2011).

2 What Is It to Vote?

List of countries by GNI (nominal, Atlas method, millions of US$,[1] top 10) [edit]

Rank	2012[2]		2010		2009		2008	
1	United States	15,734,567	United States	14,600,828	United States	14,223,686	United States	14,506,142
2	China	7,748,903	China	5,700,018	China	4,857,623	Japan	4,853,005
3	Japan	6,105,798	Japan	5,369,116	Japan	4,785,450	China	4,042,883
4	Germany	3,603,895	Germany	3,537,180	Germany	3,473,814	Germany	3,504,510
5	France	2,742,891	France	2,749,821	France	2,750,418	United Kingdom	2,799,960
6	United Kingdom	2,418,464	United Kingdom	2,399,292	United Kingdom	2,538,578	France	2,700,770
7	Brazil	2,311,147	Italy	2,125,845	Italy	2,114,668	Italy	2,115,482
8	Italy	2,061,253	Brazil	1,830,392	Brazil	1,563,126	Spain	1,449,186
9	India	1,890,363	India	1,566,636	Spain	1,472,046	Canada	1,446,669
10	Russia	1,822,654	Spain	1,462,894	India	1,405,064	Brazil	1,433,699

Fig. 2.1 List of countries by GNI, "Gross National Income" http://data.worldbank.org/indicator/NY.GNP.ATLS.CD?order=wbapi_data_value_2012+wbapi_data_value&sort=asc, quoted from en.wikipedia.org/wiki/Gross_national_income

ism, a part of all secondary education, the textbook interests defeated it. I am therefore absolutely not suggesting that it is easy. I cannot promise you a rose garden.

Currently, there is so little understanding of the value of qualitative education in producing and sustaining an electorate that these absurd remarks are made in the 2013 HDI Report, in all innocence:

> It is difficult to use the HDI to monitor changes in human development in the short-term because two of its components, namely life expectancy and *mean years of schooling change slowly*. To address this limitation, components that are more sensitive to short-term changes could [be] used for national purposes, possibly under a different name. For example, the rate of employment, the percent of population with access to health services, or the daily caloric intake as a percentage of recommended intake could be used in place of the traditional indicators of the HDI. Thus, the usefulness and versatility of the HDI as an analytical tool for HD at the national and sub-national levels would be enhanced if countries choose components that reflect their priorities and problems and are sensitive to their

development levels, rather than rigidly using the three components presented in the HDI of the global HDRs.[5]

According to this concluding remark on the 2013 Report—*The Rise of the South*—education, the kingpin of human development, is not useful for human development analysis because it moves too slowly. No analytical tool that is committed to speed as a measure of efficiency can actually get a grip on human development, and certainly not on the process of "developing", as in "developing societies". It is instructive in this connection to remember that it was the Fascists who made the trains run on time. As for the human development measurers, their only standard, "when adjusting the HDI to reflect additional concerns", *can* only be to "a commitment to data integrity and rigorous attention to statistical protocol", not to an existentially rich idea of development which might show the limits of their power and demand supplementation to produce mindsets equal to the task at hand.[6]

Supplemented, not replaced or opposed, because the impulse toward achieving greater flexibility is already there. The world of nongovernmen-

---

[5] http://hdr.undp.org/en/2015-report (my emphasis).

[6] We are constantly obliged to ask questions about the fact that more and more measuring tools are produced. How does this phenomenon relate to the human development of the largest sectors of the (sometimes potential) electorate? Who has access to these claim-rights initiatives? An example:

Dear Gayatri Spivak,

I am Raj Singh, CEO and Co-Founder of Governance Data International (GDI). GDI is a Berkeley startup that is revolutionizing the way we obtain governance data in India. GDI is focused on generating and compiling governance data through its RTI filing engine (YourAdhikar) and its online RTI database (RAACI).

How it works:

We receive strategic questions from the customer regarding what they want to know from any public authority in India. GDI leverages the RTI* Act to bulk file strategic questions to PIOs* throughout India and compile custom datasets. GDI licenses the right to use these datasets created for your academic work.

If you are interested in working with us please fill out below the Google form online. A GDI consultant will get in touch with you shortly after submission.

Google Form

Yours Sincerely,

Raj Shekhar Singh

CEO, Co-Founder

GDI

http://raaci.in/

http://youradhikar.com/*RTI Act:

http://en.wikipedia.org/wiki/Right_to_Information_Act

*PIO: Public Information Officers designated by every public officer under RTI Act

Human Development Report 2013 team

Director and lead author
Khalid Malik

Research and statistics
Maurice Kugler (Head of Research), Milorad Kovacevic (Chief Statistician), Subhra Bhattacharjee, Astra Bonini, Cecilia Calderón, Alan Fuchs, Amie Gaye, Iana Konova, Arthur Minsat, Shivani Nayyar, José Pineda and Swarnim Waglé

Communications and publishing
William Orme (Chief of Communications), Botagoz Abdreyeva, Carlotta Aiello, Eleonore Fournier-Tombs, Jean-Yves Hamel, Scott Lewis and Samantha Wauchope

National Human Development Reports
Eva Jespersen (Deputy Director), Christina Hackmann, Jonathan Hall, Mary Ann Mwangi and Paola Pagliani

Operations and administration
Sarantuya Mend (Operations Manager), Ekaterina Berman, Diane Bouopda, Mamaye Gebretsadik and Fe Juarez-Shanahan

The Human Development Report Office
The *Human Development Report* is the product of a collective effort under the guidance of the Director, with research and statistics, communications and publishing staff, and a team supporting national Human Development Reports. Operations and administration colleagues facilitate the work of the office.

Fig. 2.2 UNDP *Human Development Report 2013, The Rise of the South: Human Progress in a Diverse World* (New York: UNDP, 2013), p. iii.

tal organizations is too deeply folded in with capitalist globalization to be permeable to supplementation by the humanities' approach.

However carefully honed this might be, it does not touch the *quality* of education. And that is what produces class apartheid, rape culture and bribe culture, forcing election results by way of violence, and, at best, violence as the only recourse to a kind of wild social justice. When, on the other hand, all those wonderful people who prepare these reports send their children to school, considerations of quality, one would surmise, become paramount (Fig. 2.2).[7]

---

[7] I cite the names of the team in a spirit of auto-critique. I myself, and the academic class that could participate in the Ida Blom conference, belong generally to the class whose children can afford well-vetted campuses. I write in the hope that one and all on this list are engaged in a sustaining involvement with equal rights of information and choice in education of subaltern education. Let this

An example, alas, of sustainable underdevelopment, and even then too slow to be useful. There is no development until the index is supplemented by a spirit of equality. "Other people's children" is a democratic intuition that travels across class, as I daily find at the rural schools.

Such ideas are inconvenient. But, given that democracy is the development of abstract judgment for the sake of all (including others with different interests, who must themselves be trained in such abstract judgment), there is no way around it. Democracy lets in the element of the incalculable, because it must remain hospitable, in theory, to the most extreme positions, if managed by mere reason. Only with the electorate understanding the right to intellectual labor (not just information) can sustainable underdevelopment possibly be interrogated and combated through the political process, a larger gendered development can perhaps be claimed, and the ongoing flow of development not remain, one hopes, an account of the oppositional being nurtured destructively by the feudal left as an alternative while, on the other side, it is an account of the displacement of what used to be called petty bourgeois ideology, the involvement of more and more people—statistically numerable—into the management of underdevelopment-as-development.

W.E.B. Du Bois has given a masterful account of such a process, admittedly in terms of the mid-nineteenth-century conjuncture in the USA, as the development of so-called democracy in the USA in his *Black Reconstruction: 1860–1880* (Du Bois 1935/1962). It is a pity that we stop with de Tocqueville, no doubt because Du Bois is seen as belonging to the African-American interest alone.

Top-down state philanthropy does not work either. The Government of India gave free electricity BPL—below poverty line. I wish I had the time to tell you how BPL and APL (above poverty line) have entered Bengali creole. But, of course, there is no training in citizenship, only a desire for "tolerably good schools"; I quote Amartya Sen and Jean Drèze's recent book *An Uncertain Glory: India and Its Contradictions* (Sen and Drèze 2013). So the BPL keep lights on day and night, illiterate women

---

marginal gesture remain the essence of making public (publication), as in the agora, the necessary double bind between the secrecy of the ballot (what is it to vote?—the political) and the unconditionality of the hospitality called for by a just society (the ethical)—an empiricization of the relationship without relationship between law and justice.

speak of "current disturbed" in creole, the grids are overloaded, the BPL are being charged, there are more power cuts. On a recent visit to the schools, Ben Baer and I, Princeton and Columbia, wrote for a couple of hours by the light of a hurricane lantern across from such an electric light burning on empty space.

How do we represent them to ourselves, as members of the international civil society, so that we can represent ourselves as people acting on their behalf?

At the end of the last book published by Derrida in his lifetime, *Rogues*, or *Voyous*, he proposes something that marks out the impossibility of the taking on of world-saving projects by metropolitan intellectuals or indeed governments. In the detail I quote: "It remains to be known, to save the honor of reason, how to translate. For example, the word *reasonable*"—for us, the word "democracy"—"and how to greet beyond its Latinity"—for us, Hellenicity—"in more than one language the fragile difference between the rational and the reasonable"—for us between the capital D word and the word in small d, the work with the subalterns, the intuitions of democracy, small d in the World's Largest Democracy capital D (Derrida 2005: 159). In the last public performance that we did together, Derrida was kind enough to name me as "the task of deconstruction", doing a pun on the word *tache/tâche*, which I had used to mean the "stain" that would not go away in deconstruction, and he had said very kindly, "No Gayatri, it's the other meaning". Fulfilling, then, that task given to me by my friend, I say that although his is an excellent lesson for the elite, from the point of view of the subaltern, even the elite learning to translate globally, a fearsome responsibility, does not necessarily help anything but elite pride. These translations are not accessible at the subaltern level. It is the creole that passes into the language because English, and occasionally French these days, remains the dominant language. The completely accepted translation of the word "democracy" in my mother tongue and indeed, supposedly, in the national language of India, *ganatantra*, which my coworkers and most male voters know, gives no clue at all to them as to a possible meaning, although—and of course—they vote, and as I have said many times, their intelligent analysis is that voting is like competitive sports: who promises most, performs least, wins. And now, of course, the public flaunting of breaking the law by the party in power is eroding even that little bit of intelligent analysis.

Within this frame of the inaccessibility of the concept-metaphor of democracy as power to the people except as violence, I say to my subaltern teachers and supervisors in the villages—that when I'm called upon to speak about matters of social justice in the outside world—and try explaining social justice convincingly to these people from the most backward area of Birbhum, it's a challenge—what I have learned from my own mistakes with them in the last 30 years: For example, the keynote at the University of Utrecht, the 300th anniversary of the Treaty of Utrecht. Let me say to you that before I went, I actually shared this in Bengali—the thing about social justice—with my subaltern supervisors and teachers. "You see", said I, "what we talk about is what I'm going to say". And then I tried to explain what the cultural self-representation of the Treaty of Utrecht was in the Netherlands; that's another story. As a result—because I do tell them about the cultural self-representation offered to them by various kinds of parties and so on, I do talk about it, and as a result of our association, they at least have a sense of the map. And then I read the sentences to them in English, that I will read now. They don't understand that sentence, but before that, I said it to them in Bengali, and then I said, "Look, this is the same sentence, right, listen to it". The same sentence I said at the Center for Development and Study of Societies, that was another visit, this whole thing for a second time, that I was going to submit the wisdom I had received from them, and which, because of historical cognitive crimes I was unable yet to act on, after 30 years. I was able to report this in Delhi, which my associates in the villages know is a remote place of absolute control and glamor, most of them have never been to Calcutta, which seems to them to be a grand metropolis.

But let me get on here on the material from Utrecht. Keep in mind that Israel is described times without number as, quote, again, CNN, "the only democracy in the Middle East", although it plays the retaliation game energetically. Democracy is now equated with an operating civil structure, the functioning of a hierarchized bureaucracy and "clean" elections. We have plenty of examples around the world that unrelenting state violence on the model of revenge and retaliation can coexist with so-called democracy. Revenge is indeed a kind of wild justice that proves that no retribution is just to the outlines of the tribute. It has nothing, absolutely nothing, to do with the vision of social justice—and here now is what I said, first in Bengali, as a lesson learnt from them, to my rural coworkers—a vision which nests in all children's and therefore all people's capacity to use the right to intellectual labor. Cut off at the top because of digital idealism, cut off at the bottom because of millennial cognitive damage. The understanding of the right to intellectual labor, not just ease and speed of learning.

Many years ago, in "Can the Subaltern Speak?", just before the actual work of trying to learn from the subalterns, lessons that are just now emerging, began, I had spoken about the fact that representation has at least two meanings, as in a portrait and as in a proxy. I give you two examples.

First, Niyamgiri. This is an area in Orissa where the Supreme Court of India asked the local tribals to testify against Vedanta Resources plc, a global diversified metals and mining company headquartered in London, the largest mining and non-ferrous metals company in India with mining operations in Australia and Zambia, listed on the London Stock Exchange and a constituent of the FTSE 100 Index. The tribals testified successfully. Now, even the devoted middle-class activists see the Supreme Court as the rule of law, the Vedanta group as the bad modern, and the tribes as tradition. In fact, *niyam* means law, and the so-called god of the Niyamgiri tribals is not a god but a sovereign—*Niyamraja*—who gives the law that protects the rivers and the mountains, a preemptive critique of the anthropocene. Imaginative activism will change itself epistemologically in order to claim complicity with this.

Second, Bidhi, as in the subaltern song, in Bengali creole, *mon kore uribar torey, bidhi dey na pakha*—mind makes as if to fly, *bidhi* gives no wings. Here "bidhi" is the transcendental intuition of the rule of law, which romantic elitism cannot access. Imaginative activism will change itself epistemologically in order to claim complicity with this as well. A supplement, not a global directive.

"Gendered citizenship" was mentioned in the Ida Blom conference description. It must be crosshatched with classed citizenship and racialized citizenship and the absurdity of global citizenship when every decision of military intervention is nation state by nation states, as well as every decision of development is nation state by nation states. When you use the phrase "a member of society in the world today", you are thinking of yourselves. I have already developed this. Here, I am making the separate point that if you think of these examples as "culture", there is no democracy in the cultural sphere, only the alternative between tolerance and the incalculable.

This is the humanities-style work that can supplement, in solidarity, the tremendous desire coming from feminists in Europe to be aware of the entire world. As Ida Blom writes: "large-scale comparisons may serve as points of references for more detailed investigations". Comparisons are always political. We are most appreciative of the important generalizable work of the Internal Federation for Research in Women's History. Culture is not generalizable. The subaltern is not generalizable. Our kind of work is the slow work of acknowledging the historicity of desire. Change is needed, epistemologically, at both ends. Here, I offer my labor because I am thoroughly engaged at both ends of the spectrum.

In the 30 years that I've been working in this area, I have heard of witch killings but never seen one. I have seen no dowry deaths, though teenage marriages are the rule rather than the exception and dowry is usually paid.

The human interest stories are not typical of the place—imagine how horrified you would be if people said that the Utøya rightwing mass murderer Anders Behring Breivik was typical of Norway. Just as with Kant, here also I tried to use what is there rather than either excuse or accuse, or simply solve problems top-down. I would give you some examples, but I believe you will find them somewhat unacceptable, because this kind of effort is counterintuitive.

I am not a romanticizer and, as a teacher, it is my obligation to rearrange desire. I am simply not sure that our incredible fixation on staying alive as long as possible, or that my probiotics-fancying doctor with his cultural queries, is the answer. Time will not permit me to give these counterintuitive examples of intervention the kind of deep-focus explanation that they deserve.

My dream is that this work can lead to post-theoretical practice. This is, of course, a denial of history and I think of this as a dream to be undone by the future anterior. I offer it here, in all its vulnerability, because of my immense respect for Ida Blom.

Gendering is our first instrument of abstraction. Psychoanalysis does not give us a description of what really happens. It is therefore very important that such an imaginative psychoanalytic thinker as Lacan imagines the construction of the possibility for self-conscious socio-genetic abstraction in the pre-subjective drive falling upon the anatomical trace of a margin or border: "lips, 'enclosure of the teeth', rim of the anus, penile fissure, vagina, fissure of eyelid, indeed hollow of the ear…Respiratory erogeneity…comes into play through spasms" (Lacan 2006: 692). In other words, gendered border-thinking—the kingpin of globalist feminism—is an undecided and primary constituent of our perception of reality itself, where reason is fashioned out of what precedes it. I have spoken to Professor Ida Blom to be open to our dream.

References

Ackerman, B. (1993). *We the people. Volume one: Foundations*. Cambridge: Harvard University Press.

Barro, R. J., & Lee, J.-W. (2011). A new data set of educational attainment in the world, 1950–2010. Revised November 2011, from http://www.barrolee.com/papers/Barro_Lee_Human_Capital_Update_2011Nov.pdf

Blom, I. (1998). Women, men, and socialism in Norway. In H. Gruber, & P. Graves (Eds.), *Women and socialism, socialism and women. Europe between the two world wars*. New York: Berghahn Books.

Collins, K. (2006). *Clan politics and regime transition in Central Asia*. Cambridge: Cambridge University Press.

Derrida, J. (2005). *Rogues, two essays on reason* (P.-A. Brault, & M. Naas, Trans.). Stanford: Stanford University Press.

Du Bois, W. E. B. (1935/1962). *Black reconstruction in America*. New York: Free Press.

Kant, I. (1991). The metaphysics of morals. In *Political writings* (H. B. Nisbet, Trans.). Cambridge: Cambridge University Press.

Lacan, J. (2006). The subversion of the subject and the dialectic of desire. In *Ecrits* (Bruce Fink, Trans.). New York: Norton.

McGillivray, M., Carpenter, D., & Iamsiraroy, S. (2013). Monitoring progress towards narrowing the development gap. In M. McGillivray & D. Carpenter

(Eds.), *Narrowing the development gap in ASEAN: Drivers and policy options*. New York: Routledge.

Sen, A., & Drèze, J. (2013). *An uncertain glory: India and its contradictions*. Princeton: Princeton University Press.

Wollstonecraft, M. (1995). *Vindication of the rights of women*. Cambridge: Cambridge University Press.

3

Troubled and Secure Gender Identities in a Changing Society: Norway at the End of the Long Nineteenth Century

Ida Blom

Introduction

The enacting depiction of gendered citizenship is closely connected to different understandings of gender identities and to a different understanding of the private–public divide. This chapter will analyze changing gender identities in Norway at the end of the long nineteenth century. In this period, important processes concerning women's enfranchisement and access to education transformed their possibilities of representing themselves. Given the patriarchal structure of Norway at that time, it was men who granted permission and rights. In order to grasp the wider gendered implications of these changes, it is thus necessary to explore the ways in which the different masculinities and femininities were presented.

I. Blom (✉)
University of Bergen, Nordeievegen 38, 5251 Søreidgrend, Norway

Shifting Gender Identities

According to the American sociologist Michael Kimmel, gender identities are mainly formed within private life, family relations and marriage. Changes in these spheres thus pose special challenges to understandings of gender, and potentially disrupt normative definitions of femininity and masculinity. In their study of English middle-class families, Leonore Davidoff and Catherine Hall argue along similar lines, yet also point to the importance of juridical, economic, social and political structures in relation to changes in gender identities (Blom 1990a; Davidoff and Hall 1987; Kimmel 1987; Rose 2010). No doubt, the new social activities opened for women during the last decades of the nineteenth century had fundamental effects on understandings of gender. How can we categorize such understandings in order to grasp these transformations?

Neither masculinity nor femininity is a homogenous concept. As the Australian sociologist Raywyn Connell has shown, masculinity manifests itself in a variety of shapes, forming and conforming to a power hierarchy between different masculinities (Connell 1987, 1995). In the specific historical context of Norway in the nineteenth century, the hegemonic position within this power hierarchy was defined by the role of the male breadwinner and the male politician. These positions were challenged by the changed social, economic and political opportunities for women. As this chapter aims to show, some men defended traditional gender relations by maintaining male superiority over women. This understanding of masculinity expressed itself both by insisting on male prerogatives and by pretending to protect women from challenges and burdens unsuitable for the female sex (Bengtsson and Frykman 1987). Other men were skeptical, even fearful, of the consequences of accepting women in influential positions, warning against the loss of male prestige and advantages in society.

However, in this complex interplay, not only masculinity but also femininity was divided. The two dominant concepts of femininity at the time were *difference femininity*—which stressed the different qualities attached to femininity as compared with masculinity—and *equal rights femininity*—which stressed that women should have the same rights as men (see

Hernes 1982, 1987 for a similar analysis). In order to analyze the ways in which these different notions of masculinity and femininity interacted, I shall suggest a new term: *secure gender identity*. I use the term secure gender identity to denote the situation where both women and men accept their proscribed gender identities; thus, what counts as secure gender identity takes very different forms in different historical contexts. During the greater part of the nineteenth century, a secure gender identity demanded the combination of a dominant, patriarchal "breadwinner-masculinity", with difference femininity. At the end of the century, however, secure identities were rather expressed by those who saw equal rights for women and men as desirable in the construction of society.

It is important to note that the various positions taken up with regard to the different understandings and enactments of gender—whether secure or not—are not unchangeable but shift with the circumstances. Sometimes, one understanding of gender, sometimes another, might be expressed by the same person. Yet as analytical categories, the dominant expressions of femininity and masculinity, as well as the notion of a secure gender identity, may help us understand how gender identities were influenced by changes in society.

In order to analyze how different gender identities were formed and expressed in discussions at the end of the nineteenth century in Norway, I shall pay special attention in this chapter to the topics of women's access to academic studies and to suffrage. A short presentation of how gender was perceived at the beginning of the nineteenth century serves as the starting point for analyzing later changes.

Perceptions of Gendered Citizenship During the Early Nineteenth Century

In 1814 an autocratic monarchy was replaced by a more democratic society. Sovereignty shifted from the Danish to the Swedish king, and a national Constitution was adopted. The paragraph that detailed the conditions for obtaining suffrage rights was clear, and limited such rights to citizens with a certain economic status. It did not, however, explicitly state the gender of the citizen granted the vote, and when parliament gathered four years later, in 1818, anxiety was expressed that the term "citizen" might be understood to cover both men and women. Consequently, it was suggested to change the phrasing to: "Suffrage rights are only for Norwegian citizens *of the male sex*..." (Kolstad 1963: 5–6). The proposal was rejected on the grounds that it was evident that the term "citizen" could not mean a woman. It was also pointed out that women had not made any claims to take part in the running of the state (Kolstad 1963). It was, in other words, seen as a precondition for discussing women's suffrage that women themselves claimed this right. They did not do that until the 1880s. Obviously, accepting superior masculinity and difference femininity constituted a secure gender identity that reigned during the early nineteenth century.

Yet this version of a secure gender identity did not mean that women had no rights. Rather, male and female citizens had different rights and duties: Men were responsible for the economy of the family and the nation; they were also responsible for national defense. In return, they were entitled to take part in decisions concerning the whole of society. Thus, suffrage and representation were reserved for men—and, for a long time, only for men with a certain economic position, preferably heads of households. They were then seen as representing other members of the household: women, children and servants. Female citizens had other duties and rights. They earned their right to protection and subsistence by doing domestic work, bringing up children and caring for the sick and the elderly. This perception of gendered rights and duties was most pronounced within the middle class, who increasingly proposed similar ideals to working-class people and to peasants.

The long reign of this version of secure gender identity, which placed men in the public sphere and women in the family, made it difficult for women to gain access to important education that would qualify them for achievements in the public world, and to political citizenship through suffrage. If women gained access to the public world, it was believed, important aspects of genuine masculinity would be weakened and women might lose their feminine qualities.

However, during the long nineteenth century, there was a fundamental change in Western societies. Two parallel developments—the gradual transformation of agrarian societies into an urban industrialized world, and a slowly developing democratization of politics—had a great influence on the understanding of citizenship, and consequently of gender identities.

Changes in Economic Citizenship

Citizenship is a multifaceted concept. As the British political theorist T.H. Marshall argues, citizenship is composed of three interlocking components: the civil, the political and the social (Marshall and Bottomore 1992). The British historian Alice Kessler-Harris adds economic citizenship to Marshall's triad, pointing to the fundamental importance of rights such as occupational choice, access to education and training as well as wages adequate to support oneself and the family (Kessler-Harris 2001). The duties and rights of citizenship vary with the wealth of the citizen as well as with gender, ethnicity and race (Blom 1996, 2000; Hagemann 2012; Halsaa et al. 2012, 50; Le Feuvre et al. 2012).

The development from mainly agrarian to industrialized urban cultures during the nineteenth century changed the understanding of economic citizenship, and temporarily widened the divide between the private and the public. Work increasingly meant paid work outside of the domestic sphere. Emigration from many European countries to the USA influenced the ratio of men to women and augmented the number of unmarried women who increasingly looked for economic independence. The beginning of a reduction in fertility rates also influenced the size and the importance of the family. At the same time, institutional care, such as hospitals, and new technologies, such as the telegraph and telephone, opened for new professions, offering unmarried middle-class women the possibility of being self-sufficient. These changes in the economy lessened the burden previously placed on fathers and brothers to provide for unmarried daughters and sisters. Such possibilities, however, depended on some form of schooling and theoretical knowledge, which was mainly accessible to middle-class women (Smith 2008).

In the agrarian society, women and men were equally important for the family economy. Men often took on duties further away from home, such as fishing or lumbering, while women—in addition to doing domestic work—were responsible for economically important activities near the home, like milking, producing butter and cheese, taking care of livestock, etc. In fact, during the 1860s, examples from Norway show that urban middle-class men considered the work of agrarian women to be so important that they reproached farmers for leaving the main responsibility for the family economy to their wives. To a middle-class man, the shared workload in agrarian society seemed to express a most unmanly attitude (Blom 1990b).

The family economy was also a shared responsibility between men and women in the growing working classes. At the same time, working-class families aspired to a division of work similar to the one proscribed as the ideal within the middle class: The aim was to save wives from exhausting work in factories in order that they could concentrate on work in the family. Thus, the working-class policy—which was also supported by working-class women—aimed at a decent wage for men, which would enable them to become respectable providers, and to save working-class wives from the double burden of both paid and unpaid work (Blom 1990b).

From the middle of the century, changes in economic citizenship gradually occurred and typically were important mainly for middle-class women. In 1854 inheritance rights became the same for both genders, and women would no longer have to be content with half of what men might obtain. In 1863 widows and unmarried women gained their independence and were no longer dependent on approval of fathers or brothers for their conduct. In 1878 women got the right to sit for middle school exams, thus easing their way into work as telegraph- or telephone operators. In 1882 after some discussion, women got the right to academic studies; in 1884 they also got the right to sit for exams at the university. They had, however, to wait until 1912 before they got access to most jobs requiring an academic education. In 1890 education at teacher training colleges was opened for women. And in 1888 married women, who until then had been completely dependent on a husband's guardianship, got the right to dispose of their own income—a right which was mainly of importance for married women of the working class. Of all these changes, men seemed to find sharing academic education with women the most unsettling to masculine identity. The same was true for changes in political citizenship (Agerholt 1973; Blom 1985; Hagemann 2010; Larsen 2013a, b; Ohman Nielsen 2011).

Widened Political Citizenship

The American Revolution in 1776 and the French Revolution 13 years later inaugurated the growth of nation states and a burgeoning democracy. Concurrently, the relations between the head of state and the individual inhabitants were altered. The individual had until then been understood as a subject subordinated to the authority of the prince. Now, gradually, the subject became a citizen. Whereas the prerevolutionary subject had many duties and few rights, a number of laws and regulations would offer citizens both duties and rights (Anderson 1983; Hobsbawm and Ranger 1983; Smith 2001). As we have seen, these duties and rights were gendered. The patriarchal structure dictating that men were the heads of the family as well as of the state also made changes in political citizenship such as suffrage rights easier to obtain for men than for women.

Men's suffrage was reformed in 1884 to include men who paid taxes on a certain income. The same year the adoption of parliamentarism strengthened the power of Parliament in relation to the government. Political parties were formed. The Liberal and the Conservative Parties were both founded in 1884, the Labor Party in 1887. The class character of masculine reign was weakened when in 1898 all men gained suffrage rights, independently of economic means.

Women's claims to admission to public decision-making institutions were only slowly welcomed. From 1889 women could be elected to school boards, and from 1900, they could become members of Poor Law commissions. Significantly, as for suffrage rights, women often gained these rights in situations where decisions concerned questions near to home. Norwegian women with a certain economic status got municipal suffrage in 1901, and this was extended to all women in 1910. National suffrage was attained a little later, in 1907 for women with a certain income or married to a man with a certain income and only in 1913 for all women. A similar gradual expansion of women's rights is found in other countries (Blom 2012, 2013b; Yuval-Davis and Anthias 1989; Yuval-Davis 1999).

As already mentioned, in 1818, it was claimed that women themselves had to demand suffrage rights before the question could even be discussed. The reigning form for secure gender identity was challenged when during the 1880s women started the long battle against the then hegemonic view of masculinity in order to obtain full political rights. This happened when women started organizing themselves.

The Norwegian Women's Rights Association (*Den norske Kvindesagsforening*) was established in 1884 to work for better education and for opening a number of occupations for women that had until then been reserved for men. The following year the Women's Suffrage Association (*Kvindestemmerettsforeningen*) was formed. Headed by Gina Krog this association demanded votes for women on the same conditions as for men. Another important organization, Norwegian Women's Sanitary Organization (*Norske Kvinners Sanitetsforening*), followed in 1896, headed by Frederikke Marie Qvam. Disagreements within the Women's Suffrage Association two years later prompted Qvam, in cooperation with Gina Krog, to start the National Association for Women's Suffrage (*Landskvindestemmerettsforeningen*), continuing to work for women's suffrage on the same conditions as for men. In 1905 these two organizations initiated a large-scale signature campaign supporting the dissolution of the Norwegian–Swedish Union, marking women's strong engagement in public matters (Blom 2005).

An important blow to the notion of superior masculinity came between 1901 and 1913 when all women gradually acquired the same suffrage rights as men. By then, women had the same rights as men both to academic studies and to suffrage (Agerholt 1973; Blom 1980, 2012, 2013a, b; Hagemann, 2010, 2012; Larsen 2013a, b; Ohman Nielsen 2011; Owesen 2013). The long discussions on these two reforms reveal a variety of competing understandings of gender identities.

The Question of Masculinity in Discussions of Academic Education and Suffrage Rights

The arguments of those who were against women's new rights feature a number of examples of the belief in the superiority of masculinity. The economic aspects of women's access to academic studies effectively eliminated class as a challenge to middle-class masculinity. Thus, gender constituted the fundamental difference. Opponents of women's access to academic studies were found especially among physicians and theologians. In the following I shall point to some of the many examples of the belief in the superiority of masculinity in these discussions.

This understanding of masculinity was especially prominent within the medical faculty. In a letter to the Academic Senate in 1882, the medical faculty maintained that only men had the quiet and balanced approach and the character and will that were needed as a physician. Only in exceptional cases would the necessary ability for abstract and theoretical reasoning be found in women. When this occurred, "you would often get the impression that these women have a somewhat abnormal character, that does not leave any doubt, that here the woman is outside her natural field" (Frøhlich 1984: 10–11).[1] Consequently, only men had the qualities needed for a physician, so in 1884, the Church Department recommended that decisions concerning women's access to medical studies should be postponed. Instead, it was recommended that women should be educated as midwives, a profession controlled by male physicians (Frøhlich 1984). Still, that same year, academic studies were opened for women, and gradually more and more women qualified for the medical profession. But they were not always welcomed.

In 1914 when a female physician applied for a job at the maternity hospital in the capital, one of the counterarguments for appointing her was that "purely natural processes" would now and then weaken the mental strength needed for an obstetrician. This danger was especially prevalent at the time when a woman reached the age that she might qualify for a responsible position. The head of the maternity hospital saw menstruation and menopause as special handicaps for women (Blom 1987; Frøhlich 1984). Again and again, it was also argued that women's special duties as mothers and wives made it impossible for them to assume the kind of responsibility necessary for a physician. These understandings of femininity made it obvious that women had neither the biological nor the psychological dispositions deemed necessary for a physician. Women belonged in the private sphere, men in the public (Blom 1994).

Somewhat surprisingly, there were no strong expressions of male opposition to female students at the theological faculty. Such opposition was, however, clearly expressed through other channels. In 1909, the journal

---

[1] All quotations are translated from Norwegian by the author.

Luthersk Kirketidende reminded readers that "[t]he veil will always remain on women's heads...we demand from the Christian woman that she shows the female discretion, that prevents her from publicly playing the same role as a man" (*Luthersk Kirketidende* 1909: 251). A similar attitude was found in another Christian journal, *Kristelig Ugeblad*, in 1912: "It feels repulsive for our churchly feeling that a woman should command the pulpit, the bridge of the church so to speak" (Klokkersund 1986: 74, 90; Blom 1990a: 138).

In the field of theology, the notion of the superiority of masculinity was protected by other restrictions. Although women who passed exams at the theological faculty could work at the institutions of the Inner Mission, in Christian work among young people or as teachers, they did not gain access to the most important theological position—that of a vicar. Until 1938 women were excluded from the office as a vicar, and until 1956, they could only obtain this office where the parishioners did not object. The first female vicar was not employed until 1961 (Blom 1994). The notion of the superiority of masculinity was long-lived within the church.

Expressions of the superiority of masculinity were also found in discussions of women's suffrage. When in 1890 the question of women's suffrage was discussed in Parliament for the first time, the conservative MP Bishop Heuch reminded Parliament that the Bible commanded women's subordination to men (Agerholt 1973). This meant that women should remain in the private sphere, within the family. According to Heuch, it was unthinkable that respectable women should act in public. He painted a frightening picture of how he saw a woman taking part in a parliamentary debate and argued that no one could "at the same time aim at building the home in the silence of private life and serve one's fatherland in public life" (Kolstad 1963: 32). To do so entailed the risk of changing women into "deformed monsters...into neutras. And woe to societies no longer consisting of masculinitities and femininities, but of masculinities and neutras" (Kolstad 1963: 32).

However, the belief in the superiority of masculinity—restricting women to their "proper place"—was not necessarily presented as men's domination over women. Swedish psychologist Margot Bengtson and ethnologist Jonas Frykman have pointed to the possibility of expressing hegemonic masculinity as a voluntary choice made by both women and men, out of love or loyalty (Bengtsson and Frykman 1987). This attitude might be expressed as a way of demonstrating true masculinity by attempting to protect women from the burdens of public activities. Although this strategy does not change gender relations, it might be seen as a more democratic approach.

An example of this strategy is found in a letter from the medical faculty to the Academic Senate in 1882. The faculty warned against admitting women to medical studies by arguing that coeducation was harmful to women's shyness (Frøhlich 1984). However, this attitude was even more pronounced in the question of votes for women. In discussions of this issue in Parliament in 1890, it was said that in the world of politics, women would lose in competition with men. The conservative MP Dean Niels Christian Hertzberg proclaimed: "It is the task of men to carry the biggest and heaviest burdens…we do not want to load these burdens on women's shoulders" (Kolstad 1963: 26–27). In 1907 another conservative MP, Ole Malm, claimed that "the woman question is not solved by women's vote, nor by offering women the same wages as men or by giving them access to certain posts and offices, but by offering them an…economically carefree marriage" (Kolstad 1963: 101). Malm's belief in the superiority of masculinity surfaced when he continued: "in other words" what was in question was "to ameliorate the man's life… For the woman her happiness does not depend on being free, but on being bound to the man. Her dependence is a law of nature" (Kolstad 1963: 101). Malm had no doubt about how masculinity and femininity should be understood.

Thus, the belief in the superiority of masculinity could be expressed both through stating that only men, not women, possessed the required qualities for the reforms in question and by presenting this idea as a way of protecting women, fulfilling the obligation of a respectable man. In this way superior masculinity complied well with difference femininity. Accepting this situation could be seen as an expression of the form of secure gender identity that reigned during the early part of the nineteenth century. It was however challenged by changes during the later decades of the century.

Fearful Masculinity Among Opponents of Women's New Rights

Not all opponents of women's access to vote and to academic professions expressed themselves as securely as those mentioned above. Quite the contrary, these challenges to the belief in the superiority of masculinity made several men feel weak and worthless; a democracy that enhanced women's power over men was seen as a threat to proper masculinity. Yet, as we shall see, these challenges also gave rise to a different conceptualization of masculinity.

Such fearful reactions were not dominant among men within academia, nor among MPs, but they do sometimes come to the fore. Fear of the consequences of new rights for women was expressed in 1884 when the Medical Faculty discussed the possibility of admitting women to be educated as physicians. It was feared that, should this happen, the result would be a lowering of the income of physicians. It was seen as obvious that women would not demand the same wages as men, yet the important male quality of being the (main) provider was nevertheless in danger. It was also feared that the very fact that women might be able to do the same work as male physicians might reduce the social status of the medical profession. Women physicians were thus a threat to "proper" masculinity (Blom 1987; Frøhlich 1984).

This kind of fearful masculinity was most clearly expressed in discussions of the women's vote. In line with difference femininity, the perception was that women already wielded great authority within the family. Consequently, it was argued that it would be unacceptable to also give them influence in the public world. In 1890 the conservative MP Hertzberg claimed that "it happens more often than we may like to admit that…when you ask: from where does this man get his political opinions? I think you may quite often get the answer: you will have to ask his wife" (Kolstad 1963: 28). Believing that men's power was already not as absolute as one might assume, women would gain too much influence if they were allowed into the public sphere. Here a touch of fearful masculinity may be observed.

This fear of women's authority came out even more clearly in 1907 when the conservative MP Ole Malm exclaimed that "if—in addition to the influence women already have behind the scenes—and which unfortunately she will always retain—we now have to give her civil rights, the situation will be intolerable" (Kolstad 1963: 103). A world where women had a say both in the private and in the public was out of the question. Malm conjured up a frightening picture of how this world might look:

> It is not without reason that clear-sighted men see the women's movement as a memento mori and maintain in the noise of feminism to hear the gnawing of a beetle on the carcass of society…In reality the women's movement is a sign of disease, a symptom of the dissolution of society. A people adhering to feminism will inevitably experience a decrease in population… loose national power and reputation among nations. To allow women suffrage rights and take the full practical consequences of this will quite simply be to commit national suicide. (Kolstad 1963: 101)

Malm expresses a strong fear, one might say panic, of what it might mean if women got political power. There seemed to be no limits to the damages that would result from such a reform. His attitude is a clear expression of fearful masculinity.

Thus, the opposition to new rights for women in the public sphere found expression both in securely proclaiming the superiority of masculinity and in a more fearful warning of the consequences, noting how the very idea of a "proper" masculinity was under fire. And men were not alone in fearing the consequences of changing understandings of gender.

Women Defending the Traditional Understandings of Gender

Some women too preferred to defend an earlier form of a secure gender identity by maintaining the traditional gender order. As such, the notion of *difference femininity* complied very well with the then hegemonic idea of masculinity.

Difference femininity sees women as a special species, different from men. Women who were defending the traditional understandings of gender invoked women's special duties to care for children and other individuals in need. They also highlighted women's special characteristics, such as the ability to express love and thoughtful consideration. According to this understanding of femininity, a democratic society where women would assume responsibility in the public world would be a threat to feminine identity as such.

Defenders of this kind of femininity did not express themselves in public very often, but some examples are found. In 1890 an anonymous woman wrote in the conservative paper *Morgenbladet* that "this unhealthy modern stream of temptations…to want to share men's work, will destroy our homes and remove all beauty and poetry from our lives…Let us fight the temptation to be dragged into the whirlpool of public life" (Agerholt 1973: 142). And as late as in 1910, the leader of the Norwegian Housewives Association (*Norges Husmorforbund*), founded in 1898, warned that a woman's participation in public life "would endanger her deepest and purest instincts and thoughts… all of her feminine being would suffer…the motherly love, the reconciling will be in danger" (*Husmoderen*, 1910, cited in Blom 1980: 117).

It may not come as a surprise that the leader of the Housewives Association feared the effect of women's activities outside the home and family. It is easy to perceive this understanding of femininity as complying with the then hegemonic notion of masculinity, accepting male dominance as a form of protection and opposing new rights for women. Those who saw women and men as two different species feared the weakening of the differences between femininity and masculinity. Thus, the opposition to the reforms found expression both in secure gender identities and in fearful gender identities.

However, difference femininity was also used as an argument for demanding the same rights for women as for men. When this was the case, it could be understood in line with what Helga Hernes has termed *complementary argumentation*, that is: an argumentation that indicated that women had different experiences and different values than men and consequently might be seen as an extra resource (Hernes 1982, 1987).

In discussions in the early 1880s of admitting women to medical studies, difference femininity was expressed by stressing the caring character of the medical profession. The work of a physician could be seen as a natural prolongation of women's work in the home and family. It was also said that, especially where women's diseases were concerned, it would be a great advantage for female patients to consult a female physician. Information on what had happened in other countries was quoted to show that male physicians had exploited female patients, and that women did not dare to admit what had happened because that would subject them to gossip (Frøhlich 1984). In the feminist paper *Nylænde*, it was claimed that many women postponed visiting a physician because they feared indecent exposure. This delay sometimes had serious consequences for women's health (Svello 1980). Thus, a democratization of academic education would highlight the importance of the special and precious character of femininity for the medical profession. Contesting the notion of the superiority of masculinity would also weaken the dangers of a male-dominated health service.

Those who defended women's suffrage also used the argument of women's special characteristics in favor of this reform. It was sometimes argued that precisely *because* women were different from men, it was important to include them as voters and MPs. When proposing votes for women in the Norwegian Parliament in 1890, it was argued that

> (…) just by being present in Parliament women would improve men and take the sting out of party passions…through their stronger compassion and stronger patience [they would] add a new animating element…first and foremost in two important matters, which pressingly demand a solution, namely the social question and the cause of peace; these matters would not…be solved in a satisfactory way without the help of women. (Kolstad 1963: 14–15)

This argument in defense of women's suffrage is witness of a belief in the value of women's special qualities. It would, however, soon be demonstrated that not all women shared the same attitude to the social question and to the cause of peace (Blom 2005). But those who defended women's suffrage were not afraid of what might happen if women as well as men were present in Parliament.

Although difference femininity was not very prominent with those who worked for new rights for women, even an ardent promoter of these rights, Gina Krog, sometimes used arguments stressing women's special qualities as a value for society. In her speech to the Norwegian Women's Association in 1885, she—although a little hesitatingly—admitted that society needed "women, people with the motherly hearts" (Hagemann 2012: 282). Krog seemed more convinced of this point of view when in January 1886 she confronted feminists who did not include women's suffrage in their program. She now maintained that society needed the quality that was so pronounced in women, namely "maternal love, liberated from the monkeylike, working greatly and spiritually in a life-giving, nurturing, embracing way...the one-sided maleness, the warrior-adventurous spirit, cannot alone advance humanity" (Moksnes 1984: 82).

Two years later, a similar understanding of femininity was expressed by Fernanda Nissen, an ardent member of the coming Labor Party. She maintained that working-class women had the right to expect support from working-class men, since women had worked very hard to assist men in acquiring political influence (Blom 1980). Nissen did not stress votes for women as a means to advance women's interests, but as an instrument to strengthen men's work for socialism. However, in this case, it may be said that gender and class cooperated to fight middle-class superior masculinity. It should, of course, not be forgotten that the question of women's suffrage was above all a problem of party politics, a theme for which there is no room to discuss in this paper. Suffice it to say that allowing women from wealthy families to vote could be used as a strategy to strengthen the conservative party, while general female suffrage might mobilize voters supporting the social-democratic party (Blom 2013b).

Accepting difference femininity in the fight for women's access to academia and to suffrage might be seen as an expression of secure gender identity. Concepts of femininity and masculinity might indicate different qualities, but both genders should have the same rights in society. The idea of the superiority of masculinity should not be accepted.

Equal Rights Femininity

However, arguments in favor of new rights for women build mostly on another understanding of femininity, which insisted that women and men were equals, that women had the same rights as men in any field and that male dominance was unacceptable in a democratic society.

3   Troubled and Secure Gender Identities

When women's access to academic exams was discussed in Parliament in 1884, an argument in favor of this reform reminded the MPs of the French Revolution, claiming that "all human beings are created equal when it comes to the ability to understand truth it all its forms" (Agerholt 1973: 63). Here, it was not doubted that women's ability to acquire theoretical insights was equal to men's. And it was added that: "the need to provide for yourself is the same for women as for men" (Agerholt 1973: 63). Although this last statement was a reminder that admitting women to academic professions might ease men's burden of providing for unmarried family members, it could still be seen as a provocation for those who saw men as providers and women as housewives and mothers.

It comes as no surprise that equal rights femininity was at the core of the arguments used by Gina Krog, the leader of the Association for Women's Suffrage. From the very first discussions on this theme in 1885, Krog argued that "(w)hat we most of all have to remember is this: women as human individuals, women's rights to free personal development… Consequently, as human beings we have interests to defend, and because we as women have interests to defend, we claim our right" (Moksnes 1984: 82–83).

Her point of view was echoed by the Liberal MP Viggo Ullmann in 1890 when he reminded MPs that society consisted of women as well as of men, that women had the same human value as men, and should have the same access as men to take part in public life and influence all matters of importance for society (Kolstad 1963). This understanding of femininity left no doubt about women's identity as quite simply human beings with the same rights as men. It was repeated again and again by promoters of women's suffrage. And in 1895 the Liberal MP Ole Anton Qvam maintained that the word "citizen", used in the paragraph of the Constitution concerning suffrage rights, quite simply meant women as well as men (Agerholt 1973). The understanding of the concept "citizen" as limited to men as expressed in 1818 was now seen to be wrong. Qvam's way of formulating the defense for women's suffrage was almost an echo of Gina Krog's words ten years earlier: Gender differences should disappear in a democratic society.

Thus, both in the fight for women's access to academic studies and in the fight for women's suffrage, the notion of the superiority of masculinity was overcome and equal rights femininity carried the day. The troubled gender identities resulting from fundamental changes in society throughout the nineteenth century and surfacing in debates on women's access to academia and to suffrage may be said to be put to rest by the emergence of new secure gender identities. But the understanding of this version of gender identity had changed fundamentally during the last decades of the century.

Secure Gender Identities

The coexistence of the notion of the superiority of masculinity and difference femininity had been almost unchallenged during the greater part of the nineteenth century. Men's responsibilities as providers and as defenders of the nation, as well as their ensuing rights to certain advantages in the question of education and political citizenship were not questioned. During the same period, women's duties as wives and mothers, as well as their right to maintenance and protection, had been accepted almost without protest. This understanding of a secure gender identity paved the way for cooperation between men and women in protecting traditional gender identities. It was not until the later decades of the century that fundamental changes in society resulted in extensive discussions of women's claims for new rights. These discussions led to, and were expressions of, new understandings of secure gender identities.

While enemies of women's claims clung to the traditional understandings of secure gender identities, those who defended new rights for women—women and men alike—expressed new definitions of the term. They had no fear of accepting women on an equal footing with men, both in the private and in the public spheres. Cooperation across gender divides was now possible, grounded in equal rights feminism, and expressed as a voluntary choice made by both women and men.

Secure gender identities came to the fore in numerous cases of cooperation between spouses and near relatives defending women's rights. An important example is the cooperation between John Stuart Mill and his wife, Harriet Taylor. Together they worked on *The Subjection of Women*, a book that since 1869 has inspired many supporters of women's rights. A similar cooperation between spouses may be found in Denmark, where MP Fredrik Bayer worked closely with his wife Mathilde on the question of women's suffrage (Larsen 2010). In Sweden, too, women working for suffrage deliberately engaged male relatives and friends as supporters in their fight (Florin 2006, 2013). In Norway, Frederikke Marie Qvam, leader of the National Association for Women's Suffrage (*Landskvinnestemmerettsforeningen*), cooperated closely with her husband, Ole Anton Qvam. He was an MP, and for some years at the turn of the century, also acted as Prime Minister (Folkvord 2013). Another Liberal MP, staunchly defending women's rights, was Viggo Ullman, brother of the feminist Ragna Nielsen. In 1885 Nielsen opened the first coeducational school in the Norwegian capital. Their mother, Wilhelmine Ullmann, had divorced in 1854 and since then lived as a single mother. She ran a childcare center and was a well-known literary person, actively taking part in public discussions and supporting women's rights (Jonassen 2011). For all these people, and probably many more, a new secure gender identity allowed them to defend a democratic society where equal rights for women and men would be accepted.

The Slow Change in Understandings of Gendered Identities

But changing gender identities was a slow process. The new understandings of gender that surfaced around the end of the long nineteenth century did not immediately work perceptible changes in the function of women and men in society. One thing was acquiring new rights. Another thing was to make use of such rights. Attempting to reformulate secure gender identities took time.

As the conservative MP Emil Stang said in 1907, when women of a certain economic status obtained the vote:

> I do not understand why family life would be disturbed because women get access to public life in the same way as men. It might of course be the case where a wife acts as an MP, but that will certainly not happen very often…and how could the home be disrupted because a wife accompanies her husband to vote every three years? (Kolstad 1963: 102)

He was so right. The fight for women's suffrage had primarily been concerned with the right to vote. That it also meant the right to be elected as an MP was less in focus. True, for a short while in 1911 and again in 1912, Anna Rogstad, as the first woman ever, served as an MP for the Liberal Left party. The next time a woman was elected to Parliament was in 1921. Until the Second World War, at the most three women, representing the Labour Party and the Conservative Party, were elected as MPs. Until the 1970s women never made up more than between 1 and 10 % of MPs as well as of representatives to municipal councils (Skard 1980). An MP seemed, for a very long time, to be understood almost exclusively as a man.

Where women's access to academic studies was concerned, the notion of the superiority of masculinity and difference femininity continued to reign for a long time. Between 1907 and 1931 32 % of male students finished their academic education, while this was only the case for 31 % of female students (Backer 1932, Table 2). It was soon recognized that an academic degree was not enough to be accepted within the professions opened by this degree. No wonder that for long, only very few women showed an interest in academic studies.

Despite the formal democratization of society, the public—understood as access to channels for political influence or to top positions in the academic world—for long remained a primarily masculine arena. In practice, it seems that an earlier understanding of a secure identity had returned.

Explanations for this situation may be found in the increased importance attached to the work of housewives and of voluntary organizations. The Norwegian Housewives Association grew from 94 local units in 1927 to 1400 in 1960 (Danielsen 2013). This organization implemented new knowledge on the importance of cleanliness and healthy food for the family and assisted in teaching women how to run a healthy home (Blom 1997; Danielsen 2013).

Simultaneously, uniting difference femininity and equal rights femininity women might build on women's importance in establishing voluntary organizations. Since 1896 the Norwegian Women's Sanitary Organization had been an important channel for efforts to attain women's suffrage. At the same time, it efficiently and with impressive results inaugurated a systematic fight against the widespread and deadly disease tuberculosis. The Sanitary Association assisted women's work in the homes and built sanatoria and nursing homes for people suffering from tuberculosis. It also successfully resisted attempts from male physicians to take over the leading role in this important work. In 1972 this organization still ran more than half of the health stations in the country. Since then, public authorities have, to an increasing degree, taken over that responsibility (Bjarnar 1995; Blom 1998).

It seems that an active engagement in politics or an academic career was not seen as a necessary condition for influencing the construction of a democratic welfare state. It may be said that—although weakened—versions of the superiority of masculinity and difference femininity continued to be dominant in academia as well as in political life until the 1970s. By then, further changes in society and the growth of the new women's movement ushered in renewed discussions of gender identities. Gradually, the new understanding of secure gender identities grew in importance. But that is another story....

References

Agerholt, Caspari A. (1973/1937). *Den norske kvinnebevegelses historie.* Oslo: Gyldendal Norsk Forlag.

Anderson, B. (1983). *Imagined communities: Reflections on the origin and spread of nationalism.* London: Verso.

Backer, J. E. (1932). Kvinnelige studenter 1882–1931. En statistisk oversikt. In *Kvinnelige studenter 1882–1932.* Oslo: Gyldendal.

Bengtsson, M., & Frykman, J. (1987). *Om maskulinitet: Mannen som forskningsprojekt.* Stockholm, Rapport Jämfo, hefte nr. 11.

Bjarnar, O. (1995). *Veiviser til velferdssamfunnet. Norske Kvinners Sanitetsforening 1946–1996.* Oslo: Norske Kvinners Sanitetsforening.

Blom, I. (1980). The struggle for women's suffrage in Norway 1885–1913. *Scandinavian Journal of History, 8*(1), 3–22.

Blom, I. (1985). Nødvendig arbeid – skiftende definisjoner og praktiske konsekvenser. *Historisk Tidsskrift, 1,* 117–141.

Blom, I. (1987). "Hjernen kan ikke utvikle sig samtidigt med ovariene..." Kvinnelige pionerer i den medisinske profesjon omkring 1900. In B. Sawyer

& A. Göransson (Eds.), *Mannliga strukturer och kvinnliga strategier. En bok til Gunhild Kyle* (pp. 238–254). Göteborg: Historiska Institutionen, Göteborgs Universitet.

Blom, I. (1990a). Changing gender identities in an industrialising society. *Gender and History,* 2(2), 131–147.

Blom, I. (1990b). "Hun er den Raadende over Husets økonomiske Anliggender". Changes in women's work and family responsibilities in Norway since the 1860's. In P. Hudson & W. R. Lee (Eds.), *Women's work and the family economy in historical perspective* (pp. 157–182). Manchester: Manchester University Press.

Blom, I. (1994). *Det er forskjell på folk – nå som før. Om kjønn og andre former for sosial differensiering.* Oslo: Universitetsforlaget.

Blom, I. (1996). Nation – class – gender: Scandinavia at the turn of the century. *Scandinavian Journal of History* 2(Spring), 1–16.

Blom, I. (1997). World history as gender history: The case of the nation state. In S. Tønnesen et al., *Between national histories and global history.* Konferanserapport til det 23. Det Nordiske Historikermøte, FHS Helsingfors 1997, 71–92.

Blom, I. (1998). *Feberens ville rose – Tre omsorgssystemer i tuberkulosearbeidet 1900–1960.* Fagbokforlaget: Bergen.

Blom, I. (2000). Gender and nation states: An international comparative perspective. In I. Blom, K. Hagemann, & C. Hall (Eds.), *Gendered nations: The long eighteenth century* (pp. 3–26). Oxford: Berg Publishers.

Blom, I. (2005). 1905 – et gledens eller et sorgens år? In Ø. Sørensen & T. Nielsson (Eds.), *1905 – Nye perspektiver* (pp. 101–116). Oslo: H. Aschehoug & Co.

Blom, I. (2012). Structures and agency. A Transnational comparison of the struggle for women's suffrage in the Nordic European Countries during the long 19th century. *Scandinavian Journal of History,* 37(5), 600–620.

Blom, I. (2013a). "Det bliver ikke til at holde ud". Den lange vei til kvinnestemmeretten. *Historie,* 1, 46–56.

Blom, I. (2013b). Hva er en borger? Nasjon, borgerskap og mobilisering i Norden. *Historisk Tidskrift,* 92(4), 513–526.

Connell, R. (1987). *Gender and power.* Cambridge: Polity Press.

Connell, R. (1995). *Masculinities.* Cambridge: Polity Press.

Danielsen, H. (2013). Den kjønnsdelte arbeidsdagen. In H. Danielsen, E. Larsen, & I. W. Owesen (Eds.), *Norsk likestillingshistorie 1814–2013* (pp. 221–274). Oslo: Fagbokforlaget.

Danielsen, H., Larsen, E., & Owesen, I. W. (2013). *Norsk likestillingshistorie 1814–2001*. Oslo: Fagbokforlaget.
Davidoff, L., & Hall, C. (1987). *Family Fortunes. Men and Women of the English Middle Class 1700–1850*. London: Hutchinson Education.
Florin, C. (2006). *Kvinnor får röst: kön, känslor och politisk kultur i kvinnorna srösträttsrörelse*. Stockholm: Atlas Akademi.
Florin, C. (2013). Män som strategi. Rösträttskvinnornas informella vägar till det politiska medborgarskapet. (Norsk). *Historisk Tidskrift, 92*(4), 541–555.
Folkvord, M. (2013). *Frederikke Marie Qvam: rabaldermenneske og strateg*. Oslo: Samlaget.
Frøhlich, A. (1984). Norges første kvinnelige leger 1893–1920. Unpublished master thesis, University of Bergen.
Hagemann, G. (2010/2005). Fra de stummes leir? 1800–1900. In I. Blom & S. Sogner (Eds.), *Med kjønnsperspektiv på norsk historie. Fra vikingtid til 2000-årsskiftet* (pp. 157–254). Oslo: Cappelen akademisk forlag.
Hagemann, G. (2012). Er det noe nytt å si om stemmeretten? Foredrag på fellesmøte den 13. september 2012. In *Det Norske Videnskaps-Akademi, Årbok 2012* (pp. 273–290). Oslo: Novus forlag.
Halsaa, B., Roseneil, S., & Sümer, S. (Eds.). (2012). *Remaking citizenship in multicultural Europe: Women's movements, gender and diversity*. Basingstoke: Palgrave Macmillan.
Hernes, H. (1982). *Staten – kvinner ingen adgang?* Oslo: Universitetsforlaget.
Hernes, H. (1987). *Welfare state and woman power: Essays in state feminism*. Oslo: Norwegian University Press.
Hobsbawm, E., & Ranger, T. (Eds.). (1983). *The invention of tradition*. Cambridge: Cambridge University Press.
Jonassen, M. (2011). *Livet er et pust. Ragna Nielsen – en biografi*. Oslo: Aschehoug.
Kessler-Harris, A. (2001). *In pursuit of equity: Women, men and the quest for economic citizenship in twentieth century America*. Oxford: Oxford University Press.
Kimmel, M. S. (Ed.). (1987). *Changing men. New directions in research on men and masculinity*. London: Sage
Klokkersund, R. (1986). "…hjemmet først og fremst, men det andet ikke forsømmes…" Kirkens kvinnesyn belyst med utgangspunkt i debatten om kvinners adgang til prestembetet i perioden 1891–1912. Unpublished master thesis, University of Bergen.
Kolstad, E. (Ed.). (1963). *Stortinget om Stemmerett for Kvinner 17. mai 1814-11. juni 1913*. Oslo: A/S Fredr. Arnesen Bok- og Akcidentstrykkeri.

Larsen, J. (2010). *Også andre hensyn: dansk ligestillingshistorie 1849–1915*. Århus: Aarhus Universitetsforlag.
Larsen, J. (2013). Kvindevalgret, kvindebevægelse og politiske partier. En analyse af danske strategidiskussioner 1901–1915. (*Norsk*). *Historisk Tidskrift, 92*(4), 527–540.
Larsen, E. (2013). Stemmerett til alle. In H. Danielsen, E. Larsen, & I. W. Owesen (Eds.), *Norsk likestillingshistorie 1814–2013* (pp. 159–218). Oslo: Fagbokforlaget.
Le Feuvre, N., Ervik, R., Krajewska, A., & Metso, M. (2012). Remaking economic citizenship in multicultural Europe: Women's movement claims and the 'commodification of elderly care'. In B. Halsaas, S. Roseneil, & S. Sümer (Eds.), *Remaking citizenship in multicultural Europe: Women's movements, gender and diversity*. Basingstoke: Palgrave Macmillan.
Luthersk Kirketidende. (1909) Nr. 16, oktober 1909.
Marshall, T. H., & Bottomore, T. (1992). *Citizenship and social class*. London: Pluto Press.
Moksnes, A. (1984). *Likestilling eller særstilling? Norsk kvinnesaksforening 1884–1913*. Oslo: Gyldendal Norsk Forlag.
Ohman Nielsen, M.-B. (2011). *Norvegr. Norges Historie Bind III, 1840–1914*. Oslo: H. Aschehoug & Co.
Owesen, I. W. (2013). Fra lukkede til offentlige rom 1880–1900. In H. Danielsen, E. Larsen, & I. W. Owesen (Eds.), *Norsk likestillingshistorie 1814–2013* (pp. 113–155). Oslo: Fagbokforlaget.
Rose, S. O. (2010). *What is gender history*. Cambridge: Polity Press.
Skard, T. (1980). *Utvalgt til Stortinget*. Oslo: Gyldendal Norsk Forlag.
Smith, A. D. (2001). *Nationalism: Theory, ideology, history*. Cambridge: Polity Press.
Smith, B. G. (2008). Industry and industrialization. In B. G. Smith (Ed.), *The oxford encyclopedia of women in world history* (Vol. 2, pp. 585–590). Oxford: Oxford University Press.
Svello, B. (1980). "Reformere os selv". Norsk kvindesagsforenings vurdering av kvinners utdannelsesmuligheter, yrkesaktivitet og hjemmearbeide i perioden 1887–1894. Unpublished master thesis, University of Bergen.
Yuval-Davis, N. (1999). *Gender and nation*. London: Sage.
Yuval-Davis, N., & Anthias, F. (Eds.). (1989). *Woman-nation-state*. Basingstoke: Macmillan.

4

Representations of Equality: Processes of Depoliticization of the Citizen-Subject

Sara Edenheim and Malin Rönnblom

Introduction

Demands for inclusion have always been part of a feminist agenda. There have been demands for the inclusion of women into male-dominated spheres such as education, paid labour, and political decision-making, as well as demands for day care and equal pay in order to make these inclusions possible. Today, the demands for inclusion are directed not only towards the society 'out there' but also towards the feminist movement itself, in particular claims that are rooted in positions articulated in relation to race and sexuality. These claims are not new; especially since the 1970s, so-called mainstream feminism has been criticized for giving white, heterosexual women a privileged position. We argue that the effects of this critique have changed due to changes in political forms of

---

S. Edenheim (✉) • M. Rönnblom (✉)
Umeå Centre for Gender Studies, Umeå University, 90187 Umeå, Sweden

© The Author(s) 2016
H. Danielsen et al. (eds.), *Gendered Citizenship and the Politics of Representation*, DOI 10.1057/978-1-137-51765-4_4

governing; that is, the logic of the market is increasingly replacing the logic of the political and this shift has consequences for feminist politics (cf. Brown 2015; Mouffe 2013). As the rationale of politics becomes increasingly dominated by an economic logic, gender becomes increasingly difficult to politicize, leaving limited opportunities for feminist claims.

In this chapter, we investigate contemporary claims for inclusion in relation to what we regard as a central aim of the feminist movement: the aim of achieving equality. Here, representation is understood in terms of inclusion; thus, demands for representation are seen as demands to be included in an already-set context. This understanding of representation is related to a liberal tradition in which the organization of politics is not challenged but is seen rather as in need of reform (e.g. Philips 1995). We discuss representation in relation to the depoliticization of the political subject, a process in which the possibilities to articulate collective conflicts in political terms diminish (Mouffe 2013). Our focus is the changing political setting in Sweden, a liberal democracy commonly representing the 'Third Way' yet also a nation that has been implementing New Public Management (NPM) since the 1990s. Today, Sweden is the most privatized country in the world (see, e.g., www.privatizationbarometer.com) and all governmental authorities are audited in new ways and with increased frequency.[1] In relation to these changes, equality has become an issue that concerns individual rights: a way of representing equality that fits with how the citizen-subject is turned into a self-regulating subject managing their own success or failure. We believe Sweden to be a useful empirical case when discussing the consequences of NPM for contemporary feminist claims. Hence, we regard Sweden as a kind of 'extreme' case; on the one hand, it is known for being one of the 'most gender-equal countries in the world' with a strong and inclusive welfare state and, on the other, it has privatized the public systems for social security and welfare faster than any other country in the Western world. Thus, different feminist articulations of political claims and goals

---

[1] NPM was introduced and supported by Social Democratic governments during the late 1980s, and was enhanced and followed up by major privatizations during periods of right-wing governance (especially 2006–2014). Hence, both Social Democrats and the various right-wing parties are part of this development (see also Edenheim and Rönnblom 2012).

in the Swedish context are used as a case study to illustrate what we regard as more general trends in contemporary feminist analysis and discussions about the aim of equality. We analyse three different forms of feminist articulations of political claims and goals to illustrate and discuss our arguments: a media debate, an analysis of the party programme of the feminist party Feminist Initiative (Fi) and an analysis of national gender-equality policy. Of course we cannot claim that our conclusions are general, but we believe that the shifts in modes of governing illustrated by the Swedish case enable us to point to some general trends in contemporary feminist discourse.

Our discussion draws on both Chantal Mouffe's distinction between politics and the political (Mouffe 2013) and Wendy Brown's articulation of the paradox of liberalism and the interrelation between economics and politics (Brown 2005). These two post-Marxist scholars have both discussed the collapse of politics as we know it, Brown by focusing on the breakdown of liberal democracy, and Mouffe by making a distinction between the established institutions and practices of politics (i.e. parliament, political parties, etc.) and the dimension of collective conflict that is needed in order to articulate power relations in politics (what Mouffe calls agonism). Further, they both discuss and analyse what could be called a neoliberal shift in government. One way of describing this shift is to talk about a collapse between the state and the market, where a market rationality of government has come to permeate all of society. The technologies of neoliberal government reach from, in the words of Wendy Brown, '…the soul of the citizen-subject to education policy to practice of empire' (Brown 2005: 39). In this context, the politics of representation and rights is no exception and can be (and has been) adapted, with little effort, to these rationalities, turning demands for rights into individualized responsibilities, and democracy and societal change into a question of values and regulated, legitimized knowledge. Inspired by Mouffe (2013) and her distinction between politics and the political, we are interested in analysing the shifts to which Brown points in terms of processes of politicization and depoliticization in contemporary forms of governing, focusing on how equality is produced within feminist discussions and practice. Is the dimension of agonism part of feminist politics or not?

In our analysis, we see the notion of individualization as important, because we regard the dimension of individualization to be crucial in how political claims are articulated. We have chosen the concept 'citizen-subject' to indicate that we are focusing on how the political subject, that is, the citizen, is produced within this discourse, and how neoliberal governance changes the conditions for citizenship.[2]

Most importantly, this chapter is an attempt to develop a theoretical framework for understanding issues of power and representation in an era when liberal democracy as we know it is about to fail. Here, representation implies both traditional political representation and representation as the production of, for example, subjects. What does it mean to claim to be represented as a citizen when liberal representative democracy works within the same logic as capitalism? How can we formulate a new understanding of the citizen-subject that begins with a different logic of the political subject?

The chapter opens with a discussion of the issue of representation, and then discusses equality in relation to rights politics, including how representation has been dealt with in Sweden, both generally and within feminist movements. We then present some empirical examples of feminist politics in Sweden and finally conclude with a discussion of the relationship between standpoint feminism, rights politics and neoliberal demands.

'Equal Representation' in a Representative Democracy

Unlike rights politics, the general idea of representative democracy is not inherently liberal. There are many different models of representative democracy both within and outside of liberal nation-states (see, e.g. Manin 2002). What they all have in common is the basic idea of com-

---

[2] Although citizenship per se is not central to our analysis, we are well aware of the existing scholarship on feminism and citizenship (e.g. Lister et al. 2007; Philips 1993), including the ambitions to challenge non-feminist and especially liberal understandings of citizenship. Because our analysis emphasizes how neoliberal rule challenges the conditions for political change, we are not focusing on the specific content of or definition of citizenship per se.

4 Equality and Depoliticization

mon elections where all citizens vote for a party or individual to whom they give the right to pass legally binding resolutions. A representative democracy makes it possible for citizens to show discontent in two ways: by guaranteeing the opportunity to form a public opinion (freedom of speech and freedom of organization) and by providing a voting system that guarantees more than one alternative and the anonymity of citizens (free elections). In Sweden, the proportional election model is mainly based on party representation, within which the Social Democrats have dominated since the 1930s, and then through a delegate model of representative democracy, where the elected representative acts in accordance with the party line and is expected by both voters and other politicians to represent the party manifesto regardless of other circumstances. From the 1990s onwards, this has slowly changed; even though the introduction of the possibility to vote for a specific party representative in 1998 has not led to the 'Americanization' of political campaigning that was feared, it is still an interesting sign of a shift from the *delegate model* to the so-called *representative model*, within which parliament is expected to be a cross-section of the population in terms of gender, class, religion, race, age and so on (Philips 1995). Equal representation, then, can mean two things: to have the *equal* opportunity to vote for a representative, or to have representatives of an *equal* (or proportional) number.

Both these versions fit a liberal subjectivity and both can serve as a depoliticizing praxis, that is, a practice where the dimension of agonism between collectives disappears, although in different manners. The central question for both is how the relation between opinion and subject position is defined.

'Can a white man represent anyone other than white men?', a rhetoric question that is often asked when representation is questioned from a feminist perspective. Even though his party adheres to feminism and anti-racism, his credibility may be questioned in relation to different aspects, for example, in relation to how many other white men are found in ruling positions within the party. The delegate model, where anyone—regardless of subject position—can and ought to represent nothing but the party line, has, of course, historically been prone to white male bias and has served as a depoliticization of normative subject positions. Feminists, activists and scholars have for a very long time challenged the idea that such a version of representation of values is possible, due to the power relations that permeate society and constitute us as subjects (Squires 1999).

One response to this assumed neutral political subject was (implicitly and explicitly) inspired by standpoint feminism. The introduction of a standpoint power analysis problematizes the idea of a possible 'pure' or 'just' representation detached from individual experience and subject formation. In relation to representative democracy, this critical move encourages the representative model, based on the necessity of the presence of different subject positions among rulers for a 'correct' representation of a population. From this perspective, parliament cannot consist only of men, even if they have different opinions and political positioning. The ideal of the standpoint version of representative democracy, we suppose, would be a numerical mirroring of all subject positions in a given population. Also, this numerical mirroring (form) has priority over opinion or values (content), since it is implicit in standpoint representation that opinions and values are already an effect of a specific subject position. In other words, 'form' will automatically give rise to a changed 'content', since the representative model guarantees that different experiences are present and these experiences will, for epistemological reasons, mirror the opinions and values of those represented (cf. Jónasdóttir 1991).

Even though standpoint feminism grew out of a critique of positivism, and hence differs from liberalism's belief in rational and objective subjects by emphasizing the importance of subjectivity in both research and politics, we will show that the identity politics to which standpoint feminism gave rise has also influenced a new version of the representative model. These two different 'standpoints' on representation and the political subject—the liberal subject who stands 'above' bodily representations and experiences (cf. Åse 1997) and the feminist standpoint subject who stresses the need for including social and bodily experiences—are frequently blurred.

We want to understand how standpoint representation has become part of a late modern liberal democracy, where the problematizing of classic liberal representation has, to a certain extent, been successful, but has not moved outside the limits of liberal democracy. Even though male bias has been questioned, it has been replaced with a multiplied identity-based representation that runs the risk of enforcing moralistic and essentialized identities. However, standpoint-inspired representation is not the only cause of this development; it also works in relation to other individualizing processes, and we would now like to focus on the use of human rights discourses in relation to equality claims. Feminist research has considered how discourses on civil rights politics both open up and limit political arenas and societal change for women and other marginalized groups (Brown 1995; Scott 1996; Spivak 2005). The simultaneous possibilities and limits of rights, which historian Joan Scott has traced back to the French Revolution, is an effect of a political paradox:

> Feminism was a protest against women's political exclusion; its goal was to eliminate 'sexual difference' in politics, but it had to make its claims on behalf of 'women' (who were discursively produced through 'sexual difference'). To the extent that it acted for 'women', feminism produced the 'sexual difference' it sought to eliminate. This paradox—the need both to accept *and* to refuse 'sexual difference'—was the constitutive condition of feminism as a political movement throughout its long history. (Scott 1996: 3–4)

Within liberal democracies, rights are presented and treated as ahistorical and natural, with universal claims that depoliticize certain local particularities and politicize others. This institutionalizes a complex codependency between normative subjectivities and those that are marginalized and/or discriminated against, where the latter need to make themselves comprehensible and heard through the discourse of rights. However, by not defining this need as inherited in each individual, but rather seeing it as a consequence of a specific political organization, an analysis of how rights discourses have formed and influenced social movements and claims for emancipation is possible (see also Scott 1996: 2).

The genealogy of rights discourses, feminist or otherwise, is intimately linked to the liberal and modern subject—constituted by assumed natural identities (i.e. apolitical and pre-social) with autonomous and rational desires. It is this subject who can both harbour and make use of 'equal rights'. Still, rights discourses have been, and still are, employed by many different groups and in many different kinds of political context, not all directly related to traditional liberal universalism. It is because of this complexity that Brown asks: 'What are the consequences of installing politicized identity in the universal discourse of liberal jurisprudence? And what does it mean to use a discourse of generic personhood—the discourse of rights—against the privileges that such discourse has traditionally secured?' (Brown 1995: 97).

Feminist politics, then, can be seen as recurring efforts to adjust to, use or transform this liberal paradox within which political equality can only be obtained through essentialized and depoliticized differences. In the 1980s, standpoint feminism was one such effort; based on a collective understanding of identity, the argument was that your experience of subordination makes you better equipped both to analyse the power processes at play and to challenge them (Harding 1986; Hill Collins 1990). It is important here to acknowledge the emphasis on group identity, that political analysis as well as political struggle was understood in collective terms. We interpret standpoint feminism as a form of identity politics, but where identity was initially understood more in collective terms than as an individual project, with less emphasis on inclusion and more emphasis on separatism.

Today, standpoint feminism has returned, but in a very different political landscape than that of the 1970s and 1980s. What happens when the ontological claim to experience, as made by standpoint feminism, meets neoliberal restructurings and redefinitions of politics? We believe an answer to that question can be found in the Swedish feminist debate of the 2010s when the concept of 'identity politics' had an unexpected renaissance (unexpected for us, as poststructuralist feminists) as classic standpoint feminist claims to experience became mixed with claims to individual rights and inclusion. Before presenting and analysing these debates, however, we need to provide a broader context, mainly concerning the relation between *representation* and *feminism* in Swedish politics.

Rights Politics, the Swedish Case: Creating the Liberal Subject

In one way, the representative model has always existed alongside the delegate model in the Swedish context. It is more a question of which model is emphasized and, most importantly, why it is emphasized and what the implications are for the political context. There is, of course,

4 Equality and Depoliticization 69

no clear shift from emphasizing one to emphasizing the other, and there are many intertwined events and organizations involved. If all these were put together, however, we believe that the latest shift can be seen to have begun during the 1990s when the question of women's representation in parliament once again came onto the agenda because of a sudden drop in the number of female MPs, the first drop since the 1920s. This led to the establishment of a 'secret' network, the Support Stockings (*Stödstrumporna*), a group of women, mainly academics and journalists, who put pressure on the political establishment, using the slogan 'Half the power and full salary!' and threatening to form a new political party (Eduards 2002). Even though most feminists knew, of course, that power is more complex than equal representation in parliament, for the Support Stockings, the demand 'half the power' meant, quite literally, half of the seats in parliament. Their claim forced the other parties to put gender-based equal representation on their agendas as well, leading to a parliament where all party leaders officially claimed to be feminists. In the following election, the proportion of women in the Swedish parliament broke the international record (43 %).

These events coincided with the consolidation of new perspectives within feminist research and activism, where women as a homogeneous category, and also to some extent the political establishment, were challenged by an academically inspired poststructuralist queer and postcolonial critique. This destabilization of categories shifted the focus away from the representation of 'women' as the sole feminist aim and opened up a critique of the identity-based representation model. However, this destabilization became entangled in ongoing identity formations with other needs and aims than a poststructuralist critique of liberal subjectivities. It is, we believe, at this point that the standpoint version of identity-based representation begins to fuse with a liberal discourse of inclusion and emancipation; a liberal discourse which had by then reached the so-called postpolitical era, where bipartisanship was preferred and argued for as the only way to overcome differences and avoid political chaos (see Mouffe 2005; Rancière 2004; Zizek 1999).

The formation of an actual feminist party (*Feministiskt Initiativ*) in 2005 followed the postpolitical logic almost to its extreme: The party presented itself as transgressing the traditional left–right coalitions by claiming to be neither socialist nor liberal, which would guarantee a more flexible agenda that focused on women's rights. To legitimately claim that the party represented *all* women, the appointed spokeswomen, individually and explicitly, each represented one group of women (working class, non-white, lesbians, etc.). The aim was to combine form and content, yet legitimacy was sought by emphasizing form.

Although feminist academics during the second half of the 1990s and onwards challenged the demands of women's representation as a priority in itself, leading feminist activists and writers began to present feminism as a fight for 'being yourself' by claiming 'your right to be included'—at first mainly in relation to gender expression and sexuality and later on also including race.

Here, we want to present three examples of such discussions on representation, inclusion and identity politics in contemporary Sweden: (1) identity politics in the media debate, (2) identity politics when articulating party political claims and (3) institutionalizing identity politics. The examples are taken from three key sectors of society: the public media, party politics and government policies, providing us with three case studies from each sector. They do, of course, overlap; for example, politicians take part in media debates as well as in regulating state institutions and policies, and activists can be found in both parties and the media debate, as well as sometimes influencing policies. We therefore see this rather as a slice of cake, showing us three layers that influence each other and cannot be completely separated but that nevertheless represent different parts of the discourse of feminism. As we will show, the different layers are surprisingly similar, each making use of the others in one way or another, where the media debate very much resembles the Fi party programme at the same time as the party programme makes use of state-regulated policies on gender discrimination.

Identity Politics in the Media Debate

If feminism, as well as postcolonial and queer critique, was seen as 'anti-identity' 15 years ago in most public debates, it is now becoming increasingly linked to an explicit identity politics. Those feminists who express concern about this development (see, e.g. Linderborg 2014; Björk 2014; Westerstrand 2015) are met with quite harsh resistance from other feminists, who insinuate that their whiteness, socialist backgrounds and/or university degrees blind them to the fact that identity politics is the new, and necessary, politics of the left. This new identity politics is commonly referred to as an intersectional feminism that does not exclude anyone and feminism, in this context, is seen as a given example of identity politics, as is anti-racism or queer activism. Here is an example from the feminist journalist Judith Kiros, in her answer to the feminist and socialist writers Åsa Linderborg and Nina Björk: 'Like feminism, other analyses or organizational methods based on identity politics are tools to make oppression and exploitation comprehensible. And just as with feminism, the goal can be practical (representation) or visionary' (Kiros 2014; our translation).

This debate has been taking place in two of Sweden's leading newspapers (*Aftonbladet* and *Dagens Nyheter*) and this setting is not without its own complications, which is not possible to address in this chapter. What we want to focus on in this quote is how representation is explicitly mentioned as the practical goal, while the visionary is less distinct. This is, of course, not unusual: The visionary is always difficult to name. However, as we will also see in relation to Fi's party programme, the critique is directed towards a structure (e.g. sexism or racism), but when forced to give examples of how to 'dissolve a system that justifies assaults and exploitation' (Kiros 2014; our translation), the example given is the practice of criticizing norms (in this case, Kiros brings up the so-called cis-norm), which in itself does not carry any ontological definitions of either gender or norm. The assumption is that it is possible to be critical of 'cis' (conformed gender identity) from a trans perspective because the trans position itself stands free of this norm: 'To criticize the cisnorm (that everyone should identify with the gender they were allotted at birth) opens up space for an understanding of gender oppression and widens the feminist analysis. This creates space for more bodies and expressions' (Kiros 2014; our translation).

In the end, the vision is of a multitude of possibilities, where the individual is supposed to be able to choose to 'be who they want to be' without any norms dictating this want. The definition of agency is reduced to the notion of a liberal subjectivity that is able to autonomously (re)create itself when free of all oppression. In this case, a trans-identity is also, somewhat paradoxically, assumed to already exist *notwithstanding* gendered norms even though the vision is not yet realized (while cis-identities are all effects of the norm). A poststructuralist definition (as well as some structuralist definition) would rather assume that trans-identity is a side effect of the same patriarchal and heterosexual structures as the cis-norm and therefore a critique of the norm would not be seen as in itself enough to either change or explain gender oppression. The identity-based approach hence runs the risk of individualizing trans-identity and moralizing cis-identity (rather than politicizing both), but it also turns feminism into a struggle for classic liberal emancipation, where again, equal representation, human rights and freedom of individual expression are the visionary goals.

The implicit argument for this identity politics is standpoint feminism, even though that concept is not overtly used. It is the idea of pure knowledge, untouched by capital, liberalism or intellectual knowledge, that is proclaimed ideal. Here is an example from the editors of the popular feminist monthly magazine *Bang*, in an article that claims to take a neutral position concerning the above-mentioned media debate on identity rights and feminism:

> From a privileged position it is unreasonable to self-reliantly make claims about being able to interpret society and what is needed. It is generally those groups that have themselves been met by oppression that can best identify needs and work for change. This pattern is completely unrelated to who has the most university credits or is able to communicate most dispassionately in the media-scape. This pattern only follows the material logic on which our society is built. (Echeverría and Palmström 2014; our translation)

The similarities to classic standpoint feminism, and also some Marxist versions, are quite evident here, giving credibility only to those who have 'true experience' and disqualifying any other position of argumentation. The same can be seen in other feminist debates and articles in Sweden (e.g. Martinsson and de los Reyes 2015; Ramnehill 2014).

Identity Politics When Articulating Party-Political Claims

The Fi party platform[3] (Fi 2013) is presented as a holistic approach to politics in relation to all aspects of human relations and society, an approach which the platform calls 'feminist politics'. The main goal of this politics is defined as 'the building of a society that generates space for all humans to develop their full potential, in an equal co-relation with others, regardless of gender, gender identity, age, functionality, sexuality, religious belief, skin colour, ethnicity or citizenship' (Fi 2013: 3).

The main way to achieve this goal is anti-discrimination laws, which is a recurring feature in all areas of political interest in the platform. Likewise, great stress is given to the importance of 'observing human rights' to enable the political vision of an equal and non-discriminatory society.[4] At the same time, inequalities based on gender, sexuality and ethnicity are defined as structural, and the platform stresses the importance of making sexist and racist structures visible. Undoubtedly, the platform provides a structuralist definition of discrimination and inequalities. Yet there is a gap between this initial position (where 'patriarchy', 'heteronormativity' and 'racist structures' are common terms) and the political reforms defined as necessary to change these structures.

Interestingly, there are no corrective measures suggested in relation to labour rights or conditions; rather, those reforms are based on extended surveys, action plans, visibility, rehabilitation and knowledge production. Perhaps corrective measures are seen as the responsibility of unions rather than political parties. Fi presents itself as a radical party that works for economic redistribution, yet there are no examples of how redistribution itself will take place; perhaps there is a presumption that it will happen

---

[3] In this chapter, we are only analysing Fi's party platform as an example of feminist party politics. We believe that a broader analysis, including different sets of material, could have given a more complex picture of their political claims, and we would like to stress that we use the party platform as one of several examples of a trend in feminist politics.

[4] For example, 'The Feminist Initiative has a vision of a society where everyone can travel well through life. This requires that society in all aspects observes human rights and secures the right to health, work, home, education, social care, and safety. […] Human rights will apply to all humans residing in Sweden. People without documents and people applying for asylum will have the same rights as citizens or as people with a permanent residence permit' (Fi 2013: 4).

automatically when discrimination has ended and therefore it does not have to be forced or sanctioned? If so, it makes sense that force, sanctions and corrective measures are instead found within the section on equal treatment and anti-discrimination (Section C.2). The structural position is evident from the beginning, where it is stated that '[s]exism [*könsmaktsordningen*], racism, inaccessibility, and other structures of power generate conditions that lead to workplace discrimination' (Fi 2013: 9). To solve this problem, the platform suggests that it is necessary to focus on 'those who discriminate' (Fi 2013: 9) by both punishing them and preventing them from discriminating. Action plans for gender equality, equal treatment and so on are part of the strategy too, but here they are enforced by a mandatory anti-discriminatory clause in all public procurements, making the employer liable if workplace discrimination is not acted upon, higher compensation in court cases, sanctions directed towards companies and a so-called code of conduct giving 'a more detailed description of how employers should act in accordance with the laws on anti-discrimination' (Fi 2013: 9).

Thus, the proposed measures suggest that a structural problem should mainly be handled by punishing those who discriminate and forcing them to act in accordance with a code of conduct. The assumption is that structural discrimination based on gender, race, functionality and so on will disappear through the correction and punishment of individuals. Since there is no other definition of *what* causes discrimination, discrimination is more or less individualized and the solution is seen as enforced reforms on equal treatment, based on checklist procedures with moralist sanctions.

Overall, the main discourse within the party platform is based on human rights and identity politics, where human rights are seen as able to secure an equal relationship between already-constituted identity positions. This tendency is most pronounced in the sections concerning gender identity and sexuality, where sexual freedom and the right to define one's own gender identity are prominent (Sections E2, F1, and all through the recurring stress on 'LGBTQ-education'). Since there is no ontological definition of gender or sexuality, it is possible for the platform to suggest reforms based on gender as sometimes pre-discursive (as in reforms concerning transsexualism) and sometimes implicitly 'socially constructed' (as in reforms concerning intersexualism). This generates a mishmash of ontological assumptions, mostly following an elusive assumption of the individual right to freedom of choice. It is such recurring arbitrary and non-explicit ontologies that, in relation to the dominance of reactive and corrective legal reforms (such as mandatory codes of conduct), could lead to a moralist politics where neither political adversaries nor supporters can be sure about where the party stands or, most importantly, why it stands there. As already suggested in the media debate, such inconsistencies can create insecurity and nervousness, especially since 'wrongful behaviour' (including pointing out inconsistencies) is punished, but not explained.

The poststructuralist and postcolonial critique of the homogeneous white, middle-class, heterosexual woman, which was intended to point out the limits and paradoxes of identity-based politics, has here been superseded and instead we see a new form of identity politics coming in through 'the back door', where representation in relation to bodily experience is put forward as one of the most important feminist claims, in combination with a splitting of these experiences into a multitude of identities. It is hence possible to see how a liberal subjectivity has (re-)entered the political agenda and been allowed to (re-)write it, along with the poststructuralist definitions of power and subject.

How was this 'mixing up' of power definitions and subject ontologies enabled? We believe that the substitution of a public discourse of equality with a public discourse of rights has been one important part of this process. Therefore, we now turn to Swedish gender-equality policies, where NPM has long been implemented, and hence seems to foretell the destiny of other claims to equality and representation.

Institutionalizing Identity Politics: Mainstreaming Gender Equality

The Swedish concept of 'gender equality' (*jämställdhet*) carries the same connotations as the French *parité* and implies an assertion that gendered differences are essential and must be preserved, while the *rights* of women should be made equal to men's. Joan Scott and Wendy Brown have already pointed out the inherent paradox in this specific case, but for some reason, Swedish feminist researchers have never made the obvious parallel with the Swedish concept—a concept willingly chosen in the late 1960s as a *better* alternative than 'equality' (*jämlikhet*), because as the leading feminist debater Eva Moberg famously argued: 'women and men are as different as blueberries and lingonberries and they shall not be equal as in the same, but equally positioned next to each other, equivalent' (Moberg 1961). This fear of erasing gendered differences is still explicit in gender equality policies, for example, in this quote from a national report on gender equality in schools: 'It is hence not the case that boys should be made into girls and girls should be made into boys' (SOU 2010:83, Rapport XI; Delegation for gender equality in school: 61).

This preservation of gendered differences is today also connected to an idea of freedom of choice and even to the preservation of democracy:

[S]ince difference constitutes the foundation, and is an asset, for a democratic school, it is perhaps not advisable that boys and girls become more alike. The main problem is rather that girls and boys are met and valued in different ways in school, which leads to unequal terms. (SOU 2010: 83, Rapport XI Delegation for gender equality in school: 53)

An earlier study of Swedish gender equality policy (Rönnblom 2011) shows that ambitions to include some kind of power analysis in public policy on gender equality seem to stay at a rhetorical level, not reaching the implementation of policy measures. While, in a national Swedish policy document of 2005, gender equality is represented as a problem related to men's domination and women's subordination, and as a problem that concerns the unequal distribution of power between men and women ten years later, the problem that is to be solved through gender mainstreaming is a lack of administrative routines. The main results show that gender equality is transformed into administration and into different forms of administrative techniques. Prominent forms of governing include different forms of auditing, through checklists, evaluations and methodological tools for change. In addition, it is also possible to discern a gap between how the problem of gender equality is represented in overall policy goals and when the policy is to be implemented. A representation of the problem as related to issues of gendered power relations is transformed into a representation of the problem that fits the rules of auditing.

From this point of view, it is not surprising that gender equality politics is so easily assimilated into neoliberal discourse and regulations. Political issues have been replaced by moralism, and issues that started off as collective demands have been reduced to an individual responsibility to make oneself employable and be clear about which anti-discrimination category is relevant to your specific identity.[5] It is hence to these kinds of policy regulations that the Feminist Party turns, along with most other parties in Sweden (including the Left Party), when arguing for equal representation and anti-discrimination measures as a means to end not only the exclusion of women and minorities but also patriarchy and structural racism.

Through these three empirical 'layers', our intention has been to illustrate how neoliberal governing processes permeate politics in different spheres, from public debate to feminist party politics to institutionalized national policy; although there are exceptions and some dissident voices, the depoliticizing processes create few opportunities for articulating claims beyond this frame of depoliticized reactionary foundationalism. In agreement with Brown, we thus believe it possible to claim that the recent (re)turn to identity politics in Sweden on both the left and the right sides of the (non-acknowledged) spectrum is part of a general Western reaction to the postpolitical state, where political activism has been redefined as a struggle for inclusion in liberal democracy and human rights. Discursive alternatives are limited by both radical and liberal forces and delegitimized as anti-human rights and hence discarded as part of a patriarchal and/or racist agenda. In the end, this is not as surprising as it may look:

> As much a symptom of a certain powerlessness as a redress of it, identity politics may also be read as a reaction to postmodernity's cross-cultural meldings and appropriations, as well as its boundless commodification of

---

[5] The current official grounds for discrimination are 'gender', 'ethnicity', 'gender identity or gender expression', 'religion or other belief', 'sexuality', 'disability' and 'age'.

cultural practices and icons. Identity politics emerges partly as a reaction, in other words, to an ensemble of distinctly postmodern assaults upon the integrity of modernist communities producing collective identity. (Brown 1995: 35)

It is in the light of this development that human rights discourses and anti-discrimination policies seem to fill a never-ending soothing, but self-affirmative, satisfaction for those who can prove an injured identity.

Feminism as Equal Rights, Representation as Mirroring, Inclusion as Acceptance of the Forms of Rule

To accept that feminist demands are articulated in terms of human rights and anti-discrimination—which sadly is seen as one of the most radical versions of what the concept of equality implies today—ironically runs the risk of foreclosing differences (gendered and others) and their connections to bodies that matter (the Butlerian connotation is intended). A redefinition *and* redistribution of power are equally important, and in that process, there is neither a liberal win-win solution nor room for the preservation of (some) identities: 'For the political making of a feminist future that does not reproach the history on which it is borne, we may need to loosen our attachments to subjectivity, identity, and morality and to redress our underdeveloped taste for political argument' (Brown 1995: 51).

In accordance with this position, we would like to point to the feminist need to recognize neoliberal rationalities of government, and to understand how these are related to processes of depoliticization. Neoliberal forms of government involve the translation of marketized processes, relationships and values into arenas previously considered social and/or political, rather than economic. They also involve 'responsibilization', that is, the discursive strategy of locating responsibility for problems and their solutions in individuals and institutions at some distance from the state. In this way, technologies of the self are involved in governing the subject (see also Brown 2015). Neoliberal rationalities of government also include technologies of government like the so-called audit culture, in which processes and practices need to be arranged in an auditable way. As shown by Spivak in this volume, this form of audit culture is also present within human development analysis: only including what can be measured in a specific way, what can be auditable, leaving out the importance of education. Within gender equality policies in Sweden, political demands are turned into administrative or bureaucratic techniques, depoliticizing gender by turning gender-equality policies into checklists and tool kits in order to fit the policy to the prevailing systems of audit and quality assessments (Rönnblom 2011). Among feminist activists, the reaction to such depoliticizing moves seems to be a retreat to a stable and 'safe' identity that is always 'right' and whose political activity consists of infinite demands for ever-more-specific recognitions and inclusions into this very audit system, based on moralist codes of conduct. These are processes of individualization and depoliticization that could be regarded as a global phenomenon, although one that takes specific and situated forms in different contexts. As feminist activists make claims that fit neatly into a liberal rights discourse, even the activist-subject is turned into a self-regulating subject managing its own success or failure—only here success and failure are based on identity, and hence, different identities are cast into a struggle against each other, where all sides claim to have the correct experience to support their legitimacy. The depoliticized production of rights claims does not generate challenges to the prevailing political order; rather, there is a risk of re-producing of this order, where right-wing identity politics is mobilized as a response to left-wing identity politics, and vice versa.

Coming back to Chantal Mouffe's distinction between politics and the political, we therefore believe that the politics of equality needs the *political* in order to work as a potential tool for change and that this in turn demands new forms of feminist methodological approaches. To enable this, claims of equality need a strong positioning in an ontological politics, as defined by the political philosopher Annemarie Mol. She points to a position on reality as produced in ongoing processes. Or, in her own words from a 1999 article:

> Ontological politics is a composite term. It talks of ontology—which in standard philosophical parlance defines what belongs to the real, the conditions of possibility we live with. If the term 'ontology' is combined with

that of 'politics' then this suggests that the conditions of possibility are not given. That reality does not precede the mundane practices in which we interact with it, but is rather shaped within these practices. So the term politics works to underline this activity mode, this process of shaping, and the fact that its character is both opened and contested. (Mol 1999: 74)

To demand 'one's rights' has, ever since the dawn of liberalism, been a demand to be included in the universal. The paradoxes this creates for those deemed 'particular' have been pointed out by numerous poststructuralist feminist theorists. It also implies a claim to be part of a normative formation (legal or social). For example, claiming the right to vote has hitherto implied a desire to be a recognized part of a democratic nation-state and being able to take part in that specific political formation. Historically, this claim has been difficult to separate from nationalism (even though it may not be a necessary condition). Our point is that any claim to inclusion must be carefully thought through—achieving the right to vote may be important enough to be worth having to overlook (other) normative claims that come with it. However, this does not mean that 'achieving the right to vote' overrules the normative connotations that such a right implies; these connotations remain the same and are now also the responsibility of the newly included voter.

Liberalism as that 'which we cannot not want' (Spivak 1993: 45–6) is hence a difficult feminist insight that must be taken seriously and calls for careful consideration of *what* we are claiming and *why*. Among other things, it calls for an articulated agenda that can identify the universalities we need alongside a definition of power and subjectivity that can account for this need. In other words, it calls for a very cautious approach to claims for inclusion. For this reason, content (political demands) must always be prioritized over form (as in the representative model)—not because content will automatically manage to change the form so that it becomes more representative of a population's different subject positions, but because the content can be changed when and if it turns out that it does not lead to a less hierarchical relation (economic as well as symbolic) between these subject positions. While form can be regulated to become an almost perfect reflection of the population, it is a grave mistake to assume that this in itself will change the content. Form cannot

4 Equality and Depoliticization

be trusted to change anything by itself. This does not mean that form is unimportant—or that it should not be regulated. On the contrary, political demands should always be wary of a homogeneous form since it quite often implies an unfair distribution of power in the very structure of society, yet it is the content that needs to change to achieve a better form—not just the form itself.

Perhaps this is a complicated way to explain how we interpret Wendy Brown's call for a political agenda that asks not who we *are* but what we *want* (Brown 2005).[6] In order to move from moralism to the political, we need to rely on both an awareness of our own dependency on liberalism and the formulation of alternatives that make ontological political claims. It is only such claims that can reveal the implicit claims made by liberalism, and only in this way can a political option become available.

To clarify, to claim one's rights as 'female', 'gay', 'black', 'trans' is not an ontological political claim. It may be many other things, and indeed it may be absolutely necessary in certain contexts for survival. But it is not political in Mouffe's sense of the word. Because the right that we claim ('right to marry', 'right to work', 'right to equal pay', 'right to be part of Swedish feminism') is not given as an option, it presents itself as natural, apolitical and hence impossible to criticize. Be careful what you wish for—once you have been given your right (given, of course, by a righteous universal that expects gratitude in return), you will find yourself not only married, at work, and part of a capitalist, nationalist system, but also part of a system that only recognizes identity-based rights claims, since anything else would be incomprehensible, and most likely, deemed undemocratic. What then?

Therefore, whenever someone articulates the right to be included, this articulation must be driven by something other than moralism; it is not a good enough argument to claim that it is universally *wrong* to exclude. Moralism has the tendency to use guilt rather than politics to change people, but this is a change that can only consist of confession

---

[6] 'Surrendering epistemological foundations means giving up the ground of specifically moral claims against domination—especially the avenging of strength through moral critique of it—and moving instead into the domain of the sheerly political: 'wars of position' and amoral contests about the just and the good in which truth is always grasped as coterminous with power, as always already power, as the voice of power' (Brown 1995: 45).

and redemption—not changed subject positions. Guilt produces fear. And fear leads to a longing for safety, a safe and righteous identity based on who you *are*; this goes for everyone, regardless of who you are, and right now, in present-day Europe, this is not a road we want to walk down, again. Instead, we see the need for articulations that are driven by political arguments, arguments tied to an idea of what is needed in order to create what we mean to be an equal society.

References

Åse, C. (1997). Individ utan innehåll. *Statsvetenskaplig tidskrift, 96*(2), 138–152.
Björk, N. (2014). Ingen makt är större än den ekonomiska makten. *Dagens Nyheter*, 12 November.
Brown, W. (1995). *States of injury: Power and freedom in late modernity*. Princeton: Princeton University Press.
Brown, W. (2005). *Edgework: Critical essays on knowledge and politics*. Princeton: Princeton University Press.
Brown, W. (2015). *Undoing the demos: Neoliberalism's stealth revolution*. New York: Zone Books.
Echeverría Quezada, M., & Palmström, J. (2014). Drama i repris. *Bang, 4*.
Edenheim, S., & Rönnblom, M. (2012). Tracking down politics and power in neo-liberal society. *Nora – Nordic Journal of Feminist and Gender Research*, Special issue "Neo-liberalism and Tolerance – Scrutinizing Politics and State Regulations", *20*(4), 227–229.
Eduards, M. (2002). *Förbjuden handling: Om kvinnors organisering och feministisk teori*. Liber ekonomi.
Feministisk initiativ. (2013). *För en feministisk politik*. FI Party Platform.
Harding, S. (1986). *The science question in feminism*. Milton Keynes: Open University Press.
Hill Collins, P. (1990). *Black feminist thought: Knowledge, consciousness and the politics of empowerment*. Hyman.
Jónasdóttir, A. G. (1991). *Love, power and political interests: Towards a theory of patriarchy in contemporary western societies*. Göteborg: Studies in Politics.
Kiros, J. (2014). Identitetspolitk och vänterpolitik är inte antipoler. *Dagens Nyheter*, 10 November.

Linderborg, Å. (2014). Det ska fan vara politiskt korrekt. *Aftonbladet*, 7 November.

Lister, R., Williams, F., Anttonen, A., Bussemaker, J., Gerhard, U., Heinen, J., et al. (2007). Gendering citizenship in Western Europe: New challenges for citizenship research in a cross-national context. Bristol: Polity Press.

Manin, B. (2002). *The principles of representative government*. Cambridge: Cambridge University Press.

Martinsson, L., & de los Reyes, P. (2015). Största problemet är diskriminerande strukturer. *Feministiskt perspektiv*, 28 February.

Moberg, E. (1961). Kvinnans villkorliga frigivning. *Unga Liberaler: Nio inlägg i idédebatten*. Stockholm: Bonnier.

Mol, A. M. (1999). Ontological politics: A word and some questions. In J. Law & J. Hassard (Eds.), *Actor network theory and after* (pp. 74–89). Oxford and Malden, MA: Blackwell Publishers/The Sociological Review.

Mouffe, C. (2005). *On the political*. New York: Routledge.

Mouffe, C. (2013). *Agonistics: Thinking the world politically*. London: Verso.

Philips, A. (1993). *Engendering democracy*. Pennsylvania: Pennsylvania State University Press.

Philips, A. (1995). *The politics of presence*. Gloucestershire: Clarendon Press.

Rancière, J. (2004). Introducing disagreement. *Angelaki: Journal of the Theoretical Humanities, 9*(3), 3–9.

Ramnehill, M. (2014). Som en plusmeny, *Bang* (4).

Rönnblom, M. (2011). Vad är problemet? Konstruktioner av jämställdhet i svensk politik. *Tidskrift för genusvetenskap* (2–3), 35–55.

Scott, J. W. (1996). *Only paradoxes to offer: French feminists and the rights of man*. Cambridge, MA: Harvard University Press.

SOU 2010: 83. (2010). *Rapport XI från Delegationen för jämställdhet i skolan* (Delegation for gender equality in schools). Stockholm.

Spivak, G. C. (1993). *Outside in the teaching machine*. New York: Routledge.

Spivak, G. C. (2005). Use and abuse of human rights. *Boundary 2, 32*(1), 131–189.

Squires, J. (1999). *Gender in political theory*. Cambridge: Polity Press.

Westerstrand, J. (2015). Egofokus försvårar universitetsstudier. *Dagens Nyheter*, 10 February.

Zizek, S. (1999). *The ticklish subject: The absent centre of political ontology*. London: Verso.

Part II

Gendered Participation in Representative Democracies– Working from Below and/or Above?

5

The Costs and Benefits of Descriptive Representation: Women's Quotas, Variations in State Feminism and the Fact of Reasonable Pluralism

Cathrine Holst

Should women represent women, and blacks represent blacks? Are the disabled better represented by people that are themselves disabled, and farmers better represented by other farmers? Should Buddhists represent Buddhists, and Brits represent Brits? What about sexual minorities, or the working class? Are we better represented by those who are similar to us? Descriptive representation is hotly contested. Conservatives and right-wing liberals have traditionally opposed it, while left-wing political parties and social movements often regard quotas for marginalized groups as decisive progressive measures in struggles for democracy and justice.

In scholarly terms, descriptive representation is the idea that representatives resemble or "stand for" the represented (Mansbridge 1999, 2001,

---

C. Holst (✉)
Arena Centre for European Studies, University of Oslo, Sognsveien 68, 0855 Oslo, Norway

2005; Pitkin 1967/1972): "representatives are in their own person and lives" supposed to be "in some sense typical of the larger class of persons whom they represent" (Mansbridge 1999: 629). Which resembling characteristics are singled out as "typical" can vary a lot. A distinction is often made between functional representation, which focuses on the occupational correspondence between representatives and represented, and social representation, which concerns social characteristics such as race, ethnicity, class and gender (Norris and Franklin 1997). The chapter concentrates on the latter, and on the key example of gender, or more specifically, on the arguments for and against letting women represent women. Women's descriptive representation and quotas for women, in parliaments and other political bodies, but also on other institutional arenas,[1] have been firmly on the feminist agenda for decades, the argumentative exchanges, also among feminists themselves, have been immense, and general discussions of descriptive representation and demands for quotas for other groups (ethnic or sexual minorities, people with disabilities, etc.) have them as a central frame of reference.

However, a problem with much of the descriptive representation controversy so far has been its notorious circling around general pro and con arguments, and so its relative disregard for how the descriptive representation calculus will "vary greatly by context", to quote Jane Mansbridge's (Mansbridge 1999: 652) seminal article on the topic. Accordingly, the proper answer to whether women should represent women, black should represent blacks and so on is not "yes" or "no" ("a dichotomous approach"), as descriptive representation should be supported on "contingent" grounds, in "historical contexts" in which the benefits exceed the costs, and dismissed in contexts in which it is the other way around (Mansbridge 1999: 638).

Different contextual factors may be relevant. The following will concentrate on a particular institutional setting, namely a context in which so-called "state feminist machineries" are in place (Krizsan et al. 2012; Lovenduski 2005a; Stetson and Mazur 1995). It was the Scandinavian political scientist Helga Hernes (Hernes 1987: 153) who first introduced

---

[1] For discussions of gender quotas in corporate boards, see, for example, Engelstad and Teigen (2012).

the term "state feminism" in 1987 to describe how feminism might be promoted "from above in the form of gender equality and social policies" (see also Holst 2010: 278–308). Hernes' thesis was that feminist interests had been institutionalized on state level during the 1970s and 1980s in Scandinavia: The Scandinavian welfare states had gradually developed distinctively feminist characteristics (Hernes and Skjeie 1997: 373). Along with women's entry in the welfare state professions and "the feminization from below among women activists in political and cultural activities", state feminism had thus contributed to the development of relatively "women-friendly" societies in Scandinavia (Hernes 1987: 153).

Hence, originally, state feminism referred to a broader vision of feminist social democracy. Today, when "state feminism" is analysed and compared, the focus is primarily on the characteristics and role of women-friendly bureaucratic structures or "femocracy" (see, e.g. Lovenduski 2005a, b; Stetson and Mazur 1995). State feminist institutions show an organizational variety similar to what we know from other policy fields (Olsen 2013; Vibert 2007): Included in the "machinery" can be governmental offices, agencies, ministries, ombudsmen, permanent or ad hoc expert advisory committees, and more or less institutionalized government–civil society partnership structures. The distinguishing feature is the substantive focus and normative aims. Whereas, say, monetary regulation machineries are set up to ensure goals such as low inflation and fiscal stability, the overall task of femocracies are to develop, improve on and implement legislation and policies to facilitate gender equality, or even women's empowerment (Walby 2011).

The question is how the calculus of descriptive representation fares in a context where such machineries are in place. One hypothesis could be that descriptive representation is *less* needed and more difficult to defend in a state feminist setting. Defenders of descriptive representation argue typically that it triggers substantive representation, meaning a better representation of women's interests: "The theory of the politics of presence suggests that female politicians are best equipped to represent the interests of women; thus, the theory predicts a link between descriptive and substantive representation" (Wängnerud 2009: 52; see also Phillips 1995). Hence, state feminism and descriptive representation can be thought of, and is often thought of (Lovenduski 2005b; Wängnerud 2009: 65), as different paths towards the very same goals—gender equality, women's empowerment, the realization of women's interests and so on. If so, and we take it that state feminism succeeds and fulfils its promises effectively, or at least more effectively than descriptive representation, as argued by some commentators (e.g. Sawer 2002; Weldon 2002),[2] it would arguably be unnecessary to institutionalize descriptive representation in addition, and even un-recommendable: Descriptive representation has a set of costs—they will be listed shortly—and it is not obvious how state feminism would make all of them disappear.

However, the general anticipation could also be the opposite, namely that femocratic "feminism from above" strategies have limitations and blind spots of a kind that makes descriptive representation *more* needed, as far as descriptive representation facilitates "from below" perspectives, communication and legitimacy (see next section's list of descriptive representation pro arguments).

What is the most apt interpretation? Is descriptive representation no longer necessary or desirable if a relatively efficient femocracy is in place—or is it rather more needed under such conditions? This chapter argues that the effects of state feminism on the costs and benefits of descriptive representation are mixed, and that a considered assessment will depend decisively on the more detailed characteristics of state feminism's organization and its institutional environment, but also on the choice of normative criteria. Feminist theorists have aptly pointed out the contested character of terms such as "woman", "women's interests" and so on (see Young 1990, 1994, 2000 for instructive discussions). Arguably, this is a special case of the more general situation of normative contestation in politics and policy-making. Still, commentators tend to discuss the costs and benefits of descriptive representation as if normative evaluations were beyond disagreement. However, something is a cost or a benefit relative to what one wants to achieve, and different normative positions may approach, define and rank benefits and burdens differently. Any discussion of the merits of descriptive representation needs to take

---

[2] The point of this chapter is neither to define the threshold level of "effective state feminism" nor to argue that state feminism actually delivers "better" than descriptive representation. The question here is what happens to the calculus of descriptive representation under the condition that state feminist machineries are in place and work relatively efficiently.

this into account; it must relate to the fact of empirical "contingency" (Mansbridge), but also to the equally persuasive fact of value pluralism.

The chapter starts out with giving flesh to the pros and cons of descriptive representation as we know them from political and feminist theory discussions. The section that follows contrasts participatory, women-centred state feminism in the context of a social democratic welfare state, in accordance with Hernes' original conception, with alternative notions of state feminism—intersectional state feminism, state feminism within less ambitious welfare regimes, and state feminism disconnected from broader processes of democratization, and discusses the more detailed relationship between these variations in the institutionalization of state feminism and the pros and cons of descriptive representation. It is argued that descriptive representation, when approached from the cost side, is more recommendable in a democratized, intersectional state feminist regime than in a women-centred technocratic one. The effects of the welfare state variable on descriptive representation costs are more mixed. On the benefit side, intersectionality, a social democratic welfare state and democratization seem to deliver several of the same goods as descriptive representation, raising the question of whether descriptive representation is at all recommendable, given what we know of its costliness. In the end, there is however a set of remaining pro arguments suggesting that descriptive representation produces some exclusive benefits. The closer assessment of pros and cons will however vary with normative position. The third section explores this variation on the basis of three central normative distinctions: between equal opportunities and equality of outcome, and between aggregative and deliberative, procedural and outcome-oriented democracy. The final section sums up and highlights some implications for further analysis.

Costs and Benefits of Descriptive Representation[3]

First, what have worried critics with descriptive representation? A key problem is how quota policies can contribute to "essentialism"—*the increased essentialism argument* (see, e.g. Phillips 1995; Young 1990,

---

[3] This section relies heavily on Mansbridge (1999), but with some modifications and additions.

1994; but also Kymlicka 1993). Essentialism refers here to the idea that members of certain groups, such as women, have a common core identity; a highly misleading idea, as far as it fails to recognize cleavages cutting across groups, how women's identities and interests vary depending on, for example, class and ethnicity, but also individual variations in preferences and life projects. Essentialism is moreover accompanied, typically, by more or less subtle cultural marginalization and insufficient political representation of the substantive interests of the marginalized: A hierarchy occurs where the women on top are those who best meet the standard of how women are supposed be like and behave, and therefore get to represent what all women want.

A second worry is related to the increased risk of reduced community and trust across the groups that are the targets of descriptive representation—*the weakening of political ties argument*. It may be that descriptive representation increases group ties among, for example, women, but this will often happen at the expense of solidarity and community between women and men in broader political settings, be it a political organization such as a political party or the polity at large (Phillips 1995: 22).

A third common criticism is that descriptive representation produces political representatives that are less qualified and so less able to perform the substantive representation of interests—*the reduced competence argument* (see Pennock 1979 for a classical statement). This argument has historically been accompanied by claims about women's inferior abilities and lesser political expertise, but can also be formulated without any claims or assumptions about gendered group differences. The point then is simply how "adding any criterion"—for example, gender—"to a mix of criteria for selection will always dilute to some degree the other criteria for selection"—for example, political competence (Mansbridge 1999: 633). Descriptive representation and the concern for competence can go hand in hand, but there will also be genuine trade-off situations where the candidates "just like you", descriptively speaking, are not necessarily the ones that are most skilled and effective in pursuing your substantive interests, and so competence concerns and descriptive representation draw in opposite directions.

The fourth critical point takes up the random element in who are picked as target groups for descriptive representation and who are excluded—*the random privileging of target groups argument* (Grofman 1982: 98, see also Barry 2002; Gutmann and Thompson 1996; Pitkin 1972; Voet 1992): There are "few guidelines for selecting which social characteristics merit representation" (Morone and Marmor 1981: 437). The characteristics should be significant, of a kind that substantially shape people's experiences and interests, but still there will potentially be a long list of possible groups, where only some are picked out as actual target groups. Candidates may be left out for different reasons. Historically, there exist conventions concerning who quotas are for, and there are practical arguments for not making the list of target groups too long. The randomness of the selection process creates, however, political privileges for the selected relative to the unselected that are hard to justify, critics argue.

Finally, there is the danger that descriptive representation contributes to reduced accountability, for example, when female voters are lulled into believing that a female political representative is taking care of their interests simply because she is a woman—*the decreased accountability argument*. The phenomenon is thus a variant of blind loyalty. When it occurs, there is little chance that voters will try and hold their representatives to account, not because of a lack of opportunities or abilities, but because they do not really see the need to.

Factors in favour of letting women represent women are also a varied set. A key argument has already been anticipated, namely that descriptive representation is an easy and transparent way of operationalizing substantive representation: What female representatives want and need is regarded as a good proxy for what women generally want and need— *the substantive representation proxy argument*. The not so unreasonable assumption is that people with significant descriptive characteristics in common may have at least some overlapping experiences and interests, not least if the descriptive categorizations in question reflect key social and cultural hierarchies that are well known to contribute to the structuring of political interests and preferences along group lines (Fraser 2003; Nussbaum 1999; Phillips 1995; Walby 2011).

There will however always be a discrepancy between the concerns that are raised and the interests that are pursued by representatives meant to "stand for" a certain group, and the full range of concerns and interests among the members of this group. Some women from a group can never fully represent all women in the group even in cases of exceptional similarities in life situations and life chances (i.e. the problem of essentialism). The challenge for proponents of descriptive representation is thus how the discrepancy between descriptive and substantive representation can be reduced as much as possible. The second pro argument says that descriptive representation contributes exactly on this point, as far as social and cultural research show not only that people with significant descriptive characteristics may have overlapping experiences and interests shaping political preferences, but also that they communicate better among themselves—*the communication facilitation argument*: "The shared experience imperfectly captured by descriptive representation facilitates vertical communication between representatives and constituents" (Mansbridge 1999: 641), which in turn contributes to making descriptive representation less "imperfect" as a proxy for substantive representation. People with similar background or in similar life situations may forge bonds of trust, understand each other's concerns more intuitively and talk easier (Swain 1993; Tannen 1994; Williams 1998), and as a result of all this end up being better equipped to represent one another substantively.

A third common argument for descriptive representation is that it contributes to transforming our ideas of who political representatives and leaders are and can be (Mansbridge 1999, 2005; Swain 1993), and so to making cultural images of who can and cannot rule more inclusive and fair—*the weakening of stereotypes argument*. This pertains both to those who have been excluded from ruling historically and to those in the dominant groups: Quotas for women and similar measures can contribute to progressive changes in women's views on their own capacities and competences, but also, and no less important, to transforming men's perceptions of women's capabilities.

A fourth benefit often brought forward is that descriptive representation may make more and new groups of citizens more actively support and constructively engage with the government—*the increased de facto legitimacy argument*, since witnessing someone "just like you" participate in ruling may contribute to that you yourself feel that you are included (see Mansbridge 1999: 650, referring also to Guinier 1994; Kymlicka 1993; Minow 1991; Phillips 1995). This in turn reduces possibly costly tensions and conflicts and contributes to political stability.

The fifth and final argument—*the non-instrumental argument*—is that descriptive representation is intrinsically valuable (see, e.g. Phillips 2004; Teigen 2000; Walby 2011), and not only because of what may be positive effects (increased substantive representation, less stereotypes, etc.). That women and men participate on equal terms in politics is an independent good, and the participatory patterns resulting from quota and other policies contributing to including more women in politics and in public arenas generally are closer to democratic participatory patterns, as we would like to see them.

What happens with this list of pros and cons of descriptive representation under shifting variants of state feminism? This will be discussed in the next section, after a presentation of three key state feminism variables.

State Feminism: Women's Empowerment, Welfare State and Democratization

Helga Hernes' notion of state feminism was intertwined with an idea of a women-friendly, social democratic welfare state, responsive to and developing as a result of claims and input from civil society, not least the women's movement ("the feminization from below"). The notion is instructive also because it reminds us of how state feminism as it is often, more narrowly conceived of today—as bureaucratic structures with the aim of promoting gender equality—can vary along several dimensions.[4] First, at the time, Hernes had in mind a system centring on promoting women's opportunities: separate gender equality legislation, ombudsmen addressing gender-based discrimination, mainstreaming strategies focusing on integrating gender perspectives in public budgeting and recruitment practices, and civil society dialogue centred on providing inputs from women's organizations.

State feminism could however be less centred on gender and women's empowerment. An alternative variant is suggested by Kimberley Crenshaw's (1991) "intersectionality" approach, developed on the basis of experiences with a US society both more pluralist and stratified than the relatively

---

[4] The notions of women-centred/intersectional state feminism, state feminism with/without a welfare state and with/without democratization should be thought of in terms of Weberian ideal types. The actual empirical variation and the detailed characteristics of state feminism around the globe are different matters and not the topic of this chapter.

egalitarian, homogeneous, Scandinavian societies. Crenshaw points out how different axes of differentiation and hierarchy—gender, but also a set of other social, cultural and political structures in any given society—intersect and interact, creating both multiple systems of oppression and discrimination, and complex, multidimensional opportunity structures. This ought to have implications, Crenshaw argues, for how feminists conceptualize oppression and discrimination and formulate strategies and policies. The focus cannot be purely on gender, gender hierarchy and women's experiences and interests; measures must instead take into account the complexity of individuals' structural position: Gender is shaping people's life situations and life chances, but so are class, ethnicity, sexuality, generation and other "intersecting" dimensions. For state feminism, such an intersectional approach would not seem to imply separate gender equality legislation and separate ombudsmen for gender issues. Instead, it would mean general legislation on anti-discrimination and ombudsmen for all kinds of anti-discrimination, guidelines for public budgeting and recruitment. This would include a broader set of concerns and perspectives (not only gender perspectives) and civil society dialogue with a broad focus, assuming that a varied set of stakeholders would be relevant, shifting from one issue to the other, depending on which and whose stakes were involved (Krizsan et al. 2012; Reisel 2014).

Second, Hernes' notion of state feminism includes also the idea of a relatively ambitious social democratic welfare state, a large public sector redistributing income, providing citizens with substantial welfare benefits, and a range of health, educational and social services. One could however also think of a state feminism in the context of a substantially less ambitious "welfare regime" (cf. Esping-Andersen 1990). Hence, in the latter kind of state feminist regime, anti-discrimination legislation, anti-discrimination ombudsmen, and offices and agencies focusing on fostering and ensuring anti-discriminatory practices in all societal sectors and policy areas could more or less be in place. It would, however, be a state feminism without the infrastructure of welfare and redistributive arrangements characteristic of the Scandinavian social democracy Hernes had in a mind.

Third, Hernes is stressing the importance of democratization "from below". There is, however, also the option of a less democratized state feminism (see also Holst 2014). One could have in mind authoritarian regimes with certain state feminist and welfare state characteristics, but also more or less fully fledged liberal constitutional democracies without the social democratic ambition of deeper societal democratization and citizens' participation, described so vividly by Hernes in her outline of the Scandinavian social democratic citizenship ideal. Redistributive and welfare policies could be more or less in place in such a regime. One could also imagine the regime's "femocratic" machineries operating efficiently and on the basis of a formal democratic mandate—they would be non-majoritarian institutions coming into existence as a result of the democratic decisions of parliaments. However, apart from this, the outside "society", stakeholders, civil society and so on would have limited influence on the machineries' agenda, priorities and organization.

The question then is how variation in the institutionalization of state feminism along these three dimensions—with regard to women centredness, type of welfare regime and level of democratization—affects the above-listed costs and benefits of descriptive representation. Is it likely that a women-centred state feminism adds to the burdens of descriptive representation, or will it rather contribute to making these burdens less burdensome, and how does a women-centred state feminism fare relative to intersectional state feminism? How about state feminism with a social democratic welfare state relative to state feminism without, and a democratized state feminism relative to a more technocratic state feminism "from above"? When does the institutional context contribute to making the costs of descriptive representation worse; when does it more likely contribute to reducing them? Similarly with the benefits: Can we expect state feminism to deliver by and large similar benefits as descriptive representation, or does descriptive representation rather deliver unique benefits that state feminism cannot offer? And to what extent does the assessment of this vary with how state feminism is organized and its institutional surroundings?

Women-Centred Versus Intersectional State Feminism

First, a state feminism that is exclusively women-centred will have some likely costs that overlap closely with the costs of descriptive representation: the possibility of increased essentialism (when women-centred argumentation and measures reproduce ideas of an essential female identity), weakening of cross-cutting political ties (when women centredness result in more in-group focus on women at the expense of ties across groups in the polity), random privileging of certain groups (when women are put above other equally needy target groups) and reduced accountability (the explicit focus from above on women's interest can be a disincentive for women to check whether their interests actually are taken care of). Such an overlap seems to be less of a threat with an intersectional approach. Rather, it could be argued that a proper intersectional state feminism would contribute to ease some of the costs of descriptive representation, for example, reduce essentialist thinking (individuals are regarded as belonging to different groups at the same time), bolster political ties (in-group thinking and behaviour is complicated when cross-cutting cleavages and individuals' varied and shifting structural positions are recognized) and potentially even out established, unjustified group privileges (the intersectional approach ranks at the outset no particular group above others).

At the same time, we could reasonably expect both a women-centred and a more intersectionally oriented state feminism, granted that they are effective and hold at least in part what they promise, to deliver some of the same benefits as descriptive representation, namely increased substantive representation of women's interests, increased de facto legitimacy, as well as progressive changes in images of who are fit to rule (even if some take it that women centredness delivers comparatively better than intersectionality and vice versa; see Galligan 2014; Reisel 2014). This raises the question of whether descriptive representation is necessary and recommendable even under intersectional state feminism, given the known costs of descriptive representation. However, one of the benefits of descriptive representation—increased vertical communication between citizens and rulers (i.e. the communication facilitation argument)—is unlikely to grow out of state feminism just like that, be it women-centred or intersectional, that is, with nothing more said about other qualities of the state feminism in question, for example, the extent to which it is democratized (see below). And the remaining listed benefit—that descriptive representation is intrinsically valuable (i.e. the non-instrumental argument)—is, of course, a benefit only descriptive representation itself can provide, and not something a well-designed feminism from above can compensate for.

To sum up: If women representing women measures are to be implemented, it is better that they are implemented under intersectional state feminism than under women-centred state feminism, since the latter and descriptive representation most likely will have several of their costs in common, whereas an intersectional environment arguably eases on the exact same costs. However, the benefit side complicates the picture since state feminism—women-centred or intersectional—at least when it works as it is supposed to, is good for several of the same things as descriptive representation is good for. Why then opt for descriptive representation at all given its costs? What descriptive representation does seem to deliver in addition, however, is more exchange and discussion across the representatives–represented divide. In addition, some consider descriptive representation as an independent good. If so, there are at least two potential reasons for implementing it.

State Feminism With/Without Welfare State

With regard to a state feminism inside or outside a "social democratic welfare regime" (Esping-Andersen 1990)—or more roughly put, with or without a welfare state—the likely effects are harder to talk about in general terms. A welfare state can, for example, contribute to more or less essentialism—and so add to this cost of descriptive representation or rather contribute to reducing it—depending on the more exact characteristics of welfare benefits and services and the extent of "affirmative" and normalizing use of group categorizations in policies and legislation (see Fraser 2003, on the distinction between "affirmative" and "transformative" political strategies, and also Bacchi 1999; Cornell 1995, 1998). The same goes for more of the listed costs of descriptive representation; a welfare state can contribute to strengthening political unity and community across the polity by granting more citizens a stronger social and economic citizenship, but also facilitate in-group encapsulation among recipient groups; it can contribute to consolidating random group hierarchies, or to even them out. In short, the effect of adding a welfare state to state feminism depends on the more detailed characteristics of the welfare state.

When it comes to the benefit side, things are clearer, as it seems likely that a state feminism accompanied by a social democratic welfare regime will have several of the same benefits as descriptive representation. For example, the substantive interests of more citizens are arguably better served within such welfare regimes, something that in turn most likely contributes to increased de facto legitimacy. However, once more we are left with the communication facilitation argument and the non-instrumental argument for descriptive representation. Welfare states may provide citizens with material welfare and a social basis for their life projects, but they do not necessarily facilitate active participation and deliberation among citizens and between representatives and represented. Critics have rather argued that social democratic welfare regimes tend to become technocratic and have a communicative deficit (Fraser 2013; Habermas 1996). And again, if descriptive representation is an intrinsic good, something valuable will be lost without it, with or without a welfare state.

State Feminism With/Without Democratization

Finally, there is the democratization variable. State feminist machineries in a "social democracy" as Hernes conceptualized it, that citizens deliberate on and are actively involved in shaping, can contribute to soothing several of the burdens produced by descriptive representation: Essentialist categorizations are hard to sustain when more people participate and raise their voice exposing differences and disagreements; citizens' engagement and participation in public affairs strengthen cross-cutting political communities; random group privileges are difficult to uphold when exposed in processes of democratic scrutiny; and democratization generally increases accountability. If we stick to the cost side, there is thus little doubt that descriptive representation is most recommendable in democratized environments. At the same time, democratization as we think of it here seems to offer most of the same benefits as descriptive representation: increased substantive representation, improved communication structures, progressive transformation of leadership stereotypes, and increased governmental support and stability. Why then would descriptive representation at all be needed in a democratized state feminist regime? Also, here, the non-instrumental argument is, of course, remaining: Proponents would stress how descriptive representation makes sure that democratization takes place in a way that is properly gender-balanced and proportional. It may also be argued more instrumentally that quotas for women and similar measures are a key part of democratization and fundamental for its full realization and success; without it, the representation of interests and communication will be poorer, de facto legitimacy weaker and so on.

How Important Is Competence, Communication and the Intrinsic Value Argument?

Hence, if we sum up all our three variables on the cost side, descriptive representation is more recommendable in a democratized, intersectional state feminist regime than in a women-centred technocratic one. The effects of the welfare state variable on descriptive representation costs are more mixed. Moreover, on the benefit side, intersectionality, welfare state and democratization seem to deliver several of the same goods as descriptive representation. This raises the question of whether descriptive representation is at all recommendable, given what we know of its costliness. First, even if intersectionality and democratization may contribute to ease some of these costs, it is improbable that they would all vanish under the most favourable of environments. Take the problem of essentialism: Even if "essentializing features of descriptive representation can be mitigated", not least through democratization ("cultivating avenues of dissent, opposition and difference"), a certain level of essentialist dynamics will inevitably persist, due to the "tendency to assume homogeneity within a group" as a basic feature of how human beings think and perceive (Mansbridge 1999: 638, see also Martin 1994). In addition, there are arguments against descriptive representation that seem to stick under all the above-elaborated circumstances, such as the reduced competence argument. It is hard to put descriptive representation first and keep a stringent focus on the ability and political competence to pursue substantive interests at the same time. There are, on the other hand, also pro arguments suggesting that we will genuinely miss something if descriptive representation is called off. Neither intersectionality nor welfare necessarily triggers increased communication across the representatives–represented divide, and arguably democratization might not automatically do it either without stimulation from quotas and similar measures. There is, moreover, the non-instrumental argument for descriptive representation as intrinsically valuable.

Hence, the more detailed assessment of descriptive representation under state feminism will also depend on the weight put on these three "in the end" decisive arguments. How important is the reduced competence argument? Is it more or less important than the communication facilitation argument? What about the idea of descriptive representations as intrinsically valuable? The following section will show how the assessment of these three arguments depends, in the end, quiet decisively on which ideas of equality and democracy one subscribes to.

Assessing Costs and Benefits: On What Basis?

Contemporary discussions on equality and democracy introduce a set of legitimate normative positions; that is, there may be good reasons for citizens to hold them, given their more specific world views, values and value priorities, and the disagreements resulting from them are thus "reasonable" (see Rawls 1971/1999, 1993 on the fact of "reasonable pluralism"). One such disagreement circles around the distinction between equality as equal opportunities and equality as equal outcomes. The more specific idea is that of equal *group level* outcomes (Phillips 2004; Roemer 1998),[5] or proportional equality: Every group—women and men, or other relevant groups—should be granted goods and burdens ("outcomes") that stand in a proportional relationship to the size of the group in question. "Gender equality" means then 50/50 distributions of goods and burdens between women and men, whereas deviations from 50/50 distributions signal gender *in*equality or so-called "gender gaps" (Plantenga et al. 2009:

---

[5] Equal outcomes on an individual level would have implied that each and every individual got the same bundle of goods and burdens in question.

23–25; Phillips 2004). Equal opportunities can be given different interpretations, but a common idea is that of "fair" equal opportunities, or fairly equal life chances (Rawls 1993: 6), defined as a condition in which "(…) those who are at the same level of talent and ability, and have the same willingness to use them, should have the same prospects of success regardless of their initial place in the social system" (Rawls 1971/1999: 63).[6] From this perspective, it is in the end an open question whether this or that deviation from balanced distributions is unfair, under the assumption that individual women and individual men could use their fairly equal opportunities in life to act "willingly" in ways that do not add up to strict 50/50 group level distributions (Fleurbaey 1995; Swift 2004). Unequal group level outcomes can reflect unfair opportunity structures, but can also be the aggregative outcome of individuals' relatively autonomous priorities and life choices. In the latter case, equal opportunities proponents would argue, there is no unfairness involved.

Another debate turns on the distinction between aggregative and deliberative democracy. According to aggregative democracy theory, democracy is a particular way of aggregating citizens' individual political preferences to a collective choice. Collective choices can come about by different means, but the key mechanism is voting, the basic democracy norm "one person—one vote", and democratic collective choices are legitimate to the extent that each person's vote is given equal consideration. Deliberative democracy highlights also "the importance of public discussions prior to a vote" (Peter 2011: 31). Citizens' opinions and political will are not considered synonymous with their private preferences, but as the transformed outcomes of processes of argumentation and intersubjective scrutiny, and political decision-making is not considered legitimate in lack of prior deliberations (Gutmann and Thompson 1996; Habermas 1996).

Finally, there is the distinction between moral and instrumental justifications of democracy (Martí 2006; Peter 2011). The first set sees the basic legitimacy criterion and defining feature of a proper democracy as certain intrinsically valuable democratic procedures giving "power to

---

[6] The contention is that such similarity in success prospects requires social and economic redistribution and not only anti-discrimination and equal treatment (what Rawls refers to as "formal" equal opportunities).

the people". The second set connects legitimacy to good outcomes, and stresses how democracy must be "truth-tracking" or "truth-sensitive" and institutionalized in ways that increase decision quality (Christiano 2012; Estlund 2008; Lafont 2006). Whereas most democratic theorists would agree that both kinds of justifications are necessary, they will conceptualize and weigh the justifications differently: Some will be more focused on "outcomes", others will stress the normative primacy of procedures.

When these three distinctions are singled out from the broader landscape of reasonable normative disagreements in democracy and equality theory, it is because of their immediate relevance for a discussion of the costs and merits of descriptive representation under state feminism. We ended the previous section with the non-instrumental argument, the communication facilitation argument and the reduced competence argument as three decisive arguments in the final round assessment. Even under intersectional, democratized state feminism—the most favourable of conditions—the ultimate assessment of descriptive representation and whether it should be implemented or not will depend on the strength of these arguments. The strength of these arguments is however intimately connected to the closer positioning in debates on the meaning of fundamental normative categories in our political vocabulary.

First, if equality means equal group level outcomes, then descriptive representation and proportionality in the presence of groups in politics—and so women's entry in 50 % of political positions—is an intrinsic good. The more detailed pros and cons of descriptive representation may vary under shifting organizational and institutional conditions, but for equal group level outcomes proponents, the non-instrumental case remains as a persistent core argument for women's quotas and similar measures. If, on the other hand, the focus is on individuals' equal opportunities, the concern is rather to enable women to participate in politics on equal terms with men, and to achieve distributive patterns in accordance with this opportunity norm. From this perspective, balanced distribution bares little normative weight in and by itself, and if the case for descriptive representation ultimately rests on that it does, the case is weak.[7]

---

[7] This conclusion is complicated by the fact that some regard equal group level outcomes not as a good in and by itself but as the best available proxy for equal opportunities given available data and conventional statistical techniques (Phillips 2004).

Second, for aggregative democrats, the communication facilitation argument for descriptive representation is relatively unimportant. According to this branch in democratic theory, legitimate collective decision-making is the aggregative result of voters' preference orderings. People may or may not deliberate beforehand; a proper representation of their substantive interests does not depend on it. For deliberative democrats, on the other hand, the communication facilitation argument for descriptive representation is key as legitimate collective decisions depend on deliberation. They would then tend to be in favour of descriptive representation for this reason, given, of course, that this argument in fact holds water, and not least if alternative ways to trigger deliberation with presumably a smaller list of costs are hard to come up with.

And third, for defenders of outcome-oriented justifications of democracy, political competence and expertise is crucial. If we can identify some as more competent than others in the art of effective representation of substantive interests in politics, letting them represent us will arguably contribute to better decisions (Christiano 2012; Estlund 2008; Lafont 2006; Martí 2006), whereas selecting the less competent, for example, because of their descriptive characteristics, may result in reduced decision quality. This is a strong reason for those who see democracy as primarily a mechanism to achieve better outcomes to worry about the reduced competence argument against descriptive representation. Defenders of procedural democracy accounts will, on the other hand, put less weight on this argument. Outcomes matter, of course, for everyone, but proceduralists are more inclined to accept measures they regard as having democratic or egalitarian merits on independent grounds, even if there is the chance of reduced decision quality.

Implications and Precautions

A central conclusion of this chapter is that descriptive representation is more recommendable in a democratized, intersectional state feminist regime than in a women-centred technocratic one. The discussions have been based on general arguments about what is "most likely" and "reasonable to expect" that are presumably rather uncontroversial. How and the extent to which intersectional feminism *de facto* contributes to less essentialism, whether and how democratization over time results in progressive transformations of leadership stereotypes and so on are however issues in need of further investigation, to more thoroughly test the strength and more accurate shape of such relationships.

Another question is what this finding could mean for the understanding, study and assessment of descriptive representation as a real-world phenomenon. A hypothesis, based on Scandinavian historical experiences, is that women's quota arrangements are more likely to be implemented and have their firmest institutionalization and strongest support in countries where state machineries have a relatively women-centred approach to anti-discrimination and gender equity. A corresponding hypothesis would be that women's quotas are harder to implement and sustain, and have lower support or over time loose support, where state machineries are less women-centred and regulated instead by intersectionality or other norms that do not privilege women's issues. If so, the same thing that contributes to increasing the costs of descriptive representation—women-centred machineries—could be what makes implementation of descriptive representation feasible and effective. Another hypothesis could be that descriptive representation systematically triggers processes of societal democratization. If so, quotas for women and similar measures are accompanied by developments that most likely contribute to reducing the costs of such measures. If, on the contrary, there are only weakly positive, none or even negative connections between the implementation of women's quotas and broader processes of democratization, the situation toughens, however, once more for descriptive representation proponents. Generally, more and more targeted research is needed to establish how far the conclusions of this chapter are good or bad news for quota supporters.

Finally, the foregoing discussion has highlighted how the case for descriptive representation hinges on normative perspective. Depending on positions in conceptual debates on equality and democracy, the non-instrumental argument, the reduced competence argument and the communication facilitation argument will be decisive arguments for or against descriptive representation—or bare little or no weight at all. Future exchanges on descriptive representation should thus have a firmer and more explicit focus on fundamental normative discussions. What is a "cost" and what is a "benefit" is not always a straightforward issue.

References

Bacchi, C. (1999). *Women, policy and politics: The construction of policy problems*. London: Sage.
Barry, B. (2002). *Culture and equality: An egalitarian critique of multiculturalism*. Cambridge: Harvard University Press.
Christiano, T. (2012). Rational deliberation among experts and citizens. In J. Parkinson & J. Mansbridge (Eds.), *Deliberative systems: Deliberative democracy at the large scale*. Cambridge: Cambridge University Press.
Cornell, D. (1995). *The imaginary domain: Abortion, pornography and sexual harassment*. London: Routledge.
Cornell, D. (1998). *At the heart of freedom: Feminism, sex & equality*. Princeton, NJ: Princeton University Press.
Crenshaw, K. (1991). Mapping the margins: Intersectionality, identity politics, and violence against women of color. *Stanford Law Review, 43*(6), 1241–1299.
Engelstad, F., & Teigen, M. (2012). *Firms, boards and gender quotas: Comparative perspectives*. Emerald: Bingley.
Esping-Andersen, G. (1990). *The three worlds of welfare capitalism*. Oxford: Polity Press.
Estlund, D. (2008). *Democratic authority: A philosophical framework*. Princeton: Princeton University Press.
Fleurbaey, M. (1995). Equal opportunity and equal social outcome. *Economics and Philosophy, 11*, 25–56.
Fraser, N. (2003). Social justice in the age of identity politics: Redistribution, recognition, and participation. In N. Fraser & A. Honneth (Eds.), *Redistribution or recognition? A political-philosophical exchange*. New York: Verso.
Fraser, N. (2013). *Fortunes of feminism. From state-managed capitalism to neoliberal crisis*. New York: Verso.
Galligan, Y. (2014). *States of democracy: A gender perspective*. London: Routledge.
Grofman, B. (1982). Should representatives be typical of their constituents? In B. Grofman et al. (Eds.), *Representation and redistricting issues*. Lexington: D. C. Heath.
Guinier, L. (1994). *The tyranny of the majority: Fundamental fairness in representative democracy*. New York: Free Press.
Gutmann, A., & Thompson, D. (1996). *Democracy and disagreement*. Cambridge: Harvard University Press.

Habermas, J. (1996). *Between facts and norms*. Cambridge, MA: Cambridge University Press.

Hernes, H. (1987). *Welfare state and woman power: Essays in state feminism*. Oslo: Scandinavian University Press.

Hernes, H., & Skjeie, H. (1997). Mellom fag og feminisme: Kvinneforskning i statsvitenskap. *Norsk Statsvitenskaplig Tidsskrift, 13*(3).

Holst, C. (2010). *Feminism, epistemology and morality*. Saarbrücken: VDM Verlag Dr. Müller.

Holst, C. (2014). Why democracy? On the relationship between gender democracy and gender equality in the EU. In Y. Galligan (Ed.), *States of democracy: Gender and politics in Europe*. London: Routledge.

Krizsan, A., Skjeie, H., & Squires, J. (Eds.). (2012). *Institutionalizing intersectionality. The changing nature of European equality regimes*. London: Palgrave Macmillan.

Kymlicka, W. (1993). *Multicultural citizenship*. Oxford: Oxford University Press.

Lafont, C. (2006). Is the ideal of deliberative democracy coherent? In S. Besson & J. S. Martí (Eds.), *Deliberative democracy and its discontents*. Aldershot: Ashgate.

Lovenduski, J. (2005a). *Feminizing politics*. Cambridge: Polity Press.

Lovenduski, J. (2005b). *State feminism and political representation*. Cambridge: Cambridge University Press.

Mansbridge, J. (1999). Should blacks represent blacks and women represent women? A contingent 'yes'. *The Journal of Politics, 61*(3), 628–657.

Mansbridge, J. (2001). The descriptive representation of gender: An anti-essentialist argument. In J. Klausen & C. Maier (Eds.), *Has liberalism failed women?* (pp. 19–38). New York: Palgrave.

Mansbridge, J. (2005). Quota problems: Combating the dangers of essentialism. *Politics & Gender, 1*(4), 622–637.

Martí, J. L. (2006). The epistemic conception of deliberative democracy defended. In S. Besson & J. L. Martí (Eds.), *Deliberative democracy and its discontents*. Aldershot: Ashgate.

Martin, J. R. (1994). Methodological essentialism, false difference, and other dangerous traps. *Signs, 19*(3), 630–657.

Minow, M. (1991). From class actions to Miss Saigon. *Cleveland State Law Review, 39*(3), 269–300.

Morone, J. A., & Marmor, T. R. (1981). Representing consumer institutions: The case of American health planning. *Ethics, 91*, 431–450.

Norris, P., & Franklin, M. (1997). Social representation. *European Journal of Political Research, 32*, 185–2010.

Nussbaum, M. (1999). *Sex and social justice.* New York: Oxford University Press.

Olsen, J. P. (2013). The institutional basis of democratic accountability. *West European Politics, 36*(3), 447–473.

Pennock, J. R. (1979). *Democratic political theory.* Princeton: Princeton University Press.

Peter, F. (2011). *Democratic legitimacy.* New York: Routledge.

Phillips, A. (1995). *The politics of presence.* Oxford: Oxford University Press.

Phillips, A. (2004). Defending equality of outcome. *Journal of Political Philosophy, 12*(1), 1–19.

Pitkin, H. F. (1972). *The concept of representation.* Berkeley: University of California Press.

Plantenga, J., Remery, C., Figueiredo, H., & Smith, M. (2009). Towards a European union gender equality index. *Journal of European Social Policy, 19*(1), 19–33.

Rawls, J. (1993). *Political liberalism.* New York: Colombia University Press.

Rawls, J. (1999). *A theory of justice.* Oxford: Oxford University Press.

Reisel, L. (2014). Legal harmonization and intersectionality in Swedish and Norwegian anti-discrimination reform. *Social Politics: International Studies in Gender, State and Society, 21*(2).

Roemer, J. (1998). *Equality of opportunity.* Cambridge, MA: Harvard University Press.

Sawer, M. (2002). The representation of women in Australia: Meaning and make-believe. In K. Ross (Ed.), *Women, politics, and change* (pp. 5–18). Oxford: Oxford University Press.

Stetson, D., & Mazur, A. G. (1995). *Comparative state feminism.* Thousand Oaks, CA: Sage.

Swain, C. M. (1993). *Black faces, black interests: The representation of African-Americans in congress.* Cambridge: Harvard University Press.

Swift, A. (2004). Would perfect mobility be perfect? *European Sociological Review, 20*(1), 1–11.

Tannen, D. (1994). *Gender and discourse.* New York: Oxford University Press.

Teigen, M. (2000). The affirmative action controversy. *NORA – Nordic Journal of Feminist and Gender Research, 8*(2), 63–77.

Vibert, F. (2007). *The rise of the unelected. Democracy and the new separation of powers.* Cambridge: Cambridge University Press.

Voet, R. (1992). Gender representation and quotas. *Acta Politica, 4*, 389–403.

Walby, S. (2011). *The future of feminism.* Cambridge: Polity Press.

Wängnerud, L. (2009). Women in parliaments: Descriptive and substantive representation. *Annual Review of Political Science, 12*, 51–69.

Weldon, L. S. (2002). Beyond bodies: Institutional sources of representation for women in democratic policy-making. *The Journal of Politics, 64*(4), 1153–1174.

Williams, M. S. (1998). *Voice, trust, and memory: Marginalized groups and the failings of liberal representation.* Princeton: Princeton University Press.

Young, I. M. (1990). *Justice and the politics of difference.* Princeton: Princeton University Press.

Young, I. M. (1994). Gender as seriality: Thinking about women as a social collective. *Signs, 19*(3), 713–738.

Young, I. M. (2000). *Inclusion and democracy.* Oxford: Oxford University Press.

6

Substantive Representation: From Timing to Framing of Family Law Reform in Morocco, South Africa and Uganda

Ragnhild L. Muriaas, Liv Tønnessen, and Vibeke Wang

Most Constitutions in Africa include provisions granting women political and economic rights on equal terms with men. Nonetheless, citizenship rights in Africa clearly reflect gender inequality, particularly because women are not granted equal civil rights by religious and customary family laws. This chapter examines women's substantive representation, commonly understood as "acting for" women, using the specific area of family law reform as an example. Family law reforms specifying the distribution of rights and obligations within marriage shape the possibilities for women to act as full citizens of the polity. Hence, women's substan-

---

R.L. Muriaas (✉)
Department of Comparative Politics, University of Bergen, Christiesgt 15, 5007 Bergen, Norway

L. Tønnessen (✉) • V. Wang (✉)
Chr. Michelsen Institute, Bedriftssenteret, 5892 Bergen, Norway

tive representation occurs when pro-women actors undertake activity on behalf of some or many women,[1] such as seeking to change women's status and civil rights within the family. Such pro-women initiatives have, however, been met with strong resistance in most African countries (Tripp et al. 2009: 113). This resistance is tied to conceptions of national and traditional culture within religious and ethnic communities, which makes reforms in the area of family law much more difficult to achieve than reforms in other areas.

Although efforts to liberalize women's civil rights have met with resistance inside and outside of African parliaments, several countries have enacted progressive family law reforms over the past decade, including Morocco, South Africa and Uganda. The literature on the substantive representation of women commonly attributes such successes to the window of opportunity that may open following widespread societal conflict or other major political ruptures (Bauer and Britton 2006; Tripp et al. 2009). Such post-conflict situations are "critical junctures" (Collier and Collier 1991) in which pro-women actors find conditions propitious for reform.

In this chapter, we argue that while critical junctures may open opportunities for reform, another essential factor affecting the prospects of successful substantive representation of women is whether or not the protagonists of family law reform are able to frame their claims in a manner that is acceptable to both the public and the ruling elite. In other words, while the *timing* of a legal reform proposal is important, the *framing* of the reform campaign is also critical (these concepts are discussed more closely in the next section). Thinking about framing instead of merely timing shifts the analysis of reform toward a broader scope of inquiry (Celis et al. 2008: 104), as framing suggests that the legislative process is not a null-sum game between competing views, but that intermediaries can support, and even forcefully agitate, for law reform as long as claims are moderated. We therefore adopt a "thick" conception of substantive representation which takes into account how representation occurs as well as its outcome (Mackay 2008: 125). This means that we acknowledge the substantive representation of women

---

[1] The activity may include, for instance, campaigning, forming alliances, networking to advance law reform and introducing or supporting bills that address women's issues. For more information on substantive representation, see the introduction.

as a process (Franceschet and Piscopo 2008) that occurs through multiple actors, sources and sites. This includes pro-women actors, both men and women in government and civil society working to advance policy reform, for instance, by strategically framing policy initiatives.

Through a "most different" comparative strategy, we ask how and through what mechanisms family law reforms in Morocco, South Africa and Uganda occurred. We find that women's feminist claims for equality have been negotiated to gain cultural resonance through processes of framing and reframing the claims to appeal to critical audiences. Pro-women actors, such as women activists inside and outside government, took center stage in this process. Additionally, male actors—who acted as intermediaries or leveraged the key government positions they held—also played vital roles in ensuring that legislation was enacted. Hence, the term "critical actors" should not only be understood as those "who initiate policy proposals on their own" and "embolden others to take steps to promote policies for women" (Childs and Krook 2008: 734), but also as those who help create the necessary legitimacy and support for law reforms to ensure their adoption.

The degree to which a law proposal must be moderated to ensure adoption depends on whether the reform process is initiated from above or from below. In Morocco, we find that the 2004 family law reform was more comprehensive and closer to the original feminist demands because the process received the blessing of the Moroccan king and was pushed through in a top-down manner. Once the demands for reform were framed within Islam, the process of negotiation only required getting acceptance from a few elite political gatekeepers. In the case of South Africa and Uganda, however, the initial law reform proposal had to undergo more substantial changes in scope and content, as more veto players needed to be on board for the proposal to be successfully enacted.

Explaining Changes in Family Law: From Timing to Framing

The literature on both women's descriptive and substantive representation in Africa has focused particularly on the end of prolonged conflicts and on major political ruptures as circumstances that can open space in which women and their allies can assert themselves (Bauer and Britton 2006; Pankhurst 2002). Yet, for such circumstances to lead to extended substantive representation, pro-women actors must be available to make use of the political spaces that have opened. In particular, the rise of an autonomous women's movement, often with the impetus of a global women's movement, within a country is imperative.

The timing of pro-women law initiatives has frequently been stressed in relation to stable features of the policy process. Studies have dealt to a lesser extent with the interplay between structure and agency (see, e.g. Celis et al. 2008; Childs and Krook 2006; Childs and Withey 2006)—that is, how the opinions, assumptions and preconceived notions of major stakeholders limit the ways in which legislation, including family law reforms, can be presented and framed. For instance, since men outnumber women in most legislatures and hold a majority of key political positions, male as well as female decision-makers must accept pro-women legislation as vital and just. We regard "framing" as a process by which actors in multiple arenas negotiate law reforms, frequently moderating the initial feminist demands in scope and content in order to ensure legislative enactment. In this process, critical actors include both those who initiated and advocated for family law reform and those who have the power and political influence to make sure that the law reform proposal gains the necessary traction to be successfully enacted into a new piece of legislation. This is in line with a thick understanding of substantive representation, as defined in the introduction.

By presenting their demands in ways that take into consideration the larger political context in which they operate, reformers can build alliances and reduce resistance by conservative forces (Moghadam and Gheytanchi 2010: 268). That is, the presentation of reform proposals needs to achieve "cultural resonance", defined by Ferree (2003: 310) as "an interaction of a certain package of ideas with the variable structure of an institutionally anchored discourse". All three country cases show that the interaction of different ideas within the available political space tempers family law reform. Pro-women actors who are able to maneuver well in this landscape achieve cultural resonance by strategically framing their claims in ways that are perceived as less threatening to major stakeholders such as religious communities, clan leaders, traditional authorities and other ideologically conservative forces.

Location-specific, institution-specific and historically specific factors shape women's civil rights and the political room for reform. Political, cultural and religious resistance to family law reform thus varies depending on context. In Africa, family law reforms have faced strong opposition from actors arguing on the basis of religion, culture and custom. Accordingly, African women's movements working to bring about legislative changes within family law are not "free to choose just any strategy" (Moghadam and Gheytanchi 2010: 269). The *discursive hegemony* of incumbent power holders effectively restricts which claims are perceived to be feasible, limiting in turn the frames and repertoire of ideas available to women arguing for law reform (Steinberg 1999: 746–47). Because pro-women actors typically face constraints from conservative political and religious actors, they must make strategic decisions about how to conceptualize their claims in a way that enhances their chances for legislative success.

Gendered Citizenship in Africa: Family Law as a Battlefield

Family laws have a significant impact on major aspects of women's civil rights in African states. By "family law", we refer to rules governing matters of marriage, divorce, custody, inheritance and maintenance. These laws, whether state or non-state, are—with some notable exceptions[2]— "gendered", in the sense that men are as a rule legally and financially more empowered than women. This difference in status is important, not just in the private sphere but also in relation to public opportunities. Family law shapes women's rights and opportunities in many areas of life, including the right to decide whom and when to marry, to own property, to inherit from the husband, to study and work outside of the home, to travel, to access health care (in some cases), to divorce and to retain cus-

---

[2] In several Central and East African countries, customary land law applies matrilineal (as opposed to patrilineal) principles to landholding. In Malawi, for instance, matrilineal descent and devolution of land rights dominate in the central and southern parts of the country, meaning that land is passed on to female heirs (Berge et al. 2014).

tody of children upon remarriage. Thus, family law "has been a crucial site for the gendering of citizenship" (Joseph 2000: 20).

Africa has seen many legislative initiatives and some successful legal reforms in the area of family law within the past decade. Although this area of intervention is particularly resistant to change, African pro-women actors have started taking on some of the most challenging and sensitive issues, including, for example, domestic violence and marital rape, inheritance and property rights, child marriages, polygamy and widow inheritance. The record of success has been mixed and includes many failures and some setbacks. For example, attempts to reform family law in Sudan have thus far failed. Within the context of this Islamist state that has been in power since 1989, pro-women activists have successfully put family law on the national political agenda. But despite much pressure from local activists with regards to child marriage, divorce and marital rape, the ruling Islamist party continues to insist that the feminist demands for family law reform are in contradiction with Sharia.

In many other African countries, family law bills have been drafted or introduced but not enacted. Family law is particularly controversial in North Africa, given the rise of both Islamist and Salafist groups claiming that gender equality within the family is a Western principle that contradicts Islamic law (Tønnessen 2013). Nevertheless, there are examples of successful reform. In North Africa, these include limited reforms in Tunisia in 1993 (granting women the right to transmit their nationality to their children), Egypt in 2000 (changing women's right to divorce) and Morocco in 2004 (see the next section on Morocco) (Charrad 2012; Sonneveld 2011).

Sub-Saharan Africa has also seen several family law reforms, especially concerning laws on domestic violence. Efforts to pass domestic violence laws often run up against arguments by conservative religious actors, as well as customary beliefs, that wife beating is acceptable. Under Muslim family laws and in some Christian and traditional religions, women are mandated to obey their husbands. As a consequence, the concept of marital rape does not exist within the law of some countries because a wife is not allowed to say "no". Despite such obstacles, domestic violence acts have been passed in countries like Ethiopia, Malawi, Senegal, Mozambique and Uganda from 2005 to 2010.

The three cases selected for this chapter—Morocco, South Africa and Uganda—differ in regime type (Morocco qualifies as a royal dictatorship, South Africa is a democracy and Uganda may be termed a hybrid regime), in their descriptive representation of women in parliament (10 % in Morocco, 38 % in South Africa and 35 % in Uganda in January 2015) and in their initial challenges to pro-women reform. Yet, women's groups and their allies have successfully pushed for family law reform in all three countries. The cases illustrate the complexity and variability of the reform process and each highlights unique aspects of family law and its links to debates about religious law (Morocco), customary law (South Africa) and criminal law (Uganda). The context in which a reform is initiated and, consequently, the set of religious, cultural and political actors mobilizing against such reform vary based on the scope of the new laws proposed.

In the following sections, we examine the strategies pro-women actors used in Morocco, South Africa and Uganda to achieve cultural resonance. In particular, we examine how advocates moderated feminist demands during the processes of negotiation and alliance building with opponents and power holders in order to ensure legislative enactment.

Family Law Reform in Morocco

In 2004, Morocco went from having one of the most conservative family laws in the Muslim world to having one of the most progressive. The Mudawana, as the Moroccan family code is called, is based on the Maliki school of Islamic jurisprudence. It was codified after Morocco's independence from France in 1956. The original law was built on the patriarchal ideal of a male breadwinner and guardian and an obedient wife. Among other things, the law stipulated that a woman could not marry without the permission of her male guardian. It set the minimum age of marriage at 15 for women. The husband had the right to divorce by unilateral repudiation, and he could marry up to four wives.

Under the new Moroccan family law, as reformed in 2004, husband and wife share equal responsibility for the family: no longer is the man required to be the main breadwinner. Male guardianship is eradicated, and the wife is no longer legally obliged to obey her husband. The minimum age of marriage is set at 18 for both men and women. The right to divorce is now a prerogative of both men and women, exercised under judicial supervision; thus, the new law ends the man's right to unilateral repudiation of a marriage. Polygamy was not abolished by the reform, but it was quite severely restricted by subjecting it to a judge's authorization and to strict legal conditions.[3]

Pro-women actors first attempted to reform the Mudawana in 1991. The Union for Feminist Action, the women's branch of a Marxist–Leninist political party, launched a "one million signatures" campaign and delivered these signatures to the parliament and the prime minister. This made the reform drive a topic for political debate, rather than a matter to be discussed only by religious scholars.

Multiparty elections in 1997 and the appointment of a new prime minister from a socialist party provided an opening for women's groups to advance a legal reform agenda. The new government endorsed a National Plan of Action for Integrating Women in Development (PANIFD) with the support of the World Bank. Explicitly linked to international human rights and the Beijing Platform for Action, the plan included the abolition of polygamy. It came under attack from religious scholars and Islamists as well as from the Ministry of Islamic Affairs, which labeled it a "product of secularization" (Harrak 2009: 4). Thus, the action plan did not find cultural resonance among religious and political elites even though it was strongly backed by a male prime minister.

PANIFD's proponents relied solely on secular women's organizations and categorically excluded Islamic actors and even the Ministry of Islamic Affairs from involvement in its implementation. Furthermore, parliament was not even consulted about the plan (Pruzan-Jørgensen 2012: 146). PANIFD was seen as anti-Islamic and pro-Western by a range of Islamic actors. The launching of PANIFD sparked two opposing demonstrations in Casablanca. During one, 500,000 pro-women activists rallied in favor of the plan. But in the other, 2 million demonstrated against it. The opposition was spearheaded by the Islamist justice and spiritual-

---

[3] In addition, the reform expanded women's inheritance, property and custody rights. Further, it recognized children born out of wedlock and simplified proof of paternity procedures. For a detailed account of the reforms, see Ennaji (2004).

ity movement led by Abdessalam Yassine (Buskens 2003: 105). Some of PANIFD's opponents, including Yassine's daughter, were not against family law reform as such but objected to the anti-Islamic framing of it in the action plan. Nadia Yassine stated in an interview in 2006,

> They asked me: what do you think of the women who demonstrate in Rabat? I said: my thoughts are with them, but politically I have to march in Casablanca. In other words, I agree with them that we should reform the *Mudawana* but I disagree with them on the method to make this reform. (Yassine 2006)

The Islamist movement's strong resistance, coupled with the large turnout at the protest, basically signified the end of the "secular" plan. In response to this failure, the women's movement moved ahead with a shift in strategy and framing (Moghadam and Gheytanchi 2010: 274). Women's groups started to formulate arguments rooted in Islam, rather than in secular paradigms, calling for "more flexible readings of the Quranic texts" (Sadiqi and Ennaji 2006: 97). They started employing the concept of *ijtihad* (independent reasoning) to establish feminist interpretations of the Quran. These new interpretations were then used to justify demands for full gender equality within the family law. This new ideological framing based on Islam was intended to weaken opposition among conservative religious and political elites and to mobilize women who were favorable to gender equality but uncomfortable with secular arguments (Salime 2011).

King Mohammed VI inherited the throne following the death of his father in 1999, and he proved to be a critical actor in passing the Mudawana reform. He appointed a law reform committee whose recommendations to a large extent met feminist demands for gender equality in the family law. As the commander of the faithful, Islamic scholars, politicians and activists could not easily label him as acting in contradiction with Sharia, which was the strategy employed when they successfully buried PANIFD. Effective coalition building and alliances between feminists and state actors, including the king himself, set the stage for substantive representation when the reform was presented in a male-dominated parliament.

The majority in parliament, both women and men, were from the Islamist Justice and Development Party. Successful enactment of the reform in January 2004, after lengthy discussions and numerous amendments, was attributed to a shift in framing and a strategic use of Islam. Indeed, Nouzha Skalli, a socialist and a leading proponent of family law reform, who was previously minister of solidarity, women, family and social development, stated that "if we had said we were against religion, we would not have won any battle" (Moghadam and Gheytanchi 2010: 277).

The final shape of the reform allowed both feminists and moderate Islamists to regard themselves as "winners". The 2004 Mudawana is a text "that both Islamists and feminists could claim as a victory for their respective positions" (Clark and Young 2008: 345). Although the feminists were not able to prohibit polygamy, the reform represented a giant step forward for Moroccan women's civil rights. Among other things, it criminalized child marriages, abolished male guardianship and women's obedience to her husband, made the wife and husband joint custodians of the home, eradicated the husband's right to unilateral repudiation and expanded a woman's right to divorce. And although the 2004 reform did not abolish polygamy as women activists demanded, it put new restrictions on the practice. At the same time, moderate Islamists regarded it as a victory that the reform was crafted within a religious framework, showing the modern face of Islam to the world. According to a male parliamentarian from the Justice and Development Party,

> The [new] Mudawana based itself on ijtihad *within* shari'a. It respected the principle of shari'a and that led to national unity and consensus...We now count the new Mudawana among our victories. (Pruzan-Jørgensen 2012: 182)

The successful passage of the updated Moroccan family law showed the importance of strategic framing in the reform process. The earlier secular campaign failed because a lack of cultural resonance allowed conservative Islamists to build broad public opposition to the proposed reform. When proponents of family law reform made some concessions, for example, on polygamy, and were careful to place the demands within a specifically religious framework, this produced a compromise acceptable to all the political elites involved in the process, transcending the previously polarized positions of feminism and Islamism (Salime 2011). The Mudawana reform also showed that the king was an important critical actor. Without his blessing as the commander of the faithful, the feminist demands, even when presented within an Islamic frame, would have likely met a stronger religious opposition both inside and outside of the parliament.

Family Law Reform in South Africa

After the first democratic elections in South Africa in 1994, a new Constitution was negotiated that included provisions to eradicate discrimination on the basis of gender. It has been described as a watershed in support of women's rights. In the following years, several pro-women laws were enacted, including the Recognition of Customary Marriages Act of 1998. Women thus perceived the transition to democracy as an opportunity to take action and develop a successful organizational structure through which to channel their claims (Hassim 2005: 181). At this point, the South African women's movement was at its strongest. Through an umbrella organization, the Women's National Coalition, it played a role in ensuring that the Constitution provided the basis for eradicating gender discrimination. Its provisions encompassed not only a vertical but also a horizontal application of rights and duties, thereby penetrating deep into the private sphere (Bennett 2011: 1056).

Despite the favorable context, however, pro-women activists pushing for gender equality reforms of family law still had to take into account significant opposition to gender equality within the sphere of the family. Specific demands for the eradication of gender discrimination had to be negotiated in a dialogue with conservative traditional and religious leaders. In the constitutional negotiations, traditional leaders wanted to exempt customary law from the clauses on gender equality, but women successfully intervened (Geisler 2000: 614). The final wording in the Constitution, however, remained far from clear on the status of customary law vis-à-vis gender equality.

One area of contention was the status of marriages. Since the Black Administration Act of 1927, civil and Christian marriages had enjoyed a privileged position in the South African plural legal system. However, customary marriages, along with Jewish and Muslim marriages, were defined as "unions" and relegated to an inferior status because they were potentially polygamous. An African woman who had married in accordance with customary law was a legal minor under the guardianship of her male partner, and this customary union was legally nullified if the husband entered into a civil marriage. Polygamy was not just a symbol of patriarchy; it had severe consequences for women's health (HIV/AIDS) and rights (guardianship of children, divorce, inheritance, property and judicial status). The Women's Charter for Effective Equality, launched by the Women's National Coalition in 1994, therefore asserted in Article 9 that "custom, culture and religion, insofar as these impact upon the status of women in marriage…shall be subject to the equality clause in the Bill of Rights".

The government mandated the South African Law Commission (SALC) to monitor the process of harmonizing customary marriages with the new Constitution under the leadership of Professor Thandabantu Nhlapo, who became a critical actor in reframing the reform. At first, the Law Commission favored a uniform marriage law, a position also held by civil society and pro-women actors. The Gender Research Project of the Centre for Applied Legal Studies (CALS) at the University of the Witwatersrand and the national Commission for Gender Equality were against the retention of a plural marriage regime; they called it a "piecemeal" approach that failed to deal holistically with Islamic marriages, Jewish personal law, cohabitation and customary law (SALC 1998: 4). Traditional leaders, however, voiced concerns regarding the universality of the Law Commission's initial proposals, and in the consultation rounds, they argued in favor of retaining more duality (Oomen 2005: 82).

The Law Commission then changed its approach. Instead of demanding a single code, it attempted to work for reform within the paradigm of plurality in order to achieve the necessary cultural resonance among traditional leaders. At first, the Law Commission members "felt that marriage is an area where citizens should be in a position to know what their rights and duties are" (SALC 1998: 11). But after consultations and workshops with traditional leaders, they were convinced to abandon the idea of a unified marriage law. Their report noted that Sections 30 and 31 of the Bill of Rights guaranteed cultural pluralism and that the country needed to "eradicate former prejudices against African cultural institutions" (SALC 1998: 11). Consequently, they concluded that marriage reform should strive to incorporate historically marginalized legal systems and traditions. As argued by Bennett (2011: 1055–1056), the Law Commission was acutely aware that the legislation needed to secure wide social acceptance and that overly ambitious reforms would have little likelihood of being observed in practice.

Women's rights organizations also developed a more nuanced strategy toward the reform process, taking into account the need to redress the marginalization of traditional laws and institutions and to ensure the protection of constitutional rights (Andrews 2009: 310). After a study of customary cultural practices of marriages on the ground in South Africa, the Centre for Applied Legal Studies found that very few people were still practicing polygamy, and both men and women had to reconcile different legal systems. The Centre for Applied Legal Studies supported a unified law of marriage, although it also emphasized the need of synthesizing the positive elements within both modern and traditional systems (Mbatha and Fishbayn Joffe 2013: 199). Hence, CALS recommended an approach that would "permit polygyny but subject its most egregious effects to regulation" (Mbatha and Fishbayn Joffe 2013: 200).

In the parliament, the Joint Standing Group on the Improvement of Quality of Life and Status of Women wanted the bill to be fast tracked and arranged hearings outside and inside parliament (Gouws 2004). The Joint Standing Group ended up being crucial in getting the bill passed, even though legal experts like Professor Nhlapo, who also published several academic articles on the topic, wrote the final bill that became the Recognition of Customary Marriages Act. The Joint Standing Groups hearings gave the Law Commission something close to a discursive hegemony over the content of the final law, particularly when women parliamentarians fast tracked the bill in order to get the law enacted before the 1999 election. Hence, women's activists inside and outside of parliament constituted critical actors who were instrumental in initiating and getting a more women-friendly law passed. Other actors, particularly those involved in the process from the Law Commission, like Professor Nhlapo, can be understood as intermediaries who moderated the content of the bill to achieve cultural resonance.

The act provided full recognition of customary marriages, but it also clearly aimed to improve the status of wives within these marriages. Still, the act on customary marriages did not reconcile several problematic aspects of women's marital status. One problem was the legal protection of women in marriages that are not registered. The Reform of Customary Law of Succession and Regulation of Related Matters Act 11 of 2009 tried to respond to this shortcoming by stressing that the Intestate Succession Act applies not only to the spouses of the deceased but also to a woman "with whom he had entered into a union in accordance with customary law". Hence, additional amendments were needed to abolish the customary law rule of male primogeniture. Another controversial issue has been the proprietary consequences of marriages concluded before the new law on customary marriages came into force. As these marriages were still governed by customary law, the spouses in these marriages do not automatically share a community of property.

Family Law Reform in Uganda

In Uganda, reforms to laws governing land and domestic relations have been high on the agenda of pro-women actors since before independence (Tripp 2000: 42–44). It was in 1986, however, after a long period of conflict, that significant progress was made in formally reconfiguring gender relations. At this time, the Ugandan women's movement, benefiting from the momentum of the international women's movement, established itself as one of the major societal forces in the country (Tripp 2000). With the endorsement of the National Resistance Movement (NRM) regime, a widely acclaimed "women-friendly" Constitution went into effect in 1995. The next decade saw little in terms of pro-women legislative outcomes in the area of family law reform, but significant progress occurred from 2006 to 2011 (the Eighth Parliament). Most notably, enactment of the Domestic Violence Act in 2010 marked a significant advance in the area of domestic relations. It was only a partial achievement, however, indicating continuing constraints on the political effectiveness of pro-women actors. This legislation followed a decision to divide the stalled Domestic Relations Bill, an omnibus bill comprising legislation on many family-related issues, into more manageable separate bills, beginning with the one on domestic violence that became the 2010 law.

Actors promoting women's interests in Uganda operate within the context of a hybrid regime in which the presidency has an overwhelmingly dominant position. The NRM, headed by President Yoweri K. Museveni, has ruled Uganda since 1986. Women's marriage rights, including rights of access to land, have been a driving concern for the Ugandan women's movement for several decades. According to customary law, which is still widely applied, women's access to and control of land is limited (Asiimwe 2002: 124). Women parliamentarians mobilized around the land issue in the Sixth Parliament (1996–2001), concentrating on two provisions: one requiring the consent of the wife and children before family land can be sold and the other securing spousal co-ownership of family land. Yet when the 1998 amendments to the Land Act were passed, the package did not include the co-ownership clause. Technical problems and political maneuvering were later blamed for the omission (Matembe 2002: 238–251). The lack of support within government ranks for the co-ownership clause extended not only to the president but also to women ministers, who were either ambivalent toward it or openly advocated against it (Goetz 2002: 565; Tripp 2006: 125).

In the Seventh Parliament (2001–2006), the co-ownership clause was included in the Domestic Relations Bill, along with other controversial issues pertaining to the domestic sphere, including marital rape, domestic violence, age of marriage, divorce, separation, cohabitation, polygamy, bride price and inheritance. This move made it even less likely that the co-ownership clause would be enacted (Muriaas and Wang 2012: 332). Nevertheless, women's organizations and female activists in parliament continued their advocacy and in December 2003 the omnibus bill was finally tabled. But it was not well received among male parliamentarians and certain religious communities. Many protested vocally against the bill, especially those from the Muslim community. In response, the government intervened to stop the process, and the bill never entered its second reading in parliament. On several occasions, President Museveni expressed his opposition to the bill and exerted direct pressure to defeat it (Matembe 2002: 151; Tripp 2006: 125). It has been suggested that the reasons for resistance to the bill were deep-seated issues relating to the patriarchal nature of Ugandan society—and by extension, the potential for additional opposition (particularly among men)—rather than the need for more consultation (which was the official reason given) (Tripp 2004: 7).

The debacle over the amendments to the Land Act, followed by the failure of the Domestic Relations Bill to advance, marked a turning point for the Ugandan women's movement. Previously, Museveni and the NRM had been considered a relatively positive force with respect to securing women's rights. After the exclusion of the co-ownership clause from the Land Act, several activists started to question the government's commitment to women (Tripp 2006: 124–35). In hindsight, it is clear that these events spurred a reorientation among actors.

In the Eighth Parliament (2006–2011), after consultations with the Uganda Law Reform Commission and the Ministry of Justice and Constitutional Affairs, critical actors in civil society and parliament adopted a new approach to family law reform. The crucial decision was made to split up the all-encompassing Domestic Relations Bill into several pieces of legislation that could be advanced separately. This new framing was intended to make the legislation more palatable to opponents, and it also instilled renewed enthusiasm and motivation in pro-women actors (Wang 2013a: 54–55, 2013b). Initially, the minister of justice and constitutional affairs acted as a bottleneck, but the process accelerated when his deputy, the state minister of justice Fred Ruhindi, took over responsibility for the bill. Ruhindi became an invaluable ally and a critical actor in garnering support for the bill. As events unfolded, the Domestic Violence Bill was given priority as a stand-alone initiative (Muriaas and Wang 2012: 332), and members of the cross-party women's caucus in parliament and a domestic violation coalition in civil society closely worked together to coordinate the process of moving the bill toward enactment. In addition, these groups closely monitored the Law Reform Commission and the Ministry of Justice's developing stances on the issue. All partners involved engaged in community outreach, awareness raising and sensitization (Wang 2013b: 118–119).

Lobbying in parliament was customized to appeal to a male audience and emphasized that the problem of domestic violence transcends gender. This was also the rhetoric Ruhindi used when he presented the bill on the floor of parliament for its final reading. A murder of a well-known army general by his presumed mistress, only a few days before the bill was due for its final reading, reinforced this argument, pointing to the importance of unforeseen contingencies in shaping legislative outcomes (Wang 2013b: 119). The conscious couching of claims to appeal to men, the cultivation of strategic parliamentary alliances (including actively targeting those perceived as key male MPs) and the strategic adoption of a new frame to build legitimacy and support among potential opponents led to successful gains in cultural resonance for the measure, and the legislation was enacted.

The Domestic Violence Act is the major achievement to date in family law reform in Uganda. Efforts to pass other bills continue to face resistance. A case in point is the Marriage and Divorce Bill. While proponents of this bill have tried to use framing techniques similar to those that succeeded with the Domestic Violence Act, the engagement of key actors in civil society and parliament was more low-key in the Eighth Parliament (Wang 2013a: 55). In the Ninth Parliament (2011–), the Marriage and Divorce Bill eventually reached the parliamentary agenda, but it was voted down in an NRM caucus meeting in April 2013. President Museveni reportedly took a strong position against the bill, disagreeing with key provisions on divorce, bride price and cohabitation (Lumu and Kaaya 2013). As a result, the government once again pulled and temporarily shelved the bill. Despite this setback, pro-women actors continue to revise their framing of strategies and initiatives to advance women-friendly reforms to family law.

Family Law Reform in Morocco, South Africa and Uganda Compared

Because family law is one of the most stubborn types of legislation to reform in Africa, the recent successes in Morocco, South Africa, and Uganda merit in-depth investigation. They are all cases of women's substantive representation in which pro-women actors in alliance with other critical actors, including men, have successfully pushed for family law reform. The three cases illustrate important similarities, such as the strong presence of a women's movement and pro-women actors in initiating and pushing for family law reform. All three cases also show the importance of critical male actors in framing or reframing family law reform initiatives. In Morocco, the king played a critical role in ensuring successful enactment of the Mudawana within an Islamic frame. In South Africa, Professor Thandabantu Nhlapo, a commissioner of the South African Law Commission, helped change the strategy from a unified code to a pluralistic framework that took into account the perspectives of traditional leaders. And in Uganda, Fred Ruhindi, the state minister of justice, served as an invaluable ally in leveraging a new piecemeal approach to family law reform and advocating the Domestic Violence Bill in parliament.

The case studies from Morocco, South Africa and Uganda also illustrate different ways in which the framing of legal reform proposals affects the possibilities for enactment and the feminist content of a reform. In Morocco, the shift from a secular to an Islamic framework to accommodate the concerns of religious leaders and Islamist political elites worked as a catalyst for one of the most major family law reforms on the continent. The South African case shows the need to accept some accommodation to traditional values to achieve cultural resonance at the grassroots level. In Uganda, following setbacks in promoting an omnibus bill on domestic relations, pro-women actors reframed the issue in narrower terms and successfully promoted single-issue legislation on domestic violence.

Moderating feminist claims: In Morocco, South Africa and Uganda, pro-women activists had to bargain and moderate their feminist demands through political negotiation and interaction with conservative religious, cultural and political actors in order to get the reforms enacted.

For example, in Morocco, feminists had long advocated the abolition of polygamy, which reformers viewed as a basic component of Muslim women's oppression. In the end, the reformed Mudawana did not abolish polygamy, but it did impose restrictions on its practice designed to protect women. The law was seen as an advance by feminists even though it did not guarantee full gender equality.

In South Africa, arguments about cultural relativism and respect for customs and traditions convinced pro-women actors among the political elite to make less radical claims for reform. The hope was that limited reform would be acceptable to the legislature and would have a chance of implementation in practice. Aware that traditional rural constituencies would simply ignore more comprehensive reform legislation, they agreed to frame a law that respected cultural practices such as polygamy and *lobola* (bride price).

Ugandan pro-women actors soon realized that to successfully advance family law reform, they had to approach the issues in a piecemeal fashion. A comprehensive family law reform that bundled multiple controversial provisions (including those on domestic violence, inheritance, divorce, child marriages and polygamy) into one piece of legislation could not secure the necessary support, as nearly every major stakeholder could find something to object to. Adopting a new frame made it easier to negotiate common ground and contributed to the enactment of a historic domestic violence law in 2010. The same approach, however, has not yet been successful with respect to other aspects of family law.

Achieving cultural resonance: In all three cases, those advocating for family law reform found that the *discursive hegemony* maintained by power holders effectively limited which claims were perceived to be culturally resonant and therefore politically feasible. The precise character of those limitations varied in the three different cases, based on linkages to different legal frameworks: religious law in Morocco, customary law in South Africa and criminal law in Uganda. These specific contexts determined the array of opposing forces and the hegemonic discourses within which pro-women actors had to maneuver and frame their claims.

In Morocco, religious leaders and Islamist actors first mobilized against a reform advanced on the basis of secular arguments, defending the primacy of sacred Islamic texts. Reform advocates then realized that the use of a secular frame in arguing for family law reform aided their opponents by confirming accusations that the proponents of reform were un-Islamic and were imposing a Western agenda. When the reformers turned instead to making use of Quran and Islamic justifications for change, they were able to present themselves as defenders of Islam, arguing on the same terrain as opponents of reform. When the king, as the commander of the faithful, gave his blessing to Islamic family law reform, opponents had a hard time labeling the process as anti-Islamic.

In South Africa, pro-women activists agreed to adopt a more nuanced strategy to reform the law of customary marriage. Faced with the continued influence of traditional leaders, and sensitive to the concerns of women in rural areas, important spokespersons for women's rights adjusted their claims to the institutional, cultural and historical situation. Instead of campaigning to eliminate customary marriage law as a separate domain, they stressed the need to ensure that customary marriages were recognized and subject to legal regulations.

In Uganda, pro-women activists in civil society and parliament strategically advocated for a bill on domestic violence by adopting a discursive frame intended to appeal to men and to male legislators in particular. They asserted that domestic violence goes beyond gender and also affects men and children. The bill defined domestic violence broadly and cast a wide net in terms of categories of people protected under the law. By successfully arguing that domestic violence is not only a women's issue, pro-women actors were able to win the necessary support to pass the bill.

Reforming family law top-down versus bottom-up: The three cases also show two different approaches to law reform. On the one hand, the Mudawana reform in Morocco was elitist in nature (Cavatorta and Salmasso 2009), displaying clear parallels with the women-friendly reforms taking place in post-colonial Tunisia as described by Charrad and Zarrugh in this book (Charrad and Zarrugh, this volume). Based on the willingness of the monarchy to accept Islamic family law reform, the change was essentially decided on a top-down basis, largely disregarding grassroots perspectives. While Moroccan feminists made some compromises on polygamy, the Mudawana is the most comprehensive family law reform among the three. Since Moroccan society is regarded as quite conservative, a bottom-up approach might have resulted in a less comprehensive and less gender egalitarian reform (Elliott 2009: 221).

In South Africa and Uganda, in contrast, elitist reformers made the decision to take grassroots sensitivities into account, along with the views of opposing elites and power holders. This resulted in less comprehensive reforms focusing specifically on domestic violence and customary marriages. Anchoring decisions at the grassroots, with awareness raising and sensitization on the ground, meant making compromises and advancing limited legislation some reformers might consider weak. Such a gradual approach to family law reform, however, allowed activists to overcome barriers to reform.

Conclusion

While timing is important for the enactment of pro-women legislation, this chapter has brought attention to the importance of framing. Morocco, South Africa and Uganda are examples of countries which have successfully enacted family law reforms that have clearly enhanced women's civil rights. Looking at substantive representation as not only outcome but also as process, the chapter draws attention to how these successes were negotiated by multiple actors in various arenas. Feminist demands were framed in order to achieve cultural resonance through the use of religious and cultural arguments with the intent to avoid strong counter-mobilization by conservative actors; yet all the three law reform processes show that these demands were moderated in the end. The initial initiatives were subject to negotiation between pro-women actors, male intermediaries and counter actors. In Morocco, the top-down manner in which the 2004 Mudawana came about enabled a comprehensive reform within all the main areas of family law. But despite groundbreaking improvements, pro-women actors had to let go of their goal to outlaw polygamy. In South Africa, pro-women actors fought for a unified marriage law that would secure wives similar status in marriage across religions and cultural practices. Their claims were however moderated by the Law Commission that favored a dual system of law as this would pay respect to the values of the newly empowered African population. In Uganda, the decision to approach family law reform in a piecemeal fashion was made after actors realized that this was the only way to ensure the necessary support among grassroots stakeholders as well as policy elites.

By paying attention to how pro-women initiatives were negotiated and framed, we see a clear link between the process and the outcome. Successful enactment of a family law reform comes at a cost. In the bottom-up processes in South Africa and Uganda, initial demands were modified the most, while less compromises had to be made in the top-down process in authoritarian Morocco. While the bottom-up approach resulted in less radical content and less comprehensive scope of the family law, the legitimacy and trust developed by the stakeholders in the negotiation process may yield benefits with respect to implementation of the reforms in the years to come. The most wide-ranging family law reform is found in Morocco, yet its top-down nature might harvest less legitimacy within conservative Muslim grassroots, which were largely excluded from the negotiation process. Thus, the most gender egalitarian family law reform Africa has seen since Tunisia in 1956 is more likely to meet resistance in the implementation phase.

References

Andrews, P. E. (2009). Who's afraid of polygamy? Exploring the boundaries of family, equality and custom in South Africa. *Journal of Law & Family Studies, 11*(2), 303–331.

Asiimwe, J. (2002). Women and the struggle for land in Uganda. In A. M. Tripp & J. C. Kwesiga (Eds.), *The women's movement in Uganda: History, challenges, and prospects* (pp. 119–137). London: Fountain.

Bauer, G., & Britton, H. E. (2006). Women in African Parliaments: A continental shift? In G. Bauer & H. E. Britton (Eds.), *Women in African Parliaments* (pp. 1–30). Boulder, CO: Lynne Rienner.

Bennett, T. W. (2011). Legal pluralism and the family in South Africa: Lessons from customary law reform. *Emory International Law Review, 25*(2), 1029–1059.

Berge, E., Kambewa, D., Munthali, A., & Wiig, H. (2014). Lineage and land reforms in Malawi: Do matrilineal and patrilineal landholding systems represent a problem for land reforms in Malawi? *Land Use Policy, 41*, 61–69.

Buskens, L. (2003). Recent debates on family law in Morocco: Islamic law as politics in an emerging public sphere. *Islamic Law and Society, 10*(2), 70–131.

Cavatorta, F., & Salmasso, E. (2009). Liberal outcomes through undemocratic means: The reform of the code de statut personnel in Morocco. *Journal of Modern African Studies, 47*(4), 487–506.

Celis, K., Childs, S., Kantola, J., & Krook, M. L. (2008). Rethinking women's substantive representation. *Representation, 44*(2), 99–110.

Charrad, M. (2012). Family Law Reforms in the Arab World: Tunisia and Morocco. Report for the United Nations Department of Economic and

Social Affairs (UNDESA) Division for Social Policy and Development Expert Group Meeting, New York, 15–17 May. Available from http://bit.ly/1F76iSz

Childs, S., & Krook, M. L. (2006). Should feminists give up on critical mass? A contingent yes. *Politics and Gender, 2*(4), 522–530.

Childs, S., & Krook, M. L. (2008). Critical mass theory and women's political representation. *Political Studies, 56*(3), 725–736.

Childs, S., & Withey, J. (2006). The substantive representation of women: The case of the reduction of VAT on sanitary products. *Parliamentary Affairs, 59*(1), 10–23.

Clark, J. A., & Young, A. E. (2008). Islamism and family law reform in Morocco and Jordan. *Mediterranean Politics, 13*(3), 333–352.

Collier, R. B., & Collier, D. (1991). *Shaping the political arena: Critical junctures, the labor movement, and regime dynamics in Latin America.* Princeton: Princeton University Press.

Elliott, K. Z. (2009). Reforming the Moroccan personal status code: A revolution for whom? *Mediterranean Politics, 14*(2), 213–227.

Ennaji, M. (2004). "The New Muslim Personal Status Law in Morocco: Context, proponents, adversaries, and arguments". Available from http://bit.ly/1PGvrGH

Ferree, M. M. (2003). Resonance and radicalism: Feminist framing in the abortion debates of the United States and Germany. *American Journal of Sociology, 109*(2), 304–344.

Franceschet, S., & Piscopo, J. (2008). Gender quotas and women's substantive representation: Lessons from Argentina. *Politics & Gender, 4*(3), 393–425.

Geisler, G. (2000). "Parliament Is Another Terrain of Struggle": Women, men, and politics in South Africa. *Journal of Modern African Studies, 38*(4), 605–630.

Goetz, A. M. (2002). No shortcuts to power: Constraints on women's political effectiveness in Uganda. *Journal of Modern African Studies, 40*(4), 549–576.

Gouws, A. (2004). The politics of state structures: Citizenship and the National Machinery for Women in South Africa. *National Politricks, 3*, 27–47.

Harrak, F. (2009). The history and significance of the New Moroccan family code. Working Paper 09-002, Institute for the Study of Islamic Thought in Africa, Roberta Buffett Center for International and Comparative Studies, Northwestern University.

Hassim, S. (2005). Voices, hierarchies and spaces: Reconfiguring the women's movement in democratic South Africa. *Politikon, 32*(2), 175–193.

Joseph, S. (2000). Gendering citizenship in the middle east. In S. Joseph (Ed.), *Gender and citizenship in the middle east* (pp. 3–30). Syracuse, NY: Syracuse University Press.

Lumu, D. T., & Kaaya, S. K. (2013). Marriage bill: How Museveni killed it. *The observer*, 10 April. Available from http://bit.ly/1e4Sw3d

Mackay, F. (2008). "Thick" conceptions of substantive representation: Women, gender and political institutions. *Representation, 44*(2), 125–139.

Matembe, M. (2002). *Politics, gender and constitution making in Uganda*. Kampala: Fountain Publishers.

Mbatha, L., & Fishbayn Joffe, L. (2013). Recognition of polygamous marriages in the New South Africa. In L. Fishbayn Joffe & S. Neil (Eds.), *Gender, religion, and family law: Theorizing conflicts between women's rights and cultural traditions* (pp. 190–211). Waltham, MA: Brandeis University Press.

Moghadam, V. M., & Gheytanchi, E. (2010). Political opportunities and strategic choices: Comparing feminist campaigns in Morocco and Iran. *Mobilization: An International Journal, 15*(3), 267–288.

Muriaas, R., & Wang, V. (2012). Executive dominance and the politics of quota representation in Uganda. *Journal of Modern African Studies, 50*(2), 309–338.

Oomen, B. (2005). *Chiefs in South Africa: Law, power & culture in the post-apartheid era*. Oxford: James Currey.

Pankhurst, D. (2002). Women and politics in Africa: The case of Uganda. In K. Ross (Ed.), *Women, politics, and change* (pp. 119–128). Oxford: Oxford University Press.

Pruzan-Jørgensen, J. (2012). *Liberalization and autocracy in Morocco: The puzzle of the Moudawana reform*. Saarbrücken, Germany: Lambert Academic Publishing.

Sadiqi, F., & Ennaji, M. (2006). The feminization of public space: Women's activism, the family law, and social change in Morocco. *Journal of Middle East Women's Studies, 2*(2), 86–114.

SALC (South African Law Commission). (1998). *The harmonisation of the common law and the indigenous law: Report on customary marriages*. Pretoria: South African Law Commission.

Salime, Z. (2011). *Between Feminism and Islam: Human Rights and Sharia Law in Morocco*. Minneapolis, MN: Minnesota University Press.

Sonneveld, N. (2011). *Khul' Divorce in Egypt: Public Debates, judicial practices, and everyday life*. Cairo: American University in Cairo Press.

Steinberg, M. (1999). The talk and back talk of collective action: A dialogic analysis of repertoires of discourse among nineteenth-century English cotton spinners. *American Journal of Sociology, 105*(3), 736–780.

Tønnessen, L. (2013). *Marriage is politics: Prospects for women's equality after the Arab spring*. Bergen, Norway: Chr. Michelsen Institute.

Tripp, A. M. (2000). *Women and politics in Uganda*. Madison: University of Wisconsin Press.

Tripp, A. M. (2004). Women's movements, customary law, and land rights in Africa: The case of Uganda. *African Studies Quarterly, 7*(4), 7–19.

Tripp, A. M. (2006). Uganda: Agents of change for women's advancement? In G. Bauer & H. E. Britton (Eds.), *Women in African parliaments* (pp. 111–132). Boulder, CO: Lynne Rienner.

Tripp, A. M., Casimiro, I., Kwesiga, J., & Mungwa, A. (2009). *African women's movements: Transforming political landscapes*. Cambridge: Cambridge University Press.

Wang, V. (2013a). *Operating in the shadow of the executive: Women's substantive representation in the Ugandan Parliament*. Doctoral dissertation. Bergen: University of Bergen.

Wang, V. (2013b). Women changing policy outcomes: Learning from pro-women legislation in the Ugandan Parliament. *Women's Studies International Forum, 41*, 113–121.

Yassine, N. (2006). *Legal reform in Morocco: Views of a Moroccan Feminist Dissident*. Available from http://www.jspublishing.net/NadiaYassineUSTourLegalReform.htm

7

Constructing Citizenship: Gender and Changing Discourses in Tunisia

Mounira M. Charrad and Amina Zarrugh

Introduction

Citizenship means belonging to a community defined in political terms. It can be understood as involving rights and obligations as enshrined in the laws and regulations of a country. It can also be seen in its more symbolic form in terms of how different categories of people in a given political community are represented in public discourse or in culturally significant national texts such as Constitutions. This chapter uses a multifaceted conceptualization of citizenship that highlights its several dimensions. We

---

M.M. Charrad (✉)
Department of Sociology, A1700, University of Texas at Austin,
305 E, 23rd Street, 78712 Austin, TX, USA

A. Zarrugh (✉)
Texas Christian University, 4006 Scharbauer Hall, 76129 Fort Worth, TX, USA

© The Author(s) 2016
H. Danielsen et al. (eds.), *Gendered Citizenship and the Politics of Representation*, DOI 10.1057/978-1-137-51765-4_7

show how different dimensions of "being a citizen" come to the fore in national politics in different political contexts. In particular, we focus on how vocabularies of citizenship and gender can shift from a discourse on legal rights stated in formal codes to debates on representation, especially on how women's status in society is represented in foundational texts such as a Constitution. This focus situates conceptualizations of women's legal personhood as central to debates about citizenship. Leaving aside the obligations aspect of citizenship as outside the scope of this chapter, our analysis centers on the processes by which women have gained greater legal rights and achieved a more equal discourse of representation in foundational texts. As Danielsen, Jegerstedt, Muriaas and Ytre-Arne indicate in the introduction of the present volume, "citizenship speaks of inclusion and points to exclusion" (2016: 2). This chapter considers processes and struggles that have contributed to inclusion at the same time as it points to risks of exclusion.

Taking the example of Tunisia, a small majority Muslim population country that stands out in the Arab world by its long history of legislation relatively favorable to women (Ben Salem 2010; Charrad 2010; Kelly and Breslin 2010; Wing and Kassim 2007), we consider two critically important political contexts. First, we examine the postcolonial period characterized by authoritarian governance in the 1950s and, second, democratization processes that have transpired in what was termed the "Jasmine Revolution" in Tunisia following massive protests across the Middle East and North Africa since 2011, referred to throughout this chapter as the "Arab Spring". We show how the postcolonial state addressed issues of gendered citizenship in the foundational texts of the new state, namely the Code of Personal Status (CPS) and the national Constitution, with the objective of advancing formal equality for all citizens under the control of the state and the autonomy of the individual from the kin group in Tunisian society. This politics constituted a "politics from above" in which postcolonial state leaders defined citizenship for several decades. We then consider how women themselves debated issues of representation in the drafting of a new Constitution following the 2011 revolution and the ways in which autonomy of the female citizen became a contested point of debate. This ushered in a new process that we refer to as "politics from below" in which women themselves were involved in shaping citizenship for women.

Our analysis demonstrates how gendered the discourse on citizenship has been, regardless of the particular issues at stake. We show how different vocabularies of citizenship have entered Tunisian state documents over time with varied implications, illustrating that matters of women's status and citizenship have remained a politically contentious and unsettled arena of debate. Before turning to the analysis of Tunisia, let us review general and global discussions of gendered citizenship to situate our study of the Tunisian case.

Gender and Citizenship Debates Globally

Discussions of citizenship have been central to the sociological study of social stratification and democratization processes. Drawing on the classic work of T.H. Marshall (1964), scholars have understood modern citizenship primarily as a "personal status consisting of a body of universal rights and duties held equally by all legal members of a nation-state" (Somers 1993: 588). Beginning in the late 1980s and early 1990s, however, feminist scholars began to critique prevailing conceptions of citizenship for omitting gender as an important category of continued social inequality. For example, Walby states that, as "highly gendered and ethnically structured", citizenship ought to be recognized more as a contested and highly politicized process rather than simply a legal status accorded to members of a polity (Walby 1994: 391).

Significant work has been undertaken by scholars to elucidate the myriad of ways by which a close relationship exists between the nation-state and gender. Yuval-Davis (1997) regards this connection as closest in three features of a nation-state: its genealogical claims ("Volknation"), its symbolic heritage ("Kulturnation") and the rights accorded to its citizens ("Staatnation"). In each of these cases, boundaries of inclusion and exclusion are drawn and gender is a frequent marker for assignment into such categories. Far from being a universalist concept that necessarily offers greater inclusion and equality in a community, citizenship can reify and justify social inequality.

According to feminist scholars, early conceptions of citizenship are themselves masculine and have been "predicated on women's exclusion"

(Lister 1991: 66). Historically, the roots of citizenship date to the traditions of liberalism and civic republicanism, the latter of which conceptualized citizenship as a status accorded to an individual (Lister 2012). One central trouble with this particular conceptualization is that men and women were understood in the nineteenth and twentieth centuries in the relation of men as individuals and women as dependents. The private–public dichotomy bifurcated women's labor as distinct from that of men, thus distinguishing it from the public sphere realm of citizenship (Lister 1991).

Some feminist critiques of citizenship take issue with T.H. Marshall's (1964) historical delineation of three types of citizenship rights: civil rights, political rights and social rights, and the modes and order by which they are acquired. While Marshall maintains that these rights developed in that order in the eighteenth, nineteenth and twentieth century, respectively, Walby (1994) cites several ways in which the acquisition of such rights did not unfold so linearly in the case of women. She states that British and American women in the early twentieth century did not have habeas corpus rights in the exercise of their own bodies or suffrage rights as did men and, therefore, could not have acquired citizenship rights in the way concluded by Marshall. In other cases, such as in postcolonial states, all three rights were pursued simultaneously upon independence, though civil rights in particular were circumscribed, most especially for women (Walby 1994). Different social groups are included in the category of citizen at different times and through different processes of contestation, a feature of rights acquisition acknowledged by Marshall but not discussed in the case of gender.

In attempts to address gender in discussions of citizenship, several scholars have taken approaches that situate as central the terms "equal" and "different". A prominent debate in feminist scholarship concerns whether approaches to gender discrepancies, from political power disparities to unequal wages, ought to conceptualize women as equal with men or as different from men and possessive of unique qualities. Lister (2012) outlines the specific approaches to citizenship connected to these "equal/different" conceptualizations of gender.

These approaches include the "gender-neutral citizen", which conceptualizes women as equal with men and promotes equality in all matters in the public sphere; the "gender-differentiated citizen", which conceptualizes women as different from men and offers maternalist politics as exemplifying the significance of care and care work; and the "gender-pluralist citizen", which departs slightly from "equality/difference" concerns to conceptualize women and men as belonging to multiple groups and identities that must be acknowledged rather than assuming that men and women belong to homogenous groups with similar interests and experiences. According to Lister (1991), states and social movements have assumed different strategies on gendered citizenship, which have implications for issues ranging from matters of children's nationality to welfare provisions. The "equality vs. difference" debate has been important in the vocabulary of the US approach to gendered citizenship, with the US feminist movement pursuing a strategy that promotes "equality" or "sameness" (Lister 2012: 379).

The centrality of the individual and his/her status in politics has been the primary formulation of citizenship in Western liberal democracies and much of the literature has focused on the "equal/different" conceptualizations of citizenship. Several questions arise, however: Are these the salient terms used in discourses in other social and political contexts? Where does one look to examine issues of gender and citizenship in several cultural contexts? In examining the critiques of classic formulations of citizenship by feminist scholarship in different contexts, we can observe the ways in which the debates on gendered citizenship differ transnationally and what set of issues are at the center of contention.

Scholars studying the Middle East and Africa have focused in particular on the restrictions imposed by family law on women's citizenship. Writing about citizenship and gender in Morocco, South Africa and Uganda, Muriaas, Tonnessen and Wang see "reforms in the area of family law [as] much more difficult to achieve than reforms in other areas" (2016: 1) and state that "family law is one of the most stubborn types of legislation to reform in Africa" (2016: 19). Considering Lebanon, Joseph argues that sectarian family laws have been highly gendered and that "women and children have been disproportionally disadvantaged by the delegation of family law to religious sects" (2000: 131). Charrad (2001, 2010) shows how family law subordinated women to kin and husbands in the history of Tunisia, Algeria and Morocco. Maktabi examines how, in Syria, "family law accords male and female citizens a different legal status, thus ordering the distribution of basic rights and duties along gendered lines" and how it "plays a crucial role in structuring gendered citizenship in ways that limit the legal authority of female citizens as full members of the polity" (2010: 557). In a similar vein and taking the case of Iran, Moghadam argues that several "aspects of family law…undermine women's economic independence and empowerment" (2011: 115) and that "as a key element in the Islamic state's gender policy, Muslim family law requires a major overhaul if all women are to achieve equality and security within the family and the society" (2011: 127).

As the studies above indicate, family law is an important arena in which to consider limits placed on women as citizens and new opportunities that may open up in the Middle East and North Africa. Since it has adopted a liberal family law granting women important legal rights, Tunisia represents a significant case to examine in order to understand some of the processes and debates involved in lessening gender inequality. We now turn, in the next sections, to an examination of gendered citizenship in Tunisia's state documents, namely the CPS and the Constitution, under an authoritarian postcolonial state and then in the political turmoil following the Arab Spring. We elucidate how women are represented as more or less autonomous individuals in different eras and how the construction of personhood has followed from politics or been a matter of contention.

Postcolonial State: Discourse on Individual Rights

To understand how the postcolonial state constructed citizenship, it is important to consider the conditions under which the state emerged following the end of colonial rule in 1956. Tribes represented a prevalent form of social organization in Tunisia and much of North Africa prior to and during the period of French colonization, which lasted from 1881 to 1956 in the case of Tunisia. In the Tunisian and North African context, tribes are best understood as social groups united by local, kinship-based solidarities that often served as a basis for collective action in that, instead of relying on "members of a class, occupational group, or ideological movement" for political action, individuals in North Africa relied on membership in groups of extended kin (Charrad 2001: 4). Tribes were mobilized or marginalized differently by the colonial state and the nationalist movement in the French colonies of North Africa, leaving them in a variety of relationships to the state. Their degree of incorporation into the polity first during colonization and then during the process of state building differentially influenced the development of family law, a key site for the formulation of citizenship in each country after colonization (Charrad 2001).

Beginning with the colonial conquest in 1881, for historical reasons beyond the scope of this chapter and discussed in detail elsewhere (Charrad 2001, 2011a), French authorities encountered fewer powerful tribes and found a more centralized state in place in Tunisia than in the other North African colonies. Facing less tribal opposition throughout the territory and building on the administrative structure that was already there, the colonial state further developed a centralized bureaucratic apparatus reaching far into most of the territory. This bureaucratization, in turn, decreased even further the power of tribal groupings, even though some managed to retain a degree of political leverage.

In the transition from French colonization to an independent Tunisian state in 1956, disputes erupted between two major nationalist factions with different perspectives: Salah Ben Youssef's mobilization of pan-Arab, pan-Islamic and pan-Maghribi interests among tribal populations primarily in rural areas, and Habib Bourguiba's vision of a strong and centralized national state, with appeal to labor unions and professional elites located mostly in urban centers. Ultimately, Bourguiba and his supporters, who rejected all forms of tribal influence in politics, succeeded in seizing power in the newly formed sovereign state.

This political outcome set a precedent for the Tunisian political leadership after independence to develop a law that departed significantly from that of kin-based tribal groups, which had relied on kin-based solidarities as enshrined in conservative interpretations of Islamic family law (Charrad 2001, 2011b: 423). Once it occupied the seat of power in the new nation-state, the urban-based political leadership enacted a progressive family law. Promulgated on 13 August 1956, the CPS transformed the construct of kinship from tribal and extended to that of a nuclear conjugal family, as had been more prevalent in urban areas. Contributing to the process was also the fact that urban areas were the parts of the country where the victorious leadership found its constituency and basis for political support.

At issue in the formulation of the law in countries with an Islamic tradition is whether women have a place as equal citizens in the nation-state or are treated as subordinate to men in their roles as daughters, wives, mothers, siblings, nieces or aunts. Prior to the 1956 CPS, the Maliki interpretation of Islamic family law prevailed in most of Tunisia. Polygamy or the man's right to marry as many as four wives was legal, although practiced only by a wealthy minority of men since it takes resources to support several wives and their children. Husbands had the right of repudiation, or unilateral right to terminate a marriage at will without recourse to a judge or to a religious court. This made ending a marriage a private matter and sometimes left repudiated women without resources.

Marriage required the presence of a matrimonial guardian for the bride, usually her father or another close male relative, who expressed consent to the marriage on her behalf. This regulation symbolically defined marriage as an arrangement between families more than between individuals. Although, in reality, women could have a fair degree of influence over the choice of their marriage partners, the regulation also left room for child and compulsory marriages. Inequality persisted in inheritance in that a woman received a share equal to half that of a man in the same relationship to the deceased. Quite complex and spelled out in detail in religious scriptures, inheritance rules varied depending on kinship configurations and type and number of descendants. To take a simple example, however, if a man died leaving daughters and sons, the former would receive half as much as the latter.

The CPS shifted to a considerable degree the construct of self from a member of a lineage or kin group to that of an *autonomous individual* understood as the citizen of a state, owing loyalty to that state, and endowed with basic personal rights and obligations in a national legal code applicable to all Tunisians. The shift appears in the very structure of the law and the new regulations, especially those on marriage and divorce, which give more decision-making power over personal matters to individual men and women rather than to the kin group. For example, the CPS abolished repudiation and matrimonial guardianship. By suppressing matrimonial guardianship, the CPS redefined marriage and placed the woman in charge of her own marriage contract. The right to marry was shifted from the patrilineage to the individual as a basic personal right. The abolition of the matrimonial guardian's prerogative undermined the legal control that men used to have over their female relatives and removed a legal provision that could facilitate compulsory marriages.

In addition to reducing the power of kin over women, the CPS also decreased some of the prerogatives that men previously had as husbands. A divorce could now only occur in court, and the law allowed women to file for divorce on the same grounds as men, thus increasing women's ability to terminate marriages (Chater 1992: 235). In one of the most dramatic provisions in the Islamic Middle East, the CPS outlawed polygamy altogether, punishing any attempt to marry a second wife with a fine and imprisonment. In ending the unilateral privilege of the husband to terminate the marriage by repudiation, the CPS offered women some protection from the whims of their husbands in regard to the dissolution of marriage. Tunisia law thus reduced the power of men, both kin and husbands, over women and increased women's citizenship rights with respect to entering and terminating marriage.

Presenting a new image of personhood, the CPS defined the person primarily as an autonomous individual in interaction with the state, rather than as a member of a patrilineage whose family life was outside the purview of the state. The new conception of citizenship fostered by the CPS applied to both men and women. However, since the legal norms previously in effect placed women in a legal position subordinate to men, the CPS of 1956 had a particularly special significance for women's citizenship rights. At the same time, several forms of gender inequity remained in the law. For example, inheritance was left untouched and the initial text of the CPS in 1956 required that the wife should obey her husband (this clause was later dropped, as is considered below). Nevertheless, because persons were no longer defined primarily as members of extended kinship systems in the form of patrilineages, and because individual rights were expanded in the law, women gained a measure of legal autonomy.

Several features of the CPS and its promulgation help put it in perspective. If we use the typology on citizenship and gender offered by Lister (2012), the CPS is best conceptualized as a step toward the construction of a "gender-neutral citizen". It enshrined the individual (woman and man) as citizen of a state rather than as member of kin group or tribal entity. It constituted a top-down action, a reform from above, which occurred as a result of policy choices made by the newly formed national state, in the absence of any organized feminist movement and with little participation from civil society. There had been a few individual women voices in favor of changes in family law and women's status, but they did not coalesce into a social movement with a constituency, organization and platform. The CPS was an example of "politics from above" in which power holders design policy for reasons of their own interest and to enact their vision of society rather than as a response to demands from below by social movements.

Paired with the CPS, the Constitution was also a central site for the redefinition of citizenship and the establishment of individual rights. The new postcolonial Constitution was drafted and adopted on 1 June 1959. It adopted universalistic values in declaring equal rights before the law for all citizens, including women, including the right to vote. Further provisions were made to establish the equality of all citizens in amendments to the Constitution in 1988. Article 6 of the Constitution specifies: "All citizens have the same rights and the same duties. They are equal before the law" (quoted in Chamari 1991: 114). In addition, a provision in Article 20 further indicates: "Every citizen who has had the Tunisian nationality for at least five years and who has attained twenty years of age has the right to vote" (Republique Tunisienne 1998: 10–11). These amendments and provisions increasingly expanded individual rights and featured terms of "equality" to define the status of autonomous citizens, regardless of gender, although men and women were not explicitly mentioned as such (as they would be in the later period following the Arab Spring). Like the CPS, the Constitution of 1959 and again of 1988 was primarily the result of a top-down process with little collective discussion in the society at large.

The CPS was then followed by several amendments and further policies that gradually and incrementally expanded women's rights in family law.

For example, a 1993 amendment dropped the clause according to which a wife should obey her husband (Charrad and Ha forthcoming). That particular clause was dropped from Article 23, although the qualification of the husband as head of the family remained. Instead, the emphasis in the amended Article 23 was now on the cooperation between husband and wife in family affairs, the education of children, financial decisions, and trying not to inflict harm or injury.[1] Ben Salem, a Tunisian scholar, considers this a major change as it established "the equality of spouses with regard to reciprocal family obligations, cooperation in household management, and assistance in childcare" (Ben Salem 2010: 8).

These policies continued to occur essentially as the result of "politics from above" first throughout the regime of Bourguiba from 1956 to 1987 and then under the regime of Ben Ali from 1987 to 2011, with limited participation from civil society. Starting in the 1980s, some women's associations made their voices heard (Brand 1998). It was not until 2011, however, that civil society came in earnest to the fore in engaging in debates and shaping the discourse on citizenship.

Arab Spring: Debates on Representation of Women[2]

The Jasmine Revolution in 2011 and the collapse of the authoritarian Ben Ali regime opened a new era that witnessed, for the first time, a new "politics from below" and a set of debates in which civil society participated. When a broader set of actors entered the postrevolutionary political arena in 2011, we observe a new form of discourse on citizenship, one that centers on issues of representation in the foundational text of the new Constitution, and especially on the question of "equal" or "different" in reference to women and men. After years of authoritarian rule, Tunisians and many other Arab men, women and children protested against the suppression of civil liberties, financial corruption and

---

[1] See article 23 in Charrad and Ha, forthcoming: 167–168.
[2] This section draws on Charrad and Zarrugh 2014. Segments are reprinted with permission from Taylor and Francis, publisher of the *Journal of North African Studies*.

economic stagnation. A series of escalating protests began shortly after the self-immolation of a Tunisian vendor, Muhammad Bouazizi, on 17 December 2010, and ended with the resignation of then President Zine El Abidine Ben Ali on 14 January 2011. In the weeks and months that followed, Tunisians made arrangements to organize nationwide elections, to form a national constituent assembly and to redraft fundamental state documents, including the state Constitution.

A host of new political actors, including Islamist parties that had been brutally marginalized under the former regimes, entered the races for political office and garnered substantial support from sectors of the Tunisian population who had not felt adequately represented for decades. One of the strongest parties in the first elections in October of 2011 was the Ennahda party, which was officially recognized only in 2011, following the Arab Spring uprisings but had a longtime membership and a decade's long history as an Islamist movement inspired by the Muslim Brotherhood of Egypt.

Members of the National Constituent Assembly (NCA), who were popularly elected in October 2011, had the mandate to draft a new Constitution to replace the former Constitution of 1959. Following the release of the draft of the Constitution on 3 August 2012, several articles came under public scrutiny. Women activists and their male allies paid special attention to Article 28, which some regarded as compromising gender equality because the article defined women as "complementary" to men. A public debate ensued. Article 28 was supported mostly by representatives of the Islamist Ennahda Party. Nine of the twelve representatives in favor were from Ennahda; eight representatives from a variety of parties were against (Babnet 2012).

The Tunisian Constitution draft released in Arabic consisted of nine chapters and several articles within each chapter.[3] Two articles referred to women's rights explicitly; one of these articles was the contentious

---

[3] We discuss here the draft Constitution released on 13 August 2012 as this version was the catalyst for debates about specific articles, such as Article 2.28. Another draft was released on 14 December 2012. The nine chapters in the Tunisian Constitution draft of 13 August 2012 are entitled "General Provisions", "Rights and Obligations", "Legislative Power", "Executive Power", "Judicial Power", "Local Government", "Constitutional Authorities", "Amendment of the Constitution" and "Final Provisions".

Article 28 of Chapter 2, which concerned rights and obligations.[4] Entitled "Women's rights", Article 28 in that draft read as follows in translation:

> The state shall guarantee the protection of the rights of women and shall support the gains thereof as true partners to men in the building of the nation and as having a role *complementary* thereto within the family. The state shall guarantee the provision of equal opportunities between men and women in the bearing of various responsibilities. The state shall guarantee the elimination of all forms of violence against women. (International Idea 2012; emphasis added).

Much of the consternation concerning this article is situated around contestation of the Arabic term *yetekaamul* in the article.[5] The term is frequently translated as "complementary". We see an alternative translation of the term as "integrate with one another". This translation points to a sense of fulfillment and unity between men and women that suggests the essential significance of the roles of both men and women to the nation and the family. The translation as "fulfill one another" confers a slightly different meaning to the article, which, as Marks argues (Marks 2012), emphasizes the centrality of the two parts (men and women as mutually fulfilling to one another) and is situated within an Islamist ethics of collectivism more generally.

The most common translation of the term, however, is "complementary" (or *complémentaires* in French). Different organizations, from women's groups to political parties, assumed various positions on the terminology of the article, with many viewing it as a contradiction to other components of the draft Constitution that emphasized unequivocal gender equality. The term "equality" (French: *égaux* and *égalité*; Arabic: *al-masawa*) was used in multiple contexts in the draft Constitution, including in the following sections: the Preamble, Article 1.6 addressing

---

[4] The other article concerning women's rights is Article 1.10 entitled "Rights of women and the family". This article reads as follows: "The state shall protect the rights of women as well as protect family structures and maintain the coherence thereof" (International Idea 2012).

[5] An unofficial Arabic text of the 13 August 2012 draft Constitution is available online: http://www.marsad.tn/uploads/documents/Projet_Brouillon_Constit.pdf

equal rights among citizens, Article 2.21 addressing the rights of families and explicitly stating the "equality between spouses", Article 2.22 stating equality between citizens and Article 2.30 ensuring "equality between persons with special needs and other citizens" (International Idea 2012).

The absence of the term "equality" from Article 28 that directly addressed women's rights was disconcerting or offensive to several women's groups, which issued statements and proposed revisions to the draft. It is important to note that specific mention of women in the draft Constitution was a significant change from the 1959 Constitution, in which women were not specified as a group to be accorded particular and protected rights (World Intellectual Property Organization 1959).

Opposition to Article 28 surfaced particularly among some women's groups and large-scale demonstrations were promptly organized with as many as 6000 women in attendance at a demonstration in the capital city of Tunis on 13 August 2012, the day that the first draft of the Constitution was released and the fifty-sixth anniversary of the promulgation of Tunisia's CPS (Ghanmi 2012; Agence France-Presse 2012; Mamelouk 2012). Women in attendance were either unaffiliated with any organization or identified with organizations such as the Tunisian Association of Women Democrats (*Association Tunisienne des Femmes Démocrates* or ATFD), the Tunisian League for Human Rights (*La Ligue Tunisienne des Droits de l'Homme* or LTDH) and the Association of Tunisian Women for Research and Development (*Association des Femmes Tunisiennes pour la Recherche sur le Développment* or AFTURD). In addition to critiques around the term "complementary" were concerns about the specificity of complementary *within the family*. For some activists, the clause not only defined women vis-à-vis men but also only as married women, which represented another affront to women's interests (Ghanmi 2012). At issue here was women's autonomy, a feature of their status that had been well established and protected in the CPS and Constitution of the 1950s.

A specific critique of Article 28 concerned the possibility of future conservative interpretations of women's rights given that women's status in the article was presented as contingent upon their relation to men. Salma Hajri, of the Tunisian Association of Women Democrats, emphasized that point by arguing that women's individualism was compromised in the "complementary" clause of Article 28: "Women are not given rights as individuals...only in reference to men" (Farrell 2012). In this vein, a petition was created and disseminated by women who were inspired by insider critiques of the article made by Selma Mabrouk, a politician who was elected to the NCA in October 2011 as part of the centrist Ettakatol party (TKTL) but then joined the oppositional party Al-Massar (Meziou 2013). Mabrouk was at the forefront of protests against Article 28. She claimed entitlement to citizenship rights regardless of gender, "I am a Tunisian woman and before I am a woman or a Tunisian, I am a human being and a stand-alone citizen" (Ben Abdel Adeem 2012).

The online petition followed Mabrouk's widely circulated Facebook post about the article, which she helped draft as part of the Committee on Rights and Liberties, one of the constitutional committees tasked with writing sections of the document (Soufia 2012). Mabrouk's Facebook post was titled "Mauvaise journée à la commission droits et libertés" ("A bad day at the Committee on Rights and Liberties") (Ben Hassine 2012; Mabrouk 2012). This statement, made prior to the formal release of the complete Constitution draft, was quickly circulated across social media; on Twitter, the hashtag "#complementarité" was trending on Tunisian accounts (Ben Hassine 2012). The online petition, published on 2 August 2012, and entitled "Protégez les droits de citoyenneté de la femme en Tunisie!", acquired over 30,000 signatures (Avaaz 2012). An excerpt of the petition reads as follows:

> A woman is a citizen under the same title as that of a man. The state is about to vote on an article (28) of the Constitution that limits the citizenship rights of women under the principle of complementarity to men and not under the principle of equality. If this article were to be adopted in the final version of the Constitution, it would limit the principle of equality between men and women. A woman is not defined in terms of a man. We demand the repeal of Article 28 from the draft Constitution and maintain Article 22, which guarantees freedom and equality to citizens regardless of their gender. (Avaaz 2012)

This petition garnered signatures from both within the country and outside and from individuals belonging to a variety of civil society groups. The call demanded that civil society support equality between men and women by directly making demands upon the NCA to repeal the article. Furthermore, the petition gestured toward a notion of how gender equality ought to be articulated by drawing upon and endorsing Article 22 as a model. Article 22 reads: "Citizens shall, before the law, be equal in rights and obligations without any discrimination of any form" (Draft Constitution of the Republic of Tunisia 2012). Another set of civil society organizations, composed of the Tunisian Association of Women Democrats (ATFD), the Association of Tunisian Women for Research and Development (AFTURD), the Tunisian Defense League for Human Rights, the Women's Commission of the General Union of Tunisian Workers (UGTT), the Tunisian section of Amnesty International and the National Council for Freedom in Tunisia, formed a collective to denounce the article as "a violation of women" and "a paternalistic approach that gives to man absolute power while denying a woman's right to be a full-fledged citizen" (Babnet 2012).

On the other side of the debate on Article 28, some women affiliated with the Islamist party Ennahda emphasized and defended aspects of the article. Among the most popular figures in Islamist women's politics in Tunisia was Ennhada Executive Council member, and leader of the constitutional committee in charge of Article 28, Farida Labidi. A lawyer and human rights activist, Labidi was herself tortured under the authoritarian regime of Ben Ali (Labidi-Maïza 2012). She fiercely defended Article 28. Among her most circulated statements was her qualification of women's equality, "The rights and gains of women will not be touched…One cannot speak of equality between man and woman in the absolute" (Cavaillès 2012).

Labidi also accused the opponents of Article 28 of engaging in a campaign of deliberately misinforming the public about its contents. She suggested that the concerns of the average Tunisian woman differed from the attention accorded to Article 28:

> I think the Tunisian woman is rather concerned to guarantee the right to health, to education, to employment, to access positions of decision-making, to dignity, and to ensure life worthy conditions to rural women. (Babnet 2012)

Mehrezia Labidi-Maïza, Ennahda vice president of the NCA and an MP, attempted to distinguish the term "complementary" from notions of inequality. She declared: "Complementarity does not mean inequality. In complementarity, there is precisely an exchange, a partnership" (Boitiaux 2012). Labidi-Maïza also argued that a misunderstanding of language had fueled the controversy surrounding the article:

> Sharing roles between men and women does not at all mean that women are less than men or that the man has a higher position than women as is currently being popularized by some parties. (Ben Abdel Adeem 2012)

Many Islamist women drew from the experiences of hardship in their own lives as a testament to their concerns for women's issues; many women endured years of detention or served as the heads of household during their husbands' imprisonment. Another Ennahda Executive Council member, Mounia Brahim, emphasized the diversity and accomplishments of women who compose Ennahda and Islamist politics more generally, "Look at us. We're doctors, teachers, wives, mothers—sometimes our husbands agree with our politics, sometimes they don't. But we're here and we're active" (Marks 2011). Ennahda Executive Council members and women supportive of their positions were adamant in their stated commitments to preserving Tunisia's history of protecting women's rights and pledged support for the CPS. Ghannouchi himself committed the party's allegiance to the spirit of the CPS, though he maintained that

> [c]omplementation [sic] is an authentic concept, meaning that there would be no man without a woman and no woman without a man. This is an additional meaning to the notion of equality. (Ghanmi 2012)

The second draft of the Constitution was released in December 2012 and the final draft was completed at the end of April 2013. By then, during the early months of 2013, between the time of the release of the second and the final draft of the Constitution, the environment was changing significantly for Ennahda. The group lost significant credibility because it was unable to control security in the country.[6] Following a series of conflicts and compromises in favor of parties more inclined

---

[6] This was brought to the fore by the assassination of a secularist political leader, Chokri Belaid.

toward secularism, the Ennahda party lost influence. In both the second and the final draft, the clause of Article 28 that included the term "complementary" and catalyzed popular protest across the country was dropped. Several other concessions were made by Ennahda, including eschewing specific reference to Shari'a in the Constitution (Human Rights Watch 2013). On 26 January 2014, the new Constitution was formally ratified. In Article 21, the first article of the second chapter entitled "Rights and Liberties", the term of equality is present and Article 21 states unambiguously: "All citizens, male and female alike, have *equal* rights and duties, and are *equal* before the law without any discrimination" (Jasmine Foundation 2014; emphasis added). This closed the debate on equality versus complementarity in the text of the Constitution for the foreseeable future.

Conclusion

We have considered in this chapter the ways in which the law has represented and incorporated women into the rubric of citizenship in two different eras of Tunisian history, in the postcolonial period of the 1950s and in the contemporary period of revolutionary change since 2011. We illustrated how the construction of gendered citizenship in a country like Tunisia, postcolonial and with a majority Muslim population, has been different from the discourse on citizenship in Western liberal democracies. We also showed how the constructs have shifted over time in Tunisia, depending on the political system and who held power.

Unlike the focus on equality and difference that has prevailed in discussions among feminists studying Western liberal democracies, our research showed that the discourse in Tunisia focused on individual autonomy versus kin or tribal power over persons in the postcolonial state. In Constituting the new citizen of the newly sovereign state, the CPS of 1956 underplayed and, in some cases, undermined the ties within the extended patrilineal kinship network to enshrine instead a conception of legal personhood tied to individual rights and obligations.

We then found that, with the discourse shifting to representation, a new term, "complementary" came to the fore with regard to the representation of women in official texts in Tunisia when a different set of political actors, an Islamist party, acquired power in the transition from authoritarianism to a democratically elected government with an Islamist bent following the Arab Spring of 2011. Contested by Tunisian feminists and the object of debates engaging civil society, the term "complementary" was finally omitted from the final text of the Constitution, where the concept of equality between men and women prevails.

Citizenship in Tunisia shows a first step toward the construction of the "gender-neutral citizen" as the postcolonial citizen through "politics from above", as was the case during the Bourguiba era. In jeopardy for a short while in the initial draft of the Constitution, the concept of gender neutrality was then restored following the active participation of women's rights advocates and civil society in a new "politics from below", as has been the case since the Arab Spring. The history of Tunisia shows the extent to which discourses or debates on constructing gendered representation in citizenship are influenced by the political context and who holds power at any given time. It also demonstrates that, through the twists and turns of history, gendered citizenship can remerge as a contested and contentious issue at any time.

References

Agence France-Presse. (2012). About 'Equality' between men and women in the Tunisian constitution. 24 September. Translated from Arabic by the authors.
Avaaz. (2012). Protégez les droits de citoyenneté de la femme en Tunisie! Avaaz. org: Petitions Citoyennes. 2 August. Available from http://www.avaaz.org/fr/petition/Protegez_les_droits_de_citoyennete_de_la_femme_en_Tunisie/
Babnet. (2012). Tunisie: La société civile dénonce l'art 28 de la Constitution comme une régression des acquis de la femme. 13 August. Available from http://www.babnet.net/cadredetail-53060.asp
Ben Abdel Adeem, M. (2012). Calls for a National Celebration of Women in Tunisia amid Fears about the Principle of Equality. France 24. 13 August. Translated from Arabic by the authors.
Ben Hassine, W. (2012). Tunisian assembly: It's a Man's World, but Women Can Help! Naawat. Blogpost, 3 August 2012. Accessed May 15, 2013, from http://nawaat.org/portail/2012/08/03/tunisian-assembly-its-a-mans-world-but-women-can-help/

Ben Salem, L. (2010). Tunisia. Report. Freedom House. Available from https://freedomhouse.org/sites/default/files/inline_images/Tunisia.pdf

Boitiaux, C. (2012). 'Complémentarité' contre 'égalité; des sexes, la polémique enfle en Tunisie. France 24. 10 August. Available from http://www.france24.com/fr/20120808-tunisie-droits-femmes-feminisme-complementarite-contre-egalite-sexes-projet-loi-polemique-constitution

Brand, L. A. (1998). *Women, the state, and political liberalization: Middle Eastern and North African experiences*. New York: Columbia University Press.

Cavaillès, T. (2012). Amertume et colère des femmes tunisiennes. *Le Figaro*, 14 August. Available from http://www.lefigaro.fr/international/2012/08/13/01003-20120813ARTFIG00440-amertume-et-colere-des-femmes-tunisiennes.php

Chamari, A. C. (1991). *La Femme et la loi en Tunisie (Women and law in Tunisia)*. Casablanca: United Nations University and Editions le Fennec.

Charrad, M. M. (2001). *States and women's rights: The making of postcolonial Tunisia, Algeria, and Morocco*. Berkeley, CA: University of California Press.

Charrad, M. M. (2010). Tunisia at the forefront of the Arab World: Two waves of gender legislation. In F. Sadiqi & M. Ennaji (Eds.), *Women in the Middle East and North Africa: Agents of change*. New York: Routledge.

Charrad, M. M. (2011a). Central and local patrimonialism: State building in kin-based societies. In J. P. Adams & M. M. Charrad (Eds.), *Patrimonial power in the modern world. The annals of the American academy of political and social sciences series* (Book 636, pp. 49–68). New York: Sage.

Charrad, M. M. (2011b). Gender in the middle east: Islam, states, agency. *Annual Review of Sociology, 37*, 417–437.

Charrad, M. M., & Ha, H. (forthcoming). Sustained reforms of Islamic family law: Tunisia under authoritarian regimes, 1950s to 2010. In A. Wing & H. Kassim (Eds.), *Family law and gender in the modern middle east*. New York: Cambridge University Press.

Charrad, M. M., & Zarrugh, A. (2014). Equal or complementary? Women in the New Tunisian Constitution after the Arab Spring. *Journal of North African Studies, 19*(2), 230–243.

Chater, S. (1992). *Les Emancipées du harem: Regard sur la femme Tunisienne* (Emancipated from the Harem: Perspectives on Tunisian Women). Tunis: Editions la Presse.

Danielsen, H., Jegerstedt, K., Muriass, R. L., & Ytre-Arne, B. (2016). Introduction. In H. Danielsen, K. Jegerstedt, R. L. Muriaas, & B. Ytre-Arne (Eds.), *Gendered citizenship and the politics of representation*. London: Palgrave Macmillan.

Draft Constitution of the Republic of Tunisia. (2012). Chapter 2, Article 2.28. Draft of August 13, 2012. Translation (from Arabic) by International IDEA. Language: English. Accessed April 20, 2013, from http://www.constitutionnet.org/files/2012.08.14_-_draft_constitution_english.pdf

Farrell, J. (2012). Tunisian constitution: Text and context. *Jadaliyya*, 23 August. Available from http://www.jadaliyya.com/pages/index/6991/tunisian-constitution_text-and-context

Ghanmi, M. (2012). Tunisian women march for their rights. *Magharebia*, 15 August. Available from http://www.magharebia.com/en_GB/articles/awi/features/2012/08/15/feature-02

Human Rights Watch. (2013). Tunisia: Slow reform pace undermines rights. 6 February. Available from http://www.hrw.org/news/2013/02/06/tunisia-slow-reform-pace-undermines-rights

International Idea. (2012). Draft constitution of the Republic of Tunisia. 13 August. Available from http://www.constitutionnet.org/files/2012.08.14_-_draft_constitution_english.pdf

Jasmine Foundation. (2014). Constitution of the Tunisian Republic: Unofficial translation. Available from http://www.jasmine-foundation.org/doc/unofficial_english_translation_of_tunisian_constitution_final_ed.pdf

Joseph, S. (Ed.). (2000). *Gender and citizenship in the Middle East*. Syracuse: Syracuse University Press.

Kelly, S., & Breslin, J. (Eds.). (2010). *Women's rights in the Middle East and North Africa: Progress amid resistance*. New York: Freedom House.

Labidi-Maïza, M. (2012). Tunisia's women are at the heart of its revolution. *The Guardian*, 23 March. Available from http://www.guardian.co.uk/commentisfree/2012/mar/23/tunisia-women-revolution

Lister, R. (1991). Citizenship engendered. *Critical Social Policy*, *11*, 65–71.

Lister, R. (2012). Citizenship and gender. In E. Amenta, K. Nash, & A. Scott (Eds.), *The Wiley-Blackwell companion to political sociology* (pp. 372–382). Malden: Blackwell.

Mabrouk, S. (2012). Mauvaise journée à la commission droits et libertés. Facebook post, 1 August. Available from https://www.facebook.com/selma.mabroukdeputeeanc/posts/116719421806537

Maktabi, R. (2010). Gender, family law and citizenship in Syria. *Citizenship Studies*, *14*(5), 557–572.

Mamelouk, D. (2012). Article 28 of the Tunisian constitution: A problem among many others. *Jadaliyya*, 26 September. Available from http://www.jadaliyya.com/pages/index/7233/article-28-of-the-tunisian-constitution_a-problem-among-many-others/

Marks, M. (2011). Can Islamism and feminism mix? *New York Times*, 26 October. Available from http://www.nytimes.com/2011/10/27/opinion/can-islamism-and-feminism-mix.html

Marks, M. (2012). 'Complementary' status for Tunisian women. *Foreign Policy*, 20 August. Available from http://www.mideast.foreignpolicy.com/posts.2012/08/20/complementary_status_for_tunisian_women

Marshall, T. H. (1964). *Class, citizenship, and social development*. Garden City: Double Day.

Meziou, D. M. (2013). Huge Al-Massar Meeting Galvanizes Tunisian Opposition. *Al-Monitor*, 14 April. Available from http://www.al-monitor.com/pulse/ar/contents/articles/politics/2013/04/tunisian-opposition-organizes.html

Moghadam, V. (2011). Feminism and family law in Iran: The struggle for women's economic citizenship in the Islamic republic. In F. Sadiqi & M. Ennaji (Eds.), *Women in the Middle East and North Africa: Agents of change* (pp. 114–128). New York: Routledge.

Muriaas, R., Tonnessen, L., & Wang, V. (2016). Substantive representation: From timing to framing of family law reform in Morocco, South Africa and Uganda. In H. Danielsen, K. Jegerstedt, R. L. Muriaas, & B. Ytre-Arne (Eds.), *Gendered citizenship and the politics of representation*. London: Palgrave Macmillan.

Republique Tunisienne (1998). *Constitution de la République Tunisienne (Constitution of the Republic of Tunisia)*. Tunis: Imprimerie Officielle.

Somers, M. R. (1993). Citizenship and the place of the public sphere: Law, community, and political culture in the transition to democracy. *American Sociological Review*, 58(5), 587–620.

Soufia, B. A. (2012). Tunisie: La Femme, un simple complement de l'Homme. Mag 14, 2 August. Available from http://www.mag14.com/national/40-politique/782-tunisie–la-femme-un-simple-complement-de-lhomme.html

Walby, S. (1994). Is citizenship gendered? *Sociology*, 28(2), 379–395.

Wing, A., & Kassim, H. (2007). The future of Palestinian women's rights: Lessons from a half century of Tunisian progress. *Washington and Lee Law Review*, Vol. 64.

World Intellectual Property Organization. (1959). Constitution of the Tunisian republic. Available from http://www.wipo.int/wipolex/en/details.jsp?id=7201

Yuval-Davis, N. (1997). *Gender and nation*. Thousand Oaks, CA: Sage.

Part III

Challenging the Public–Private Divide

8

Representations of Women Voters in Newspaper Coverage of UK Elections 1918–2010

Emily Harmer and Liesbet van Zoonen

Introduction

The way women are depicted in news media sends out important messages about their place and role in society. If women are absent or marginalized from political news, this suggests that they are irrelevant to representational politics in its twofold sense: as representatives of the people, and as people to be represented. The first dimension of women's representation in politics has been amply researched within media studies. The majority

---

E. Harmer (✉)
Department of Social Sciences, Loughborough University, Epinal Way, LE11 3TU Loughborough, Leicestershire, UK

L. van Zoonen (✉)
Department of Sociology, Erasmus University Rotterdam, Burg Oudlaan 50, 3062 PA Rotterdam, The Netherlands

of work in this area focuses on the US and European context and tends to analyse contemporary representations, from the 1990s onwards. Many scholars have noted that the activities of female politicians receive less news coverage than those of men and, second, news descriptions refer to their appearance, or to the men in their lives, rather than to their independent qualities and achievements (Norris 1997; Braden 1996; Ross 2002; Gill 2007). These representations articulate a particular ideological view about men and women; far from being neutral, the imagery and language of mediated politics is heavily gendered and reinforces the idea of male as the norm, while women are regarded as outsiders or novelties (Sreberny-Mohammadi and Ross 1996).

The other dimension of women's political representation, that is, as people that need to be represented politically, has hardly been analysed yet in media research. This chapter therefore aims to contribute to the wider discussion, in this volume and beyond, about the ways in which citizenship and representational politics remain gendered, by demonstrating that media discourses about politics reinforce existing ideas about the roles of men and women in society. Our analysis draws upon the dual meaning of representation discussed at the beginning of this volume, by arguing that in order for women to be adequately represented in politics, they must also be represented in the public discussion of it, which takes place in the media. The chapter provides a historical analysis of the way the British press has represented the concerns of female voters, from the moment they could vote, to the present day. Our chapter explores the way the press provides particular vocabularies, images and concepts with which to make sense of the world and the place of men and women within it (Holland 2004).

Our data demonstrates how women have been consistently represented as wives and mothers whose political concerns are almost exclusively bound up with the health and well-being of their families. There is surprisingly little historical variety or progress in this respect, although there are relevant changes in *how* their interests as wives or mothers are portrayed; for example, earlier coverage focuses on women as housewives concerned about the cost of living and this declines in later years to include a wider set of policy concerns. We also analyse how women who do not conform to stereotypical political identities are represented as exceptional or deviant; their representation thus confirms the overall rule.

We will first introduce our theoretical perspective and then explain our methodological approach before discussing our findings.

Media and the (Political) Representation of Women

There is a substantial amount of general research about the portrayal of women in the media. Of special interest here is the Global Media Monitoring Project, which has been conducted by feminist media researchers worldwide every five years since 1995 (Gill 2007). It tracks the representation of women across national media. Every study has shown that nowhere in the world has women's mediated representation achieved parity with men, who continue to dominate the news. Strikingly, there is a lack of variation across countries and women were marginal to news agendas on a global scale. The latest study from 2010 shows that after 15 years of monitoring, the visibility of women as producers and subjects of news has seen some improvement, but that men still dominate the news because they receive three times the visibility of women (Ross and Carter 2011). These reports demonstrate that Tuchman et al.'s (1978) early contention that women were subjected to "symbolic annihilation" remains relevant. This term refers to the condemnation, trivialization or absence of women from mass media. Such patterns of representation are central to the means by which social inequality is maintained since they contribute to the overall impression that the public sphere is overwhelmingly male.

Feminist scholars have pointed out that the political domain and its activities have been constructed in contrast to the private, domestic sphere. Van Zoonen (1998) argues that such a distinction between "public" and "private" is a fairly recent historical construction and that it is tied to the division of labour between men and women in the family. Siltanen and Stanworth (1984) argue that this separation of public and private promotes a set of dichotomies which disadvantage women. These are defined as: political–apolitical, public–private and male–female. Such dichotomies construct the abstract public citizen as male in the sense that he performs traditionally masculine roles and has male characteristics. He is universal, rational and is concerned with the public interest. In contrast, the female, non-citizen's concerns are private and domestic and she is emotional, irrational and weak (Lister 1997). Feminists have frequently pointed out that if politics is assumed to be the prerogative of the public sphere, and women are located within the private domain, it is no wonder that women's participation in politics has been historically problematic (Siltanen and Stanworth 1984).

Landes (1998) notes that the division between the public and private spheres meant that a whole range of concerns came to be labelled private and treated as improper subjects for public discussion. The feminist movement, and the incorporation of women into the formal public sphere as politicians and voters, has meant that the boundaries between the public and the private, and the political and the personal, have become blurred: demonstrating that the line between public and private is constantly being renegotiated (Landes 1998). As a result, matters such as childcare and domestic violence, which would previously have been considered private, have become subjects of political concern and public policy. Lister (1997) argues that the exclusion of women from citizenship, which was only partially rectified by women's formal incorporation in the twentieth century, far from being an aberration, was integral to the theory and practice of citizenship. Women made the public sphere possible by undertaking the provision of care, reproduction and other unpaid (and therefore unrecognized) duties. When women were admitted to the public sphere, they did so on different terms than men, because they were still expected to fulfil their private roles. Accordingly, the nature of women's contemporary inclusion is still imbued with gendered assumptions.

While such a general understanding of women's presence in the public sphere has become a common framework in the analysis of gendered politics, there has been little attention for its empirical and historical specificities in research on media representations. In this chapter, we will therefore show exactly how the British press represented the concerns of women as political subjects and potential voters from 1918 (the first election in which women were able to vote and stand as candidates) to 2010 (the most recent general election, at the time of writing). Therefore, our contribution is empirical rather than theoretical, since, as Van Zoonen (2005) has claimed, this is a field where there is more theory than extensive empirical and historical work.

Method

The chapter draws upon a quantitative and qualitative content analysis of five national UK daily newspapers, the *Daily Telegraph*, *The Guardian*, *The Sun*, the *Daily Mail* and the *Daily Mirror*. These titles were selected because they reflect the British political spectrum, with the *Daily Telegraph* and *Daily Mail* representing the centre-right and *The Guardian* representing the centre-left, and because they were all around in 1918, allowing for an historical comparison. The content analysis sampled the week before all 25 elections which took place between 1918 and 2010. All items which were entirely about the election and featured more than one mention of a female actor were coded. This resulted in 1382 separate items about women voters. Each was coded for a number of variables; those relevant to this chapter include: the two main themes, whether the women's personal lives were mentioned and whether women were directly or indirectly quoted. A qualitative analysis was conducted on items which were typical examples of electoral coverage for each election. A constant comparison of items over time allowed us to analyse how the themes and vocabularies associated with women voters changed over time. We focused on the policy issues they were associated with and whether their familial roles were invoked as explanations for their political views. Although we looked at five newspapers, we found very few systematic differences in the representations of women voters, so we will not discuss differences between newspapers here.

"A Wife's Vote Is a Husband's Vote Times Two"[1]

An enduring aspect of the coverage of women voters is the extent to which their political choices are constructed as an extension of their husband's political concerns. During the interwar years when women were newly enfranchised, it was largely assumed by the newspapers that women would vote according to their husband's views. *The Guardian* stated in 1918 that "it is said that many of the wives of absent soldiers will not vote because their husbands cannot advise them, and this, unfor-

---

[1] This phrase is used by Goot and Reid (1984) to describe the assumption that mainstream voting studies employed when looking at women's political participation.

tunately means the double disenfranchisement of the soldiers" (*The Guardian* 1918b). We recognize an assumption here that women need male relatives to help them understand politics, but also that women failing to vote is mainly problematic because it means their men will not be represented. Women's lack of political convictions of their own was also discussed by the *Daily Telegraph* during the 1922 election. It claimed that "in the present uneducated state of womanhood…there is a disposition on the part of the married woman voter to accept her husband's view as her own" (*Daily Telegraph* 1922). Here, it is suggested that women do not understand the issues and are therefore content to accept their husband's views rather than educate themselves. The *Daily Mail* is more negative when it states that "one man who has had more than twenty years of election experience yesterday classified the women into three groups: the woman who regards a request for her vote as an impertinence; the woman who takes her politics from her husband and stands by them to the death; the woman who distrusts politics and regards a canvasser in the same light as a tax collector" (*Daily Mail* 1922b). The suggestion that all women fall into one of these groups served to construct women as difficult to communicate with and uninterested in politics and highlights their perceived incompatibility with the political realm.

A striking example of women being portrayed as an extension of their husband's political views is the *Daily Mirror's* "Vote for Him" campaign during the 1945 election, which was designed to encourage women voters to vote according to the views of their husband's and sons who had not yet returned home from the war. The campaign manifests itself as a series of readers' letters, mainly authored by women, explaining which party they intend to vote for on behalf of their male relations. The newspaper described this as a "sacred trust" (*Daily Mirror* 1945c) that women ought to fulfil in order to ensure that fighting men were represented in the election. This suggests that women's citizenship is somehow secondary to their male counterparts. It also positioned women as mere proxy voters rather than as concerned citizens with their own views. Seemingly vast numbers of women agreed however, since "wives, mothers, sweethearts from all over Britain have written to the '*Daily Mirror*' to say that they are going to vote 'for them'" (*Daily Mirror* 1945a). One letter stated that: "I am a married woman, serving in the WAAF and shall vote Labour because I know that the future politics will decide whether I can afford to bring up one child or whether or not I shall get a house at a reasonable price, whether my husband will get a job at a living wage or not" (*Daily Mirror* 1945b), suggesting that despite the increase in women's employment during the war, traditional roles would be restored after its conclusion. This parallel between women as reserve citizens and their role as a reserve workforce demonstrates that, when circumstances call for it, there can be historic fluctuations in the public–private divide, which underlines Landes' (1998) assertion that the boundaries between the two spheres are constantly under negotiation.

After WWII, some coverage focused on the fact that women no longer defer to their male relatives, who have "apparently less influence over their wives than at one time" (*The Guardian* 1951). *The Sun* uses an academic to make the same point: "Dr Durant said that a survey had shown that 12 per cent of women did not vote like their husbands" (Suich 1964). During the 1960s, women voters begin to be routinely constructed as independent voters who no longer defer to their husband's choices. *The Guardian*, for instance, claims that "women no longer automatically vote with their husbands and are quite happy to say so on the doorstep" (*The Guardian* 1964). The newspaper goes on to suggest that because "more women are going out to work" (*The Guardian* 1964), their "economic independence leads to independent thought" (*The Guardian* 1964). This is largely repeated by the other newspapers, although its repetition suggests that it is still considered surprising: "[T]he only amazement of the campaign so far has been the extraordinary number of households in which husband and wife hold opposing political opinions" (*The Sun* 1966). This change perhaps stems from the recognition that women are capable of engaging in independent thought after nearly 50 years of voting rights and, furthermore, the recognition that a wider range of political concerns have come to be considered worthy aspects of public discussion. The influence of feminist efforts to redefine what can legitimately be considered political may also be a factor (Landes 1998). This discourse therefore declined dramatically after the 1970s, although there have been rare moments where women's roles as wives have seen a resurgence, such as the debate over the Conservative Party's manifesto commitment to introducing a married person's tax allowance in 2010.

In summary, during the interwar years, the newspapers talk about women voters as though they will automatically vote according to their husband's political views. After 1945, the idea that men have less influence than they once did starts to take root, although up until the 1970s, newspapers continue to refer to there being some relationship between the voting preferences of women and their husbands'. These discourses are largely consistent across newspapers but begin to decline after the 1970s. These findings give credence to feminist scholars who argue that the public–private divide is partly based on gendered assumptions about the roles and capabilities of men and women in the family (see Lister 1997). This early focus on the familial roles of women voters being explicitly connected to their engagement with the political sphere is also reflected in the policy themes, which women are most commonly associated with throughout the sample period.

"The Price of an Egg and a Loaf of Bread and a Packet of Detergent Is Politics"[2]: Home Economics

The economy, in particular the cost of living, is constructed as the central concern for voters for most of the sample period. The economy was the main theme in 34.7 % of the total number of items about women voters and the dominant theme in 15 out of the 25 elections in the content analysis sample. This corresponds closely to the ways in which, as Bingham (2004) found, women voters were constructed during this period. Bingham argued that the press tended to portray women as thrifty housewives concerned about the prices of essential items and as caring mothers who prioritize the welfare of their families. The idea of the housewife and her concerns is visible in this example from the *Daily Mirror*: "they will scrutinise the promises and merits of competing candidates solely from the point of view of the housewife, [and] the home" (Willoughby 1922), therefore excluding the possibility that women might not have

---

[2] *Daily Mirror*, 28 February 1974, p. 17.

children or are unmarried. Such attitudes also suggest that it was assumed that women did not have any other political concerns. The economy is constructed as an important policy area because "the women are profoundly concerned at the high cost of living, and the party which is able to convince the army of housewives that it is determined to reduce taxation—and, consequently the cost of commodities—will triumph tomorrow" (*Daily Mirror* 1922). This emphasis on the economics of the home supports Lister's (1997) suggestion that when women gained the right to vote, they entered the public sphere still encumbered with their private responsibilities.

Despite the previous observation that newspapers present women as voting in line with their husbands, they are rather contradictorily also positioned as voters with special insight into the domestic sphere. During the interwar period, voters, or more specifically housewives, are flattered by constant references to their abilities to run a household and, therefore by extension, their abilities to understand how to run the country: "[T]he average mother of a family…is essentially a good manager. She has to make a pound go as far as 210 pence" (Watkins 1923). Furthermore, these women are frequently constructed as "the Chancellors of the Exchequer of the home" (*Daily Mail* 1931) and "guardians of the domestic purse" (*Daily Mirror* 1931). Housewives are constructed as central to the economic prosperity of the country because "the smashing wage reductions in the last three years have restricted her power to buy goods, thereby restricting the home market, creating unemployment, and at the same time bringing want into millions of homes" (*Daily Herald* 1923). Politicians are frequently reported appealing directly to women voters in these gendered terms; for example, in 1923, then Prime Minister Stanley Baldwin was quoted: "I am not surprised that our opponents have given up argument and have fallen back upon a dishonourable attempt to scare the housewife by talking of dear food. Women of every class find their resources straightened by the burdens which their households have to bear in taxes and rates to save the workless from destitution" (*Daily Mail* 1923). This construction of the woman voter as the household manager is particularly evident in the conservative press of the interwar period (Bingham 2004); however, our analysis did not find a strong difference between the political perspectives of newspapers and their adherence to this discourse. After the war, the cost of living becomes central to the political discourse due to reconstruction policies that maintained rationing well into the 1950s (Zweiniger-Bargielowska 2002). During this period, housewives became an even more influential political force and their discontent for austerity had important electoral consequences. This example from the *Daily Mirror* illustrates the importance of the cost of living: "[W]e repeat this regrettable truth for the benefit of any housewives who may have been deceiving themselves with the great illusion that any British Government can suddenly give them more food, or put more buying power in their purses, or slash prices without slashing the standard of living" (*Daily Mirror* 1951). Such overt criticism of women voters is rare, however, and for the most part, the newspapers throughout the 1950s to the 1970s position themselves on the side of the housewife.

The 1970s would be no different, "Tory leader Mr Edward Heath made a final attempt last night to win the housewives' vote, with a slashing attack on sparing prices and crippling taxation…he blamed Labour for Britain's economic problems and declared: 'Mr Wilson has made his biggest mistake. He has underestimated the mood of the women of this country'" (*Daily Mail* 1970a). The 1970 election is particularly relevant in this regard because the cost of living dominates the discourse about voters, for example: "[O]f course, prices are the biggest election issue for housewives, agree all the party spokesmen, and the candidates in the field" (*Daily Telegraph* 1970). Politicians of all parties place the rising cost of everyday commodities at the centre of their campaign to women voters because "the evidence is there for all to see, clear and beyond dispute. It is the evidence of the shopping basket and grocer's counter. It is the evidence every housewife knows only too well" (*Daily Mail* 1970b). The Conservative Party in particular sought to appeal to working-class women who were not receiving the benefits of their husband's improved pay packets under Labour (Day 1982).

Prices and the cost of living continued to be an important means of constructing women voters throughout the 1970s: "[F]or the housewives of Britain, the cost of the family's food bill is a major factor as they weigh up the pros and cons of this election" (Burton 1979), reinforcing the "conventional wisdom…that every election, in the end, turns out to be a Shopping Basket Election" (*The Sun* 1979) as far as women are concerned. Throughout the 1980s and beyond, this discourse gradually changes, and as such, the cost of living as the most important policy area for women declines rapidly after 1979 and the most dominant policy themes associated with women voters after this are issues related with health and welfare policies. Despite the shift, associating women with health and welfare issues still reflects the assumption that their political priorities are informed by their continued responsibility for the private sphere.

Domestic Politics

Strikingly, throughout the entire sample period, women are consistently constructed as caring more about domestic matters than other policy areas. This is clearly linked to assumptions about women's traditional role as the providers of domestic labour in the private sphere, which is reflected in the proliferation of media texts which predominantly construct women as domestically oriented household managers and mothers (MacDonald 1995). Our analysis shows that women are consistently constructed as caring more about domestic matters than any other policy areas; for example, the *Daily Mirror* claims in 1924 that voters "may not particularly care whether we sign a treaty with Albania or not because the whole thing is too distant, but every housewife cares very considerably whether the price of sugar is to be 2d per pound cheaper or not" (Wallace 1924). This discourse is consistently maintained throughout the elections so that in 1974, the *Daily Mirror* editorial asks: "[D]oes the Chancellor think the electorate is soft in the head? Does he think the British housewife is more worried about Reds under the bed than the price of bread under Ted?" (*Daily Mirror* 1974). This discourse persists even into the most recent elections: in *The Sun* in 2005, for example, a columnist complained that she had "written many times before in this column that women voters—particularly those with children—are interested in education, crime, health and all the issues that affect our families and their future…yet all these important matters seem to have been smothered into oblivion by repeated bickering over the validity, or otherwise, of the decision to 'liberate' Iraq from Saddam Hussein" (Moore 2005). This frequent assertion that women are only concerned about aspects of policy which directly impact home life demonstrates that the public sphere has clearly expanded to include discussion of aspects of private life, reflecting once again the constant renegotiation of public and private boundaries (Landes 1998).

Examples that deviate from these constructions are rare but offer an important means of challenging the prevailing discourse. An early example would be a woman voter complaining that "politicians canvassing for votes are promising jam to everyone—except the single woman. After twenty-five years at work I earn £4 16s a week…I live in a bed-sitter in someone else's house and pay a high rent. How about a little jam for me—a living wage and a council flat?" (Derby 1955). This woman directly contests dominant social expectations and emphasizes her role as an unmarried employee and tenant. The majority of the few examples offering a counter discourse come from the late 1970s onwards, such as this example from 1979: "[W]omen account for more than 40 per cent of Britain's work force—and two out of three of them married. So the true picture of women today is not one of the little wife at home who can't be bothered with anything more than the price of butter" (Cousins 1979), which emphasizes, to some extent, the diversity among women. *The Guardian* also presents a more nuanced view of women voters during the 2010 election by arguing that the focus of the election became narrowed to address certain types of women such as mothers, rather than addressing women generally. It also recognized that the outcome of the election would impact women significantly; "two thirds of public servants are women: they are the teachers, the doctors, and the much more cuts prone home helps and dinner ladies. They use public services more, and—as mothers and carers—do most of the dropping off at the schools and the surgeries that will soon feel the squeeze" (*The Guardian* 2010), which shows that later elections do begin to represent women beyond the traditional scope of housewife and mother.

Our analysis shows that up until the late 1970s, women voters are consistently represented as housewives whose political priorities revolve around the cost of living in particular. This is increasingly important during the immediate post-war period when austerity politics meant that women became an even more pronounced political force. This discourse declines however during the late 1970s and early 1980s when women voters start to become more associated with health and welfare issues. This decline in representing women as interested primarily in domestic issues perhaps reflects the expansion of the public sphere that was happening at this time, with larger numbers of women entering the public sphere by taking paid employment outside the home and feminists advocating for a wider definition of what may be considered political, newspapers may have been responding to these changes by recognizing that women have other legitimate concerns that do not necessarily stem from their position in the home.

"The Hand That Rocks the Cradle Is the Hand That Writes the Decisive X"[3]

From the very beginning of women's citizenship, their roles as mothers have been constructed as having an impact on their political views, and this discourse remains the most consistent feature of the newspaper coverage up unto 2010. In 1918, *The Guardian* suggests about women's right to vote that "having got this power, a power which they can use for improving the conditions of life for their own household, for their homes, and for their children, it is a trust which they ought to exercise" (*The Guardian* 1918a). Women are often subjected to political messages that aim to elicit an emotional response: "making a strong appeal to women electors [one campaigner] says that unemployment and decreased wages, coupled with the high cost of living, are having tragic effects on mothers, who are denying themselves to make both ends meet" (*Daily Mail* 1922a); this kind of appeal assumes that innate maternal qualities will inform women's political choices. This recurs throughout the interwar period: "[T]here was no section of the community who understood more distinctly than the mothers of the nation the need for healthy conditions in the home, school, factory, and everywhere where children and adults met and lived together" (*Daily Herald* 1924).

---

[3] *Daily Mirror*, 5 October 1959, pp. 16–17.

In his study of the popular press in the interwar period, Bingham (2004) also observes that women tend to be represented as mothers who are concerned about social conditions and the welfare of children. During the post-war period, the dominance of motherhood continues but the focus becomes much more personalized and individualized; so mothers are constructed as less anxious to improve social conditions generally, thinking only in terms of their own families. The following appeal from the *Daily Herald* demonstrates this tendency: "[I]f you have children… help the Labour party to see that they get the food they need and the education they deserve" (Allan 1945). This period sees motherhood redefined as an individual pursuit rather than a collective experience: "[I]n this election the housewife's fight is to keep what her family already have. She is fighting for family security" (*Daily Mirror* 1951). Women themselves contribute to this discourse by invoking their own roles as mothers in political discussions or reader's letters: "[M]others, said Mrs Jones junior, cuddling her baby, 'have got the future of their children to think about'" (Proops 1974). Mothers are also constructed as an important target group for politicians to win over. In 1987, "Labour hopes to woo Britain's mothers last night with the promise of a brighter future for their children" (Bradshaw 1987).

During the 1990s and 2000s, the motherhood discourse becomes even more personalized by using specific individual women and their opinions to speak on behalf of mothers everywhere. One woman suggests she will vote for "the party that will help her family the most" (*The Sun* 2001). Children and policy areas which directly affect them feature heavily in these personal accounts: "[W]ith three children in school, Allyson is *naturally* concerned about education" (*The Sun* 2001; emphasis added). Another voter's response in the same article is also focused primarily on her role as a mother: "Laura hopes Labour will stick to their election pledges of delivering pre and after school care for 100,000 children by 2004. And she is keen to see the introduction of more breakfast and after-school clubs, holiday places and weekend activities for families" (*The Sun* 2001). The journalistic conventions of personalization sometimes construct the mothers in the news as passive objects that are talked about, rather than as active political participants that have their own voice: "[D]espairing Julie Cleminson cuddled her newborn son Paul yesterday…and prayed he will be given the chance to be happy that she has never had" (Corless 1992), which further emphasizes the idea that women's main political interests are based around their familial role. Yet, when we hear women's own voices, traditional ideas of motherhood are reinforced as well: "'I'm appalled', says her mum Jeannie, 'because of these cut backs, my daughter and other handicapped children like her are going to suffer'" (Palmer 1997). Motherhood remains an important discourse in the most recent election where party strategists suggested that the election would be decided by 400,000 women in marginal constituencies, meaning that none of the main political parties would want to "risk alienating some important groups of voters, such as the young mother" (Beckford 2010).

In sum, our analysis shows that discourse of motherhood as a reason for political engagement is a historical constant in news coverage of women voters. However, the particular articulations of this discourse change over time and become increasingly personalized: While in the early twentieth century, mothers were framed as a collective concerned with the well-being of children in general, currently, they are presented as individuals caring for their own children in particular. There is little difference between the newspapers in this respect. The dominance of motherhood further demonstrates that women voters' political priorities are assumed to derive from their commitments within the private sphere. The endurance of this particular discourse is perhaps unsurprising given that the figure of the mother is the central icon of the caring person within Western culture (MacDonald 1995); consequently, women appeared predominantly in this guise in a range of different media throughout the nineteenth and twentieth centuries (MacDonald 1995).

Active Citizenship?

The extent to which women are depicted as active and engaged citizens can be assessed by analysing the extent to which they are given a voice in the newspaper coverage. During the interwar years, women's voices are relatively scarce. The content analysis showed that during the interwar years, women were directly or indirectly quoted in under 20 % of all news items about them. These were mainly confined to the occasional reader's letter, such as this example from 1935: "As a mother, I shall support the candidate who advocates a sane policy of education, infant and maternity welfare, the abolition of slum areas and the provision of more playgrounds for children. As a woman, I shall support the candidate who stands for peace abroad and improved social conditions—less taxation, less unemployment, more houses at cheaper rents, decreased living cost. As a citizen, I shall vote for the candidate who demands an adequate British Navy and Air Force to maintain collective security" (*Daily Mirror* 1935). This complex list of political concerns hints at the multiple identities that women voters may have considered themselves to occupy, but ultimately, the majority of the news coverage still remained traditionally focused on their familial roles and domestic duties.

After the war, readers' letters remain an important feature of the election coverage. One woman confessed that "I'm trembling while I write this. (I've left my wash-tub to do it)" (Roberts 1951) because she has never written to the newspaper before but is keen to express her views. The post-war years also see an increase in the number of items where women voters are directly quoted. They were directly or indirectly quoted in 30–40 % of items between 1951 and 1979. There was a marked increase in items where they spoke to politicians on the campaign trail. For example, one woman was quoted speaking to then Chancellor Rab Butler: "'[Y]ou're welcome to do my exchequer next week'. Laughing Mr Butler replied: '[I]f I could advise you after the election I would be quite glad. But perhaps you could advise me. You probably know more about it than I do'" (*Daily Mail* 1955). During the 1960s onwards, women begin to be asked for their political views directly by journalists, for example, "Maureen Price, 23, housewife of Birmingham…I get my housekeeping on Friday and I am broke by Tuesday" (*Daily Mirror* 1964). This period also sees the beginning of newspapers including items featuring panels of readers who are called upon to give their views about the election or politics generally. In 1979, the *Daily Mail* featured a "panel of housewives" (Coolican 1979) who they ask to give their verdict on the campaign. The popular newspapers in particular employ these types of items regularly: "Michelle Marsh, 18 from Oldham, Greater Manchester, is equally keen to see a change in power…I think the Lib Dems are the party of the future. I am fed up of the pathetic way this country is run. On education, health and law and order, we need a shake-up" (Bowness 2001). The content analysis showed that after 1979, women voters were quoted in 50–65 % of items about them, showing once again an increase.

Despite the increase in women being directly quoted across time, during the 1990s and 2000s, there is a marked tendency to construct women as potential and actual victims of political decisions. The popular tabloid newspapers in particular choose to highlight areas where it is felt the government is lacking by introducing such policy victims into their coverage. This not only reflects a broader journalistic trend for making stories more relevant and immediate to readers by putting a human face on political consequences, but also the importance of sensationalized human interest stories in tabloid news discourses (Conboy 2006). In 1992, the *Daily Mirror* carried a feature whereby those who were struggling under the Conservative government are interviewed about their living conditions. Examples included: "Daisy is a widow. She lives alone in a spick and span council flat that betrays no outward sign of deprivation" (*Daily Mirror* 1992) and "Karen Grant had seen iron bars go up at neighbours' windows. She'd watched helplessly as gangs of vandals daubed graffiti on walls in broad daylight. She had heard the groups of giggling teenagers sniffing glue outside her three year old daughter Leanne's bedroom window" (Young 1992). Such examples function as highly emotive appeals to the wider audience by using vulnerable people like senior citizens and young mothers to highlight the inadequacy of the incumbent government. These accounts appear most frequently in tabloid newspapers but were not completely absent from quality broadsheets. Such representations persist throughout this period around vulnerable groups. "The plight of pensioners on the poverty line" (*Daily Mirror* 1992) was a common trope: "[W]idow Alice Barham, 85, has to survive on a £63-a-week pension and lives in sheltered accommodation" (*Daily Mirror* 1997). The National Health Service (NHS) is an obvious focus for such coverage and, accordingly, "a desperate mum who cornered Mr Blair on TV about her dying daughter declared last night: '[H]er life is in his hands'. Alice Maddocks, eight, has a rare condition called severe aplastic anaemia and will die without a bone marrow transplant" (Pascoe-Watson 2001), which once again constructs voters in highly emotional terms and reinforces stereotypical assumptions about women. The NHS is also frequently commented on by women themselves as an important policy area of concern: "[T]he NHS is something I believe in and yet my experience of it is dreadful" (*The Sun* 2001). One woman whose mother died amid poor conditions in an NHS hospital appeared in the *Daily Telegraph* and *Daily Mail* on the same day during the 2010 election. Her emotive account serves to undermine Labour's claims that the NHS had improved under their administration. The newspaper accounts claim that the woman's mother had been "treated worse than an animal" (Rayner 2010) and was left to "die in squalor" (Wilkes 2010).

To summarize, the extent to which women are constructed as actively engaged in speaking about politics does increase over time. The interwar years featured very few women speaking directly apart from a few letters by specific readers. As time goes on, more women are quoted while engaging with politicians on the campaign trail, with an increase in news items which directly asked women what they thought. Despite the increase in women's voices over time, noted by the content analysis results discussed earlier, there remains a tendency for journalists to speak about women voters rather than to allow them to speak for themselves.

Conclusion

Throughout the sample period, women voters and their political views have consistently been constructed in largely domestic roles, as mothers and housewives whose political priorities are largely informed by their familial obligations. This focus on how the private lives of women inform their political priorities reflects the traditional expectations of women in patriarchal societies. Despite gaining access to the public sphere as citizens and, furthermore, the advances made by feminists who sought to challenge the legitimacy of the public–private divide and to expand our understanding of what issues can legitimately belong to the public sphere, women seemingly continue to be tied to the private sphere and its responsibilities. Furthermore, the persistence of such traditional discourses which confine women to the private sphere fails to recognize the extent to which women have made political, economic and social gains throughout the century.

Despite a surprising amount of consistency, we did find a number of important changes. First, as the century went on, journalists began to acknowledge that women were capable of voting independently of male influence. Second, the category of housewife concerned with the cost of living disappeared in the late 1970s and was replaced by an association with health and welfare policies. The final important changes were an increase in news items which included women's voices in the coverage as the century went on. The association between women voters and the private sphere remains fairly strong despite these important changes.

The newspaper coverage of women voters, therefore, seems to be lagging behind when attempting to portray the political realities of many women's lives, especially given that many more women are in the paid workforce, unmarried and childless or as single parents, than might have been the case earlier in the century, for example. This means that since media representations produce and maintain specific ways of understanding the world and the place of men and women in it (Gill 2007; Holland 2004), the modes of representation that are used to marginalize and exclude women from press coverage of politics are perpetuating a situation where women's political views are understood to be focused on domestic issues at the expense of anything else.

Despite the negative aspects of newspaper coverage of voters during elections, the historical analysis does show that journalists have made some effort to explicitly include women in the public discourse surrounding politics. Moreover, there are large numbers of women whose familial situation may play some role in their political priorities. For example, women with children may place more emphasis on policy areas which affect them directly, such as education provision, and this needs to be recognized in the public discussion about politics; but this should not be at the expense of other representations of women's priorities. The extent to which these gendered representations have persisted throughout the electoral coverage is however revealing since it shows that although women have gained much in the past century, the dominant representations of their roles in society in electoral coverage have changed very little.

There are no doubt difficulties in representing voters in all their diversity in newspaper coverage of elections due to the fact that elections tend to be dominated by politicians and also because there are so many voters with different priorities and opinions. This does not excuse the poor representation of women in electoral coverage, however, even if it might go some way to explain it. Furthermore, such explanations do not help to illuminate why women voters tend to be constructed as an undifferentiated mass. A more plausible explanation for this can be drawn from feminist theory whereby women's historical exclusion from politics is based on the assumption that the model citizen is male in the sense that he performs traditionally masculine roles and has male characteristics (Lister 1997). He is universal, rational and is concerned with the public interest. In contrast, the female non-citizen's concerns are private, partial and domestic and she is emotional, irrational and weak; hence, the main representations of women voters in our analysis revolve almost entirely around their familial roles. It should therefore not be surprising that when women finally became admitted to the political sphere, they did so still imbued with the obligations of the private sphere, which means they did so on unequal terms with men. Since women do not conform to the original masculine citizenship model, they are perceived as different (Landes 1998) and therefore become constructed as an undifferentiated mass in opposition to the ideal masculine citizen. Despite the admittance of women into the public sphere having taken place almost a century ago, the evidence presented in this chapter demonstrates that this legacy of gendered citizenship roles whereby women's political concerns are derived from their private roles has remained stubbornly persistent in the mediated representations of women in UK election coverage.

References

Allan, M. (1945). These are the issues for women. *Daily Herald*, 4 July, p. 4.
Beckford, M. (2010). The Mumsnet set must be won over to tax break cause. *Daily Telegraph*, 10 April, p. 4.
Bingham, A. (2004). *Gender, modernity, and the popular press in inter-war Britain*. Oxford: Oxford University Press.
Bowness, M. (2001). Jack's on board with us. *The Sun*, 4 June, p. 6.
Braden, M. (1996). *Women politicians and the media*. Lexington: University of Kentucky Press.

Bradshaw, D. (1987). Kids pledge woos mums. *Daily Mirror*, 9 June, p. 2.
Burton, P. (1979). Mums the Word on Prices! *Daily Mirror*, 27 April, p. 7.
Conboy, M. (2006). *Tabloid Britain: Constructing a community through language*. Abingdon: Routledge.
Coolican, D. (1979). Housewives' final choice. *Daily Mail*, 2 May, p. 4.
Corless, F. (1992). Born into Despair…Is Today a New Dawn for Julie and her Little Baby Paul? *Daily Mirror*, 9 April, pp. 2–3.
Cousins, J. (1979). Housewives' choice for a better deal. *Daily Mirror*, 3 May, p. 5.
Daily Herald. (1923). How tor-libs raided housewife's purse. *Daily Herald*, 4 December, p. 1.
Daily Herald. (1924). Women's party is labour. *Daily Herald*, 24 October, p. 8.
Daily Mail. (1922a). Costly home life. *Daily Mail*, 9 November, p. 6.
Daily Mail. (1922b). Women's power. *Daily Mail*, 14 November, p. 9.
Daily Mail. (1923). Premier and women voters. *Daily Mail*, 3 December, p. 6.
Daily Mail. (1931). Appeal to women. *Daily Mail*, 23 October, p. 14.
Daily Mail. (1955). Butler and housewife: You can advise me. *Daily Mail*, 24 May, p. 4.
Daily Mail. (1970a). Tories go for the wives' vote. *Daily Mail*, 15 June, p. 2.
Daily Mail. (1970b). Heath woos the wives. *Daily Mail*, 18 June, p. 1.
Daily Mirror. (1922). Whirlwind finale today to election struggle. *Daily Mirror*, 14 November, p. 3.
Daily Mirror. (1931). Let women consider. *Daily Mirror*, 27 October, p. 7.
Daily Mirror. (1935). Untitled letter. *Daily Mirror*, 9 November, p. 14.
Daily Mirror. (1945a). I'll vote for them. *Daily Mirror*, 30 June, p. 1.
Daily Mirror. (1945b). Untitled letter, *Daily Mirror*, 30 June, p. 2.
Daily Mirror. (1945c). Your sacred trust. *Daily Mirror*, 30 June, p. 2.
Daily Mirror. (1951). Housewives, Beware! *Daily Mirror*, 23 October, p. 12.
Daily Mirror. (1964). Look what's happened to the Tory £. *Daily Mirror*, 14 October, p. 9.
Daily Mirror. (1974). The unacceptable face of Mr Barber. *Daily Mirror*, 21 February, p. 2.
Daily Mirror. (1992). Remember me: "We Must Stop the Tory Rot before It's Too Late". *Daily Mirror*, 8 April, pp. 10–11.
Daily Mirror. (1997). My 25p Insult. *Daily Mirror*, 26 April, p. 6.
Daily Telegraph. (1922). Independent wives. *Daily Telegraph*, 10 November, p. 11.
Daily Telegraph. (1970). Votes from women… *Daily Telegraph*, 9 June, p. 13.

Day, B. (1982). The politics of communication, or the communication of politics. In R. M. Worcester & M. Harrop (Eds.), *Political communications: The general election of 1979*. London: George Allen and Unwin.

Derby, O. (1955). Who'll Help a Working Girl? *Daily Mirror*, 21 May, p. 2.

Gill, R. (2007). *Gender and the media*. Cambridge: Polity Press.

Goot, M., & Reid, E. (1984). Women: If not apolitical, then conservative. In J. Siltanen & M. Stanworth (Eds.), *Women and the public sphere: A critique of sociology and politics* (pp. 122–136). London: Hutchinson.

Holland, P. (2004). The politics of the smile: 'Soft News' and the sexualization of the popular press. In C. Carter & L. Steiner (Eds.), *Critical readings: Media and gender*. Maindenhead: Open University Press.

Landes, J. B. (1998). *Feminism, the public and the private*. Oxford: Oxford University Press.

Lister, R. (1997). *Citizenship: Feminist perspectives*. Basingstoke: Palgrave Macmillan.

MacDonald, M. (1995). *Representing women: Myths of femininity in the popular media*. London: Arnold.

Moore, J. (2005). I'll Vote…But It's Hard to Give a XXXX. *The Sun*, 4 May, p. 11.

Norris, P. (1997). Women leaders worldwide: A splash of colour in the photo op. In P. Norris (Ed.), *Women, media and politics*. Oxford: Oxford University Press.

Palmer, J. (1997). Vote for her…and a better NHS. *Daily Mirror*, 1 May, p. 3.

Pascoe-Watson, G. (2001). Docs and sirs blast blair. *The Sun*, 1 June, p. 8.

Proops, M. (1974). Which way will the middle jump? *Daily Mirror*, 25 February, p. 4.

Rayner, G. (2010). Land girl "Betrayed and Treated Worse than an Animal". *Daily Telegraph*, 28 April, p. 5.

Roberts, M. (1951). A young woman warns the women of Britain. *Daily Mirror*, 23 October, pp. 6–7.

Ross, K. (2002). *Women, politics, media: Uneasy relations in comparative perspective*. Cresskill, NJ: Hampton Press.

Ross, K., & Carter, C. (2011). Women and news: A long and winding road. *Media, Culture and Society, 33*(8), 1148–1165.

Siltanen, J., & Stanworth, M. (1984). The politics of private woman and public man. In J. Siltanen & M. Stanworth (Eds.), *Women and the public sphere: A critique of sociology and politics* (pp. 185–208). London: Hutchinson.

Sreberny-Mohammadi, A., & Ross, K. (1996). Women MPs and the media: Representing the body politic. *Parliamentary Affairs, 49*(1), 103–115.

Suich, M. (1964). A puzzle of pollsters. *The Sun*, 9 October, p. 10.
The Guardian. (1918a). Two years of progress. *The Guardian*, 9 December, p. 6.
The Guardian. (1918b). The women voters. *The Guardian*, 11 December, p. 4.
The Guardian. (1951). The undecided. Women's votes key to leicestershire. *The Guardian*, 20 October, p. 2.
The Guardian. (1964). The woman voter – A Political Enigma. *The Guardian*, 13 October, p. 2.
The Guardian. (2010). Women and the election: Fairer sex. *The Guardian*, 19 April, p. 30.
The Sun. (1966). Mr Butler taking on Mr Heath at Bexley. *The Sun*, 25th March, p. 8.
The Sun. (1979). Whose hand is in your pocket? *The Sun*, 28 April, pp. 1–2.
The Sun. (2001). Eight women tell us how they'll vote – and why. *The Sun*, 6 June, p. 23.
Tuchman, G., Kaplan Daniels, A., & Benet, J. (Eds.). (1978). *Hearth and home: Images of women in mass media*. New York: Oxford University Press.
Van Zoonen, L. (1998). The ethics of making private life public. In K. Brants, J. Hermes, & L. van Zoonen (Eds.), *The media in question: Popular cultures and public interests* (pp. 113–123). London: Sage.
Van Zoonen, L. (2005). *Entertaining the citizen*. Oxford: Rowman and Littlefield.
Wallace, M. (1924). Why women must use their votes. How politics affects life in the home. *Daily Mirror*, 29 October, p. 5.
Watkins, F. (1923). Mothers and the next parliament. Feminine influence on legislation. *Daily Mirror*, 30 November, p. 5.
Wilkes, D. (2010). Inhumane Betrayal of Land Girl Left to Die in Squalor on NHS Ward. *Daily Mail*, 28 April, p. 8.
Willoughby, F. (1922). Armistice day and its lessons: How it should inspire the voter this week. *Daily Mirror*, 13 November, p. 7.
Young, S. (1992). We have a big job to do in those inner cities. *Daily Mirror*, 6 April, pp. 16–17.
Zweiniger-Bargielowska, I. (2002). *Austerity in Britain: Rationing, controls, and consumption 1939–1955*. Oxford: Oxford University Press.

9

The Pedagogy and Practice of En-Gendering Civic Engagement: Reflections on Serial-Viewing Among Middle-class Women in Urban India

Mahalakshmi Mahadevan

Introduction

This chapter explores the everyday media practices and discourses of women in low- and middle-income families in urban India, arguing that popular representations of gender and family can limit women's access to full-fledged citizenship. The chapter argues that specific patriarchal representations of gender and family reinforce gendered citizenship in ways that stymie women's oppositional civic and political engagement. To illustrate this, I examine a new conjunctural moment in Indian television as a vantage point from which to make visible, theoretically and ethnographically, the gendered permeability between familial and civic spaces through the mediatory effects of popular representations of gender

---

M. Mahadevan (✉)
Independent Researcher, 1750 P St. NW, 301, Washington, DC 20036, USA

© The Author(s) 2016
H. Danielsen et al. (eds.), *Gendered Citizenship and the Politics of Representation*, DOI 10.1057/978-1-137-51765-4_9

and family. Extant scholarship on gender and citizenship, particularly those that utilize feminist political theory, lends considerable theoretical weight to the "inter connectedness, fluidity and permeability" between the spheres of family and civil society—largely within the public–private debate (Howell 2004). However, the ways in which the affective dimensions of specific patriarchal configurations of the family are implicated in the everyday, iterative processes that engender citizenship merits greater scholarly attention.

This chapter draws on qualitative data from multi-sited ethnographic fieldwork and participant observation in middle- and working-class neighborhoods in two Indian cities—New Delhi and Kollam—that were conducted between 2007 and 2009 as part of a doctoral research project at the Communication and Media Research Institute, University of Westminster. The project sought to explore a new conjunctural moment in Indian television characterized by the feminization of Indian television—the representational hegemony of women-oriented narratives exemplified in the rise and popularity of a new brand of television fiction called "K-serials" (Mahadevan 2010). K-serials revived traditional tropes of the extended Hindu family and ideal Indian/Hindu womanhood by idealizing narratives of domesticated womanhood, and re-centering women within the family as primary nurturer and custodian of traditional ideals of family and gender.

The popular reception of this new brand of Indian family melodramas that rose to prominence in India and the larger South Asian region in the latter half of the 1990s, signaled a new moment in Indian television in the post-liberalization period. This period was marked simultaneously by the deregulation of Indian media, the electoral ascendance of Hindu Nationalism and the competitive drive among transnational media corporations to Indianize content (Mahadevan 2006, 2010). Thus, this new moment became visible in the national circulation of traditionally inflected soap opera narratives and implicated in the feminization of television in India in the post-liberalization period (Mahadevan 2006, 2010).

Drawing on fieldwork data in four economically divergent neighborhoods in India, this chapter makes visible the ways in which the feminization of Indian television through the K-serials amplifies the discursive permeability between patriarchal ideals of the Indian family and gender and civic spaces and practices. The core fieldwork period this chapter draws from lasted over six months and included formal and informal interviews with 20 key informant families. Key informants were usually women between the ages of 18–60, who saw themselves "perform" and "learn" the roles of daughter, mother or wife from the K-serials in order to improve themselves and the lives of their families.

The relationship between family, civil society and state has served as the ground for much feminist debate, particularly in relation to the structural and discursive location of the family within the public or private realm (Pateman 1989; Dahlerup 1994; Phillips 2002). The feminist theorizations emerging out of this debate seek to effectively challenge the Longue Dure'e of political and civil society scholarship that sidelines the institutional significance of the family to the study of gendered forms of civil society and citizenship. However, the hegemonic power of affective constellations inherent in patriarchal forms of the family and their insertion into 'the everyday, iterative processes that engender citizenship' (Lister 1997, 2003) are sidelined in feminist scholarship, particularly those inspired by political science and history. Feminists working within the disciplines of Anthropology, Sociology and Cultural Studies have largely analyzed affect as an institutional phenomenon. In particular, within Media Studies, scholars like Shakuntala Banaji (2008, 2010) and David Buckingham (1987, 2000, 2008) explore a range of new media texts to study youth civic engagement. Banaji (2008) argues that while on the one hand spontaneous, passionate and often oppositional civic actions are met with "disproportionately authoritarian responses by so-called democratic states", young people's civic engagement is also not normatively democratic, but played out along a spectrum of political engagement that ranges from the authoritarian to the democratic. However, in the wake of the rise of digital media, studies that explore the mediated nature of citizenship tend to naturalize the news genre and the new media as particularly fecund arenas for exploring the notion of the "civic" and practices of democratic civic engagement, valorizing them as sites of digital learning (Buckingham 2000, 2008; Banaji 2008; Banaji and Buckingham 2013; Banaji and Cammaerts 2014). This has resulted in the increasing marginalization of fictional, melodramatic and affect-oriented genres such as the soap opera in scholarship on civic engagement and mediated citizenship.

A significant body of twenty-first-century democratic theory that seeks to foreground the affective nature of the "civic" conceptualizes affect as discrete emotional responses that are not tied to structural or institutional locations or outcomes; deliberative democracy is, at its best, an effective mix of "reason" and "passion" (Marcus and Hanson 1993: 1–32). There is little room for questions such as "To what extent are the institutions, norms and practices of civil society gendered?" (Howell 2004: 7). More crucially, as Banaji (2008) argues, in scholarly and policy discussions on civic engagement and "good citizenship" globally, there is an overarching emphasis on conformity, with group anger, cynicism and unsanctioned protest, seen as being in conflict with proper "civic pathways". "The 'political' is primarily configured as pertaining to elections and government, and civic is the implicitly pro-social and conformist field within which future citizens are educated for political engagement" (Banaji 2008: 16).

In order to highlight the normative ways in which practices of "good citizenship" are gendered, this chapter explores ways in which specific patriarchal constellations of the familial are imbricated in the "civic" and the ways in which patriarchal affect shapes the interaction between various sites of civic-democratic action. To this end, the chapter re-poses Howell's question in the following way: "To what extent are the discourses, spaces and practices of civil society familialized?"

As Howell (2004) points out, women have been active in civil society theaters across the world and yet civil society theorists, in particular, treat women's civic and community level engagement as unproblematic and fail to systematically address the engendering processes and effects of local civil societies and their relationship to the state. The robust civic participation of women at the local, neighborhood and community levels peters out in the higher political realms. Yet, few questions are asked concerning the lack of permeability for women between the associational arenas of community and civil society groups and the arena of formal politics. By investigating the representational hegemonies that reinforce the marginality of women in formal civic and political discourses and spaces, this chapter seeks to problematize the engendering processes at work in the interaction between the familial and the civic.

The Theoretical Case for Familial Citizenship

Political scientists working on postcolonial South Asia identify women's relatively low participation in formal politics but do not problematize it in any substantive way, exploring instead the impact of ameliorative measures like gender-based quotas and reservation in legislative bodies. In particular, civil society scholars normalize the exclusion of the patriarchal family from analyses of civil society processes and institutions by refusing to problematize its status as a "primordial" and "organic" part of society.

For example, in the South Asian context, Partha Chatterjee conceptualizes a space of empirically differentiated groups characterized by significant "naturalness" and "primordial ties" that he terms a separate political society (Chatterjee 2001, 2004; Sarkar 2012: 31–48). For these groups to be recognized as targets of governmentality, they must "give to the empirical form of a population group the moral attributes of a community", says Chatterjee (2004: 57). However, he (2004) fails to make explicit what might be the moral contents of such communities. As Swagato Sarkar points out, the moral content of these communities seems to derive overwhelmingly from the notion of shared kinship—the most common metaphor is that of the family (Sarkar 2012: 34).

Indeed, in the Indian context, a modern liberal democracy has, far from creating a contractual family, been realized in a state that mostly refrains from defining it as anything other than natural in its law and policy formulation. Analyzing postcolonial South Asia, Gayatri Chakravorthy Spivak (1988: 277) highlights the nature of the imagined community at the height of the nationalist struggle for India's independence from Britain as one that blends "the feeling of community that belongs to national links and political organizations" with "that other feeling of community whose structural model is the [clan or the extended] family". According to Dipesh Chakrabarty (1997: 283), the idioms through which anti-colonial struggle has been conducted in the Indian subcontinent has often been in the sphere of the non-modern, specifically the "sanctified and patriarchal extended family".

Although by the late nineteenth century, the "contractual" family became the normative model for much social theorizing in the West, feminist political scientists like Carole Pateman (1988, 1989) highlight the contradictions and antagonisms in the dialectic between the family and civil society, those that result from an early reluctance on the part of classical theorists to define family as associational, rather than organic, in nature. Pateman (1980: 114) argues that treating the family as the "foundation" of social life and as the point of procreative origin of society and locating it as a corollary to Nature has debilitating consequences on women's emergence as full-fledged citizens and their participation in civil society. By association with the "natural" family, women are seen as guardians of order and morality as well as inherently subversive (Pateman 1980: 114). "The public realm," Pateman points out, "cannot be fully understood in the absence of the private sphere … Civil freedom depends on patriarchal right" (Pateman 1988: 4).

Feminist scholarship on nationalism, particularly the work of Yuval-Davis (1997a, b), highlights the manner in which nationalist discourses naturalize the differential positioning of men and women in relation to the nation state. According to Yuval-Davis (1997a, b), the relative importance of the state, civil society and the domain of kinship have been varied, with some "cultures of citizenship" evidencing, at certain points, a bigger investment in kinship ties over that of the civil society or the state. Yuval-Davis (1997b) proposes a differentiation between three spheres—the state, civil society and the domain of family and kinship—as the relative importance of these three spheres could variously determine the construction of citizenship.

In challenging the validity of the public–private divide, feminist scholars like Pateman (1980, 1988, 1989) and Yuval-Davis (1997a, b) on the one hand and postcolonial scholars like Spivak (1988, 1996, 2005) and Chakrabarthy (1997) on the other have made a clearing space from which the historical specificity of non-Western civil societies might be addressed.

The Feminization of Indian Television: A New Conjunctural Moment

In analyzing the kinship systems and the nature of the family in India, Patricia Uberoi (2006) refers to an important dimension that must be reckoned with—this doesn't have to do with the family as it is, but as it

9 Reflections on Serial-Viewing in Urban India   191

is imagined to be through the media. Terming this realm of the imagined family "the moral economy of the Indian family", Uberoi (2006: 30) suggests that it is not just a fixed set of ideals, but a dialogic system "that is framed in terms of a set of moral dilemmas and contradictions, even as it posits the patrilineal joint family as the ideal, 'traditional' and culturally authentic form of Indian family life". Since its inception, national television, unlike any other medium, including cinema, has sought to weld together the objectives of the state with representations of womanhood and family (Mankekar 1999).

However, the manner in which discourses on Indian womanhood have evolved through popular modes of representation since the colonial period to the present reveals areas of significant continuities and disjunctures (Chatterjee 1989, 1997). The discursive conflation of gender, religion and nation was first achieved in the colonial period through nationalist and religious reform movements and invoked in visual forms such as painting and calendar art (Guha-Thakurta 1991; Freitag 1996, 2001; Ray 2000; Pinney 2001). According to Sunder Rajan (1993: 47) "in the colonial encounter the Hindu 'good wife' is constructed as patriarchy's feminine ideal: she is offered simultaneously as a model and as a signifier of absolute cultural otherness, both exemplary and inimitable".

Cinema, particularly early Hindi cinema, made use of mythological ideals of womanhood that emphasized the Sati-Sita-Savitri construct (the powerful ideological trio from Hindu mythology representing the dominant virtues of ideal womanhood—self-sacrifice, chastity and unflinching devotion to one's husband). The Sati-Sita-Savitri construct served to "emphasize with all the force of mythological inspiration ... the 'spiritual' qualities of self-sacrifice, benevolence, devotion, religiosity etc" (Chatterjee 1989: 248–249).

However, after Independence, through the decades of the 1950s and 1960s, the nationalist conflation of the Indian nation and the Indian woman/mother echoed in Hindi cinema, reaching its zenith in Mehboob Khan's *Mother India*. With the arrival of color television in Indian homes in the 1980s, the Indian state sought to construct a modern femininity by allying the image of the female subject with its development objectives through the national broadcaster, Doordarshan.

In the late 1980s, the broadcast of the *Ramayana* and *Mahabharata* on national television was a watershed in that it symbolized a harnessing of the discursive surplus of the Hindu nationalist rhetoric that had attained particular force at this time (Rajagopal 2001). By doing what the mythological film could not, namely, bringing the historic memory of the myth to the intimate and realistic realm of the family, the mythological serials on television powerfully aligned discourses of gender, nation and community, achieved through the othering of non-Hindus, particularly Muslims. While the *Ramayana* reinstated Sita, represented as self-sacrificing, chaste and devoted to her husband Lord Ram, as emblematic of ideal Hindu/Indian womanhood, the *Mahabharata* underscored the co-implication of discourses of gender and nationhood in the figure of Draupadi and the powerful narrative of her disrobing (Mankekar 1999).

In their 1986 study of 27 television programs, Krishnan and Dighe (1986) concluded that the broad pattern in the construction of femininity on television in this period was one of affirmation and denial. In the K-serials, sacrifices and self-denial on the one hand and affirmation of patriarchal duties and roles as wife/mother on the other are central to the construction of ideal womanhood. Rights versus responsibilities become the fundamental axis along which conflicts develop and are resolved in order to ultimately reaffirm the centrality of the Hindu joint family. Through the constant reaffirmation of a woman's duties to the family as wife, mother and so on over her individual rights, the contemporary soap opera determines the resolution of conflicts to ensure the unity of the Hindu joint family.

Thus familial disagreements involve expanding and reclaiming the duties of a woman rather than her rights so that the gender and power constructs that undergird the joint family structure remain intact. This approach points to a specific conjunctural revival of representations of ideal Hindu womanhood that seek to naturalize a discourse defined exclusively in familial terms as mata, pativrata or sumangali. The critical slippage from Hinduness to Indianness is routinized by locating the traditional joint family as a site of epic struggles to be continuously secured and defended by ideal (Hindu) womanhood.

Television has been instrumental not only in the collective reimagining of the private sphere of family but also in aligning everyday, common

9 Reflections on Serial-Viewing in Urban India

sense discourses of family and gender to broader ones of class and national identity. Through the decade of the 1980s, the very act of purchasing or owning a television set became an act of self-definition, an assertion of its respectable, middle-class and nuclear identity (Monteiro 1998: 164).

A new conjunctural moment in Indian television in the latter half of the 1990s saw the emergence of a new trend in the representation of ideal Indian womanhood through the "K-serials" on Star Plus, the Indian face of the Rupert Murdoch-owned transnational News Corporation (Mahadevan 2006). This emerging trend in the representation of Indian womanhood, characterized by the domestication of the female subject and her re-centering within the family and home, was symptomatic of an ongoing process of feminization of Indian television, whereby a Hinduized visual imagery is deepened and naturalized in cultural representations of Indian womanhood (Mankekar 1999; Rajagopal 2001). It may be termed what Elspeth Probyn (1997) identifies, in a totally different context, as "New Traditionalism". This return to "tradition", coming close on the heels of progressive women-oriented narratives on national and satellite television in the early 1990s, is comparable to the moment of new traditionalism in US television shows of the late 1980s which offered a "post-feminist vision of the home to which women have 'freely' chosen to return" (Probyn 1997: 128).

The patriarchal family had been the principal vehicle in the televisual discourses of "women's uplift" and national development deployed by Doordarshan prior to media liberalization (Mankekar 1999). In the post-liberalization period, older narratives about the patriarchal family are not jettisoned but reworked around anxieties regarding familial stability that permeate contemporary middle-class domesticity. The family has become the diegetic terrain on which to articulate a new middle-class (Hindu) womanhood.

The televisual representations of Indian womanhood through the K-serials drew on various facets of nationalistic and patriarchal ideals of womanhood, positing for the viewing citizen a return to "the family". The K-serials revived several features of television's hegemonic representation of womanhood, foremost among them the domestication of the Hindu woman, her re-centering within the home and enshrinement as a mother. In its construction of femininity, the serials accommodate shades of various identities that have represented ideal Hindu womanhood—that of the mata (sacred mother), the sumangali (auspicious married woman), the pativrata (supremely chaste wife), and the virangana (the archetype of the warrior woman).

The dominant discourse that underlies the ideal womanhood the first wave of K-serials such as *Kyunki Saans Bhi Kabhi Bahu Thi* (Because a mother-in-law was once a daughter-in-law) and *Kahani Ghar Ghar Ki* (The story of every household) offer for consumption is one in which women are perceived as embodiments of Matri shakti or mother power. By the very nature of the feminine power that flows from it, Matri shakthi serves to circumscribe women's potential to the domain of domestic life (Krishnan 1990: 113).

Serial Texts, Middle-class Lives and Patriarchal Affect: The Invisible Pedagogy of Indian Womanhood

Within the context of a new conjunctural moment in Indian television characterized by the feminization of the medium, contemporary family dramas reconfigure and re-imagine Indian womanhood in and through a pedagogy of domesticated Hindu womanhood. The "invisible pedagogy" of Indian television dramas draws on a set of affective ties originating in and defined by the institution of the patriarchal Indian family and grounded in ideas of middle-class respectability. I use the term invisible pedagogy drawn from the work of Basil Bernstein (1975) to draw attention to women's televisual engagement not only as a non-hierarchic process of learning but also animated by their socio-economic membership in the middle class.

At its most basic, invisible pedagogy relates to the concept of play and a personalized form of organic solidarity where there are "implicit rather than explicit hierarchical social relationships" (Bernstein 1975: 12).

Women from the Delhi neighborhoods of Kishan Nagar and Sarkar Marg spoke of serials as a source of "*seekh*" or learning about the right conduct of family life. *Seekh* is understood as wisdom through informal learning that leads to a moral stance. *Seekh* is also crucially knowledge that is circulated; it is both acquired and shared or passed on, like a family heirloom. Seekh is not visible, it is implicit. Komal, a respondent from the lower middle-class neighborhood of Kishan Nagar spoke of how the serials portrayed the complexity of a web of relationships that she herself was part of as a wife, daughter-in-law, sister and mother. The protagonist Tulsi, Komal explained, had been an *"adarsh"* (ideal) wife, daughter-in-law and mother. Tulsi knew how to perform (*nibhana*) her responsibility as wife, daughter-in-law and mother perfectly. Significantly, Komal used the word *"nibhana"* in order to explain the *seekh* she obtained from serials. In Hindi, *"nibhana"* denotes the practice of embodied performance of a role or a responsibility depending on the context in which it is used. In common parlance, a cinematic or theatrical performance of a character is referred to as *"kirdar nibhana"*. As a mother on the look-out for a bride for her elder son, Komal often spoke of the *seekh* she got from Tulsi on how to be a good mother-in-law:

> I will try to be a good mother-in-law to the daughters who come into this family just as Tulsi tries to carry everyone along… she goes to great lengths to treat the daughters-in-law as daughters… to keep the family together… only then can there be peace in the family.

According to Komal, as a mother, Tulsi is morally instructing the younger generation in the serial, trying to bring her sons who have gone astray back on track. She is distributing the *seekh* she received from the elderly matriarch Amba Virani, even as she attempts to deal with the conspiracies around her that threaten the unity and integrity of her large joint family. While Komal and the other women in Kishan Nagar recognized the enormity of the sacrifices made by Tulsi, Parvati and other serial heroines, they were evaluated not as isolated acts representative of ideal Hindu womanhood, but as those necessitated by the family and for the sake of its unity. While explaining why Tulsi, despite being an ideal Hindu woman, had universal appeal among women cutting across religious divides, Komal pointed out that family and relationships are universal themes that women can identify with:

I'm not saying I will become Tulsi or that I will imbibe all her qualities but I will try to live with my family the way Tulsi lives with hers. Only then peace can prevail in the family. Otherwise there is no peace. If someone is *ulta* (troublesome) then she also becomes *ulta*; but only to reform them… she becomes like that only for a few days.

Thus, even when Tulsi acts in a manner contrary to her ideal self, it is read as an exigency that becomes necessary to preserve peace within the family. Tulsi thus becomes a source of knowledge or *seekh* about ideal Indian womanhood in so far as her character helps nurture the ideal (middle-class) Indian family.

Another informant, Lalitha, lives in Sarkar Marg. She does not work outside the house and resides with her family in a two-bedroom apartment. When I first met Lalitha she had been a regular viewer of *Kyunki*. But when I met her four months later, she had begun watching other serials and admitted that she now preferred the new brand of romantic shows "meant for the children". In her critique of K-serials, she was primarily concerned with the "real-ness" of the extended Hindu family depicted:

> It is not possible to keep the family together all by one self; only by enlisting the support of the family and carrying the family along. Some family members are supporting her in her endeavors [to keep the family together]. It is not possible for a human being to achieve this on one's own. But she takes all the burden on herself; 'let every burden be my lot, but not the family's' seems to be her attitude. But despite this, she has suffered at the hands of her family. There have been many misunderstandings. It is difficult for her to keep track of every incident, every one's need within the family. I feel a human being just tires him/herself out after a while. It is not possible for **me** to think of every person in the house and be understanding of everyone's needs and desires and to keep the family going that way. This is perhaps not possible (emphasis in original conversation).

Here Lalitha is clearly disillusioned by a narrative that seems to place enormous responsibilities on Tulsi so that familial harmony is always restored. Yet, the realness of the serial family is judged not by the depth of the metaphoric identification it evokes with the common sense North Indian *parivaar* (family)—simultaneously ordinary and ideal—but through an evaluation of the realistic possibilities inherent in the efforts of the central female protagonist to hold the family together.

The ideal womanhood of the serials epitomizes the promise of securing peace and stability within the family. Tulsi's qualities as a woman are ultimately defined in and through her negotiation of relationships within the family. A key tool in such negotiation is giving—the fulfillment of her subject position as mother and wife comes from giving of herself because it is only by doing so that the family, the realm that defines her and is defined by her, can be preserved. But giving is not just a familial ethic, it is seen as a broader social ethic. As Amba Virani, the matriarch of the Virani family proclaims in Episode 101 of *Kyunki* which was first broadcast from July 2000 to November 2008 on Star Plus: "I am the eldest member of the Virani family. And carrying such a large family along as one is the highest form of social work. I am always busy".

As Banaji (2008) points out in her reflections on a project titled *Civicweb: Young People, the Internet and Civic Engagement*, young people are perceived as "good citizens" when they perform a list of duties that are widely acknowledged to be their foremost civic duties—including voting, watching the news, attending town hall meetings, volunteering and so on; it clearly excludes protest, conflict and anger. Women in lower middle-class families in Delhi similarly were in broad consensus about their duties as "good mothers", wives and exemplary members of their family.

While most landmark studies of the reception of popular culture refer to learning as one of the outcomes of reading the romance (Radway 1984) or women's magazines (Hermes 1995) or watching Egyptian melodramas (Abu-Lughod 2004), dealing with it progressively as learning, repertoires of knowing and pedagogy, the notion of pedagogy is not considered the centerpiece of viewer engagement with the romance or soap opera text. Radway's (1984) work on reading the romance makes the politically resonant argument that the romance teaches women to associate female identity with the social roles of mother, lover and wife—a potential dissatisfaction with which has led them to seek recourse to the romance narrative in the first place. However, her findings draw on a textual analysis of the romance's "conflicted discourse" rather than interviews with respondents (Radway 1984: 186–208).

Joke Hermes's (1995: 47) ethnographic study of the consumption of women's magazines subsumes learning under a methodological category she terms repertoires or ways of talking about reading women's magazines, where she admits "the margin between being impressed and learning, and having a good cry, is a small one". But in atomizing representational themes "reconstructed" out of her data as repertoires, critical scrutiny is not applied to the fault-lines that separate them. Yet it is precisely the inter-connectedness between repertoires that can provide insights into the discourses that animate romance reading and may in fact condition them.

In the South Asian context, a tentative beginning was made in the direction in Anjali Monteiro's (1998: 106) ethnographic study of middle- and working-class communities in Goa, India, in the 1980s where, based on her observations and interviews, she explains that "expectations of 'reality' and 'learning' combined with the ubiquity of choice associated with the televisual image give the medium a unique location within the familial space... television becomes a panopticon in reverse where watching others becomes the means for controlling oneself".

As was evident from my findings, the early discourse of State-sponsored television as a source of knowledge continues to inform, at least in part, the manner in which women in contemporary India engage with serial narratives broadcast on transnational television.

While most informants assumed that they could freely and openly discuss their interest in watching serials, given that it was a research subject, others were circumspect and anxious about how their perspective might be written up. For example, Komal, a key informant from the lower-middle-class Kishan Nagar said:

> My views may not be as good as theirs (upper middle-class informants from Sarkar Marg) but you will see that I am different from them, my ideas are different than theirs.

At a kitty party session in the upper-middle-class neighborhood of Sarkar Marg, a woman wanted to know:

> Will you write about us as flimsy women who waste their time gossiping and playing cards at kitty parties?

These anxieties reflect their positioning as housewives and subjects of a specific economic class. Women wished to be represented as well-rounded individuals for whom watching serials was meaningful activity and a source of pleasure, but nevertheless one that they did not participate in uncritically.

In this context, it is critical to understand that the producers of K-serials position their narratives within the discursive framework of middle-class "values". Ekta Kapoor, Creative Director of Balaji Telefilms, the production company that launched and popularized the K-serial brand of television dramas, identified the ethical basis of the family dramas produced by her company in an interview to indiantelevision.com (2003):

> Most of the rich people do not need values, most of the poor do not have time for them. Hence, middle class values are what my serials are about. These middle-class values are incidentally in keeping with the cultural ethos of the country. As far as I am concerned, economically I belong to the high class, but morally to the middle class…

Women cited togetherness and harmony as influential forms of affect characteristic of the traditional Indian joint family system portrayed in the television dramas, but it was clearly only realized when the central protagonist went "to great lengths" to preserve and protect familial harmony and well-being. Such self-sacrifice was seen as legitimate and normal, yet a quality that had to be continuously imbibed and cultivated. The nature of the affective investment in the ideal of the traditional Indian family is captured well in Komal's words:

> Tulsi was in the middle of criticism from all sides. She was being pulled in different directions. Her husband had gone astray, a son had gone astray; she had to deal with her mother-in-law's schemes, she had to deal with her husband's infidelity. And go through the process of understanding the son (Karan) he had out of another woman. She adopted Karan as her own son and he also soon began to love her more than he loved his own mother. Karan and Tulsi are outstanding characters. You won't find a son like Karan and a mother like Tulsi, a daughter-in-law like Tulsi or a sister-in-law like Tulsi. I have a learnt a lot from Tulsi.

Alongside the patriarchal equivalence between nature and female, male and culture, Carole Pateman (1989) identifies the disorder of women as fundamental to patriarchal and liberal thought. It is individual and social, private and public, because, as Pateman (1989: 18) says, "women have a disorder at their very centres—in their morality—which can bring about a destruction of the State. Women thus exemplify one of the ways in which nature and society stand opposed to each other. Moreover, the threat posed by women is exacerbated because of the place, or social sphere, for which they are fitted by their natures—the family".

The traditional family system, as portrayed in the soap operas, is symbolic of order and normalcy—which the viewers experience and articulate variously as harmony, togetherness or discipline. According to respondents interviewed in Delhi, the serials taught women how to conduct relationships within the family, and underlined the need to "go to great lengths" in order to lead a harmonious and peaceful family life.

Women discussed their safety on the streets of Delhi in various real-life contexts, including episodes of sexual violence portrayed in the serial narratives. In Delhi, making a case for embodying familial roles of womanhood on the street, women of all age groups and socio-economic status urged the need for self-discipline on the streets in order to avoid sexual violence.

Rimi from Sarkar Marg described her fear of the ubiquitous and mundane nature of sexual molestation on the streets of Delhi as part of the televisual experience of the rape of Nandini, a young female character in *Kyunki*:

> When Ansh raped Nandini I was so affected. I said God! It happened in a serial but I had to go with my aunt to the market to get clothes that day and I couldn't even do that. You won't believe I stood in front of Babaji [Guru Nanak, founder of the Sikh religion] and said, Babaji please let someone come and save her. Do you know how he raped her—he raised the volume of the television so her voice isn't heard outside the room... I couldn't sleep the whole night.

In a conversation on the rape of Krishna Tulsi, daughter of the ideal protagonist Tulsi, the overriding sentiment among women favored individualizing the problem of sexual violence. Rimi, the young female informant from Sarkar Marg, prescribes a bodily regime that had to be rigorously pursued in order to avoid being molested:

> I've been here [in Delhi] for two years. I've never been molested by anyone when I step out into the street or in the bus. Nobody has offered to befriend me. When I go out, ***I don't get commented on*** but the girls with me are taunted. My brother tells me, Rimi, if you are good, nobody will tell you anything. If you are wrong, if you are travelling in a bus and you look at someone, keep looking at someone, look here and there, eyes rove everywhere, if someone is in front of us and he is looking at us and we look back that seems wrong. If someone is looking, ignore it (emphasis added).

Molestation, in her account, becomes a public commentary on improper or flawed bodily discipline in the streets. Not being subject to molestation is not only rare as the girls with her are taunted, but also, as in her case, proof of having achieved normative, even ideal, bodily discipline. Her prescription reflects a street-based gender regime and performance that is reinforced by representations of the violation of the female body in the serials.

Women agreed that immodest attire and the misplaced freedom inherent in venturing out late in the evening were at the heart of the widespread problem of sexual violence in Delhi. If a woman conducts herself in the appropriate way, she will always be an exception to the rule (of being molested). According to one respondent, sexual violence can be avoided in the following way:

> One should always display one's sense of dignity and honour. One should always keep one's head covered with the pallu (tail-end of a shawl or saree). I always keep my head covered. And I always wear a Salwar-Kameez… If I wear a skirt and go out, people are going to stare at me. They will not see that I am a mother, a wife, a sister or a daughter-in-law. They will see me in the wrong way. They might even molest me. What can I do? Nothing. Because that is how I am dressed.

Implicit in women's views on sexual violence was an overarching sense of self-condemnation, self-discipline and the inevitability of violence. The street becomes a locus of disorder where one's only right to safety stems from one's ability to flawlessly embody the familial, even while walking the streets. One's seamless performance of familial womanhood can displace the disorder of the street with the order and safety inherent in the patriarchal family.

Scholars of Indian history have illustrated the manner in which discourses on body and gender are closely tied to normative ideas of aesthetics and sartorial display (Bannerji 2001; Kumar 2002; Devika 2005). In the context of television dramas, women discussed the need to discipline themselves through attire along the lines of the costume schemes employed by soap opera characters. Women's emotional investment in the dramas seemed to be grounded in the normative legitimacy of familial womanhood, even as they criticized it as unrealistic.

Conclusion: Respectable Middle-class Women Become Familial Citizens

Contemporary television dramas exemplified by the case study presented in this chapter reinforce the gendered and domestic nature of middle-class women's participation in urban India's public spaces. The orderliness of domesticity that middle-class women consent to represent through their engagement with televisual texts disallows them from performatively or discursively participating in civic spaces and practices that disrupt and challenge civic norms.

Middle-class women's appropriation of televisual narratives at the discursive and performative levels points to their active participation in invisible pedagogies of order and disorder. While the category of order is epitomized in the family and the person of the ideal woman, disorder is epitomized in challenges to the family and is manifested in the impermeability of the civic arena. In the interplay of and intersections between the patriarchal category of order and the subaltern category of 'womanly disorder', familial order, portrayed as in need of constant reclamation through the efforts of the good mother, the wife or the daughter, is set up in opposition to the disorder of the civic space. In fact, for women like Komal and Rimi, their neighborhood was safe and honorable while the world outside, the streets and civic arena outside the perimeters of the neighborhood were cantankerous and disorderly spaces, posing all manner of risks for women. Such disorderly spaces required performances of womanhood that invoke familial order and patriarchal affect; it called for the initiation of certain disciplinary rituals grounded in a woman's body and desire.

By investing the patriarchal family and women's role within it with unprecedented significance, contemporary serials set up the family both in opposition to the practices and discourses of "expressed politics" while simultaneously making women's access to civic spaces conditional on familial discourses and practices. Women in the Delhi neighborhoods saw their safe access to public spaces as possible only through an extension of and explicit display of their domestic persona as mothers, wives or daughters.

The representational hegemony of familial womanhood in the K-serial brand of television dramas reinforces the patriarchal and gendered representations that disallow women access to and visibility in civic spaces. In animating a nostalgia for the patriarchal family, its gendered practices and the constellation of affect that undergird it, these narratives reinforce the familial woman as the preferred gendered subject of (re)-presentation. Middle-class respectability becomes a key normative discourse deployed in the process of valorizing familial womanhood. Performances of familial womanhood facilitate women's disavowal of their right to safety from sexual violence and free movement in civic spaces. It works to marginalize performances of citizenship that facilitates women's full-fledged access to and engagement with the spaces and practices of citizenship, including oppositional or disruptive forms of civic engagement.

Despite women's criticism of the narratives as portraying extremes of sacrifice and devotion and their concomitant desire for alternative modes of womanly agency, there is a penury of gendered imagination, of alternative representations of middle-class womanhood among women viewers of the serials. Middle-class women who constitute the enthusiastic audience of contemporary television fiction shy away from oppositional civic practices, reinforcing familial performances of womanhood in order to secure their safety and freedom of movement. In asserting familial womanhood and patriarchal affect as the central vehicles for the representation of gender and family, contemporary Indian televisual representations of gender and family marginalizes spaces of resistance, dissent and adversarial citizenship for middle-class women in contemporary India.

References

Abu-Lughod, L. (2004). *Dramas of nationhood: The politics of television in Egypt*. Chicago: University of Chicago Press.
Banaji, S. (2008). The trouble with civic: A snapshot of young people's civic and political engagements in twenty-first-century democracies. *Journal of Youth Studies, 11*(5), 543–560.
Banaji, S. (Ed.). (2010). *South Asian media cultures: Audiences, representations, contexts*. London: Anthem Press.
Banaji, S., & Buckingham, D. (2013). *The civic web: Young people, the internet and civic participation*. The John D. and Catherine T. MacArthur Foundation series on digital media and learning. Cambridge: MIT Press.
Banaji, S., & Cammaerts, B. (2014). Citizens of nowhere land: Youth and news consumption in Europe. *Journalism Studies*. doi: 10.1080/1461670X.2014.890340.
Bannerji, H. (2001). *Investing subjects: Studies in hegemony, patriarchy and colonialism*. New Delhi: Tulika.
Bernstein, B. (1975). *Class and pedagogies: Visible and invisible*. Paris: Organization for Economic Cooperation and Development.
Buckingham, D. (1987). *Public secrets: EastEnders and its audience*. London: BFI Publishing.
Buckingham, D. (2000). *The making of citizens: Young people, news and politics*. London: Routledge.
Buckingham, D. (Ed.). (2008). *Youth, identity, and digital media*. The John D. and Catherine T. MacArthur foundation series on digital media and learning. Cambridge: The MIT Press.
Chakrabarthy, D. (1997). Postcoloniality and the artifice of history: Who speaks for 'Indian' pasts? In R. Guha (Ed.), *A subaltern studies reader, 1986–1995* (pp. 263–293). New Delhi: Oxford University Press.
Chatterjee, P. (1989). The nationalist resolution of 'the Women's Question'. In K. Sangari & S. Vaid (Eds.), *Recasting women: Essays in colonial history* (pp. 233–253). New Delhi: Kali for Women.

Chatterjee, P. (1997). The nation and its women. In R. Guha (Ed.), *A subaltern studies reader, 1986–1995* (pp. 240–262). New Delhi: Oxford University Press.

Chatterjee, P. (2001). On civil and political society in post-colonial democracies. In S. Kaviraj & S. Khilnani (Eds.), *Civil society: History and possibilities* (pp. 165–178). Cambridge: Cambridge University Press.

Chatterjee, P. (2004). *The politics of the governed*. New York: Columbia University Press.

Dahlerup, D. (1994). Learning to live with the state. State market and civil society. Women's need for intervention in east and west. *Women Studies International Forum, 2*(3), 117–127.

Devika, J. (2005). The aesthetic woman: Re-forming female bodies and minds in early twentieth-century Keralam. *Modern Asian Studies, 39*(2), 461–487.

Freitag, S. (1996). Contesting in public: Colonial legacies and contemporary communalism. In D. Ludden (Ed.), *Making India Hindu: Religion, community and the politics of democracy in India*. New Delhi: Oxford University Press.

Freitag, S. (2001). Visions of the Nation: Theorizing the nexus between creation, consumption and participation in the public sphere. In R. Dwyer & C. Pinney (Eds.), *Pleasure and the nation: The history, politics and consumption of public culture in India*. New Delhi: Oxford University Press.

Guha-Thakurta, T. (1991). Women as Calendar 'Art' Icons: Emergence of pictorial stereotype in colonial India. *Economic and Political Weekly, 26*(43), 91–99.

Hermes, J. (1995). *Reading women's magazines: An analysis of everyday media use*. Cambridge: Polity Press.

Howell, J. (2004). Introduction. In J. Howell & D. Mulligan (Eds.), *Gender and civil society: Transcending boundaries* (pp. 1–32). London: Routledge.

Indiantelevision.com. (2003). Interview with Balaji Telefilms' creative director Ekta Kapoor. Available from http://www.indiantelevision.org.in/interviews/y2k3/executive/ektakapoor.htm

Krishnan, P. (1990). In the idiom of loss: Ideology of motherhood in television serials. *Economic and Political Weekly, 25* (42 and 43), 103–116.

Krishnan, P., & Dighe, A. (1986). *Affirmation and denial: Construction of femininity on Indian television*. New Delhi: Sage.

Kumar, U. (2002). Two figures of desire: Discourses of the body in Malayalam literature. In B. Bose (Ed.), *Translating desire: The politics of gender and culture in India* (pp. 132–144). New Delhi: Katha.

Lister, R. (1997). Citizenship: Towards a feminist synthesis. *Feminist Review, 57*, 28–48.

Lister, R. (2003). Feminist theory & practice of citizenship. Paper presented at the annual conference of the DVPW (German Political Science Association).

Mahadevan, M. (2006). Sacred beings in the marketplace. *Feminist Media Studies, 6*(1), 109–112.
Mahadevan, M. (2010). *Engendering familial citizens: Serial-viewing among middle-class families in Urban India.* Unpublished doctoral dissertation, University of Westminster, United Kingdom.
Mankekar, P. (1999). *Screening culture, viewing politics: Television, womanhood and nation in modern India.* New Delhi: Oxford University Press.
Marcus, G. E., & Hanson, R. L. (1993). The practice of democratic theory. In G. E. Marcus & R. L. Hanson (Eds.), *Reconsidering the democratic public* (pp. 1–34). University Park, PA: Penn State University Press.
Monteiro, A. (1998). Official television and unofficial fabrications of the self: The spectator as subject. In A. Nandy (Ed.), *The secret politics of our desires: Innocence, culpability and Indian popular cinema.* New Delhi: Oxford University Press.
Pateman, C. (1980). The disorder of women: Women, love and the sense of justice. *Ethics, 91*, 20–34.
Pateman, C. (1988). *The sexual contract.* Cambridge: Polity Press.
Pateman, C. (1989). *The disorder of women: Democracy, feminism and political theory.* Cambridge: Polity Press.
Phillips, A. (2002). Does feminism need a conception of civil society? In S. Chambers & W. Kymlicka (Eds.), *Alternative conceptions of civil society.* Princeton, NJ: Princeton University Press.
Pinney, C. (2001). Public popular and other cultures. In R. Dwyer & C. Pinney (Eds.), *Pleasure and the nation: The history, politics and consumption of public culture in India.* New Delhi: Oxford University Press.
Probyn, E. (1997). New traditionalism and post-feminism: TV does the home. In C. Brunsdon, J. D'Acci, & L. Spigel (Eds.), *Feminist television criticism: A reader* (pp. 126–138). Oxford: Clarendon Press.
Radway, J. (1984). *Reading the romance: Women, patriarchy, and popular literature.* Chapel Hill: University of North Carolina Press.
Rajagopal, A. (2001). *Politics after television: Religious nationalism and the reshaping of the Indian public.* Cambridge: Cambridge University Press.
Ray, S. (2000). *Engendering India: Woman and nation in colonial and postcolonial narratives.* Durham: Duke University Press.
Sarkar, S. (2012). Political society in a capitalist world. In A. Gudavarthy (Ed.), *Re-framing democracy and agency in India. Interrogating political society* (pp. 31–48). London: Anthem Press.

Spivak, G. C. (1988). Can the subaltern speak? In C. Nelson & L. Grossberg (Eds.), *Marxism and the interpretation of culture*. Urbana, IL: University of Illinois Press.

Spivak, G. C. (1996). Subaltern studies: Deconstructing historiography. In D. Landry & G. M. MacLean (Eds.), *The Spivak reader* (pp. 203–235). New York: Routledge.

Spivak, G. C. (2005). Scattered speculations on the subaltern and the popular. *Postcolonial Studies, 8*(4), 475–486.

Sunder Rajan, R. (1993). *Real and imagined women: Gender, culture and postcolonialism*. London: Routledge.

Uberoi, P. (2006). *Freedom and destiny: Gender, family and popular culture in India*. New Delhi: Oxford University Press.

Yuval-Davis, N. (1997a). *Gender & Nation*. London: Sage.

Yuval-Davis, N. (1997b). Women, citizenship and difference. *Feminist Review, 57*, 4–27.

10

Vietnam Women's Union and the Politics of Representation: Hegemonic Solidarity and a Heterosexual Family Regime

Helle Rydström

Introduction

"Why ask them?" my sympathetic but firm contact persons from the local Women's Union were wondering while looking at me in bewilderment. I was about to begin conducting my first long-term anthropological fieldwork in northern rural Vietnam and was dedicated to gathering in-depth ethnographic data from families throughout the year.[1] "Just ask us, we know all the answers", they let me know. While this encounter took place in the early 1990s, in the years to come it would be followed by succeeding meetings with the Vietnam Women's Union (VWU) either

---

[1] Thinh Tri and all personal names are pseudonyms.

H. Rydström (✉)
Department of Gender Studies, Lund University, 221 00 Lund, Sweden

in connection with my research projects or when organizing workshops in collaboration with my Vietnamese colleagues.

On that particular day, though, I felt slightly confused as it was not clear to me how anybody would be able to answer questions about personal life experiences and individual opinions on behalf of others. Reluctantly, they accepted my explanations about how important people's own narratives were for my research and it was agreed that I from 1994 to 1995 should collect data *in* families rather than *about* families.[2]

Years later, I gathered data in connection with two other research projects in Vietnam, and even this time leading Union members would, with confidence, represent individual women as well as women as a collective.[3]

As an official mass organization, the Women's Union is committed to improving the conditions of the female population of the country by representing the interests of Vietnamese women to the state, and state policies to its members. Members are reached through a refined network which includes even the tiniest and most remote rural ward. By working closely on the grassroots level, the Union can identify local suggestions of importance for governmental priorities. While the central level of the Union

---

[2] From 1994 to 1995, I conducted anthropological fieldwork in Thinh Tri to study gender socialization. The fieldwork consisted of continuous observations of social interaction in five families and interviews with family members and official representatives (e.g. the WU) (see e.g. Rydström 2002, 2003). During my second fieldwork in Thinh Tri (2000–2001), I worked with four families to study violence and sexuality. Interviews were carried out with family members and official representatives such as the WU. Focus group discussions and observation also were conducted (see e.g. Rydström 2006, 2012). In 2004, I collected data in schools in the region of Hanoi to study gender and education which included observations in classes and interviews with teachers, pupils, and organizations. During these periods of fieldwork I collaborated with the Vietnam Institute of Educational Sciences and with was Bui Thanh Xuan, Nguyen Thu Huong, Nguyen Loc, and Tran Thi Kim Thuan. From 2004–2011, I was the Swedish coordinator of the Rural Families in Transitional Vietnam project; a collaboration with the Hanoi Institutes of Sociology; Family and Gender Studies; and Anthropology (among others). The project was funded by Sida and part of a bilateral research capacity building program. Data collection in 1200 households was organized in collaboration with the Vietnamese project coordinator, Trinh Duy Luan, and colleagues at the involved institutes. see e.g. H. Rydström (2011).

[3] Focus of this fieldwork was on organizations, civil society, and gender. It included in-depth interviews with Union representatives in the Ha Dong area and with national representatives of the Union. Interviews were also carried out with NGOs, research institutes, politicians, and aid agencies. In addition, focus group conversations were conducted with young women. The fieldwork was a collaboration with Nguyen T. Huong, Department of Anthropology, Hanoi University.

would offer advice in law preparatory work, for instance, local unions would organize sightseeing excursions, information meetings, or run small clubs in which women meet to mend clothes or discuss special concerns such as reproductive health care issues and domestic violence (Hakkarainen 2015; Rydström 2010; Waibel and Gluck 2013; WU 2015a, b).

Proficiently oscillating between its role as a governmental mass organization and a grassroots movement, the Union emerges as a kaleidoscopic body with a dual representative role. Initiatives taken by the Union revolve around women and their lives as organized in the predominant family constellation in Vietnam; the heterosexual family in either its nuclear or extended form.[4] Construed as a congenital point of departure, this family regime[5] provides a platform from which the Union pursues a hegemonic solidarity with women and their lifeworlds by dealing with female-specific issues such as intimate partner violence, child rearing, and income generating activities (Hakkarainen 2015; WU 2015a, b).

In this chapter, I consider the dual representative role of the Union and the ways in which it has become the voice of a hegemonic solidarity with heterosexual women and their families. The Union's characteristic politics of representation, as I will show, is particularly epitomized in regard to current contestations in Vietnam over the legal recognition of same-sex marriage.

Dual Representation

The comprehensive grassroots network of the Union indicates the horizontal nature of the organization and its more informal qualities, not unlike those found in a typical Non-Governmental Organization (NGO). This impression, however, is obscured by the vertical political structure into which the Union is engrained (WU 2015a, b). Integrated into the state[6] apparatus as a governmental body under the guidance of

---

[4] For details about the patrilineally organized heterosexual family see H. Rydström (2003).
[5] Following Foucault, a regime is like a grid of intelligibility that establishes "a certain division between truth and error" (2003: 164).
[6] The state is composed of the Party and the government which together comprise the National Assembly and the legislative and administrative bodies (Thayer, 2008; Vasavakul 2014).

the Communist Party of Vietnam (*Dang cong san Viet Nam*),[7] the Union is under obligation to contribute to the drafting and implementation of laws of significance for women and their families, collaborate with Vietnamese and international NGOs, encourage and support activities of relevance for women in the family and facilitate initiatives taken from below by local Union leaders and members. The Union is thus constrained to represent strategies of the Vietnamese state to its members and simultaneously represent women as a unified collective to the state and the public (Chiricosta 2010; W. Duong 2001; Endres 1999; Le 1989, 1997; Mai and Le 1978; Study Report 2008; Tai 1996).

By virtue of its dual representative role, the Union is engaged within all of the societal spheres that usually are defined as state, private, and civil society.[8] In a one-party society like Vietnam, these spheres, though, appear as rather indistinguishable (London 2014; Study Report 2008; Taylor et al. 2012; Vasavakul 2014). In such a context it is particularly clear that state acceptance, as Antonio Gramsci (1971) has argued, is a precondition for the fostering and perpetuation of a societal sphere of contestations, also known as civil society.[9] Within this vaguely demarcated sphere, struggles are taking place between various interests and agents including the state, unions, organizations, and the family to gain power and influence in what can be seen as an ongoing "war of position" (Gray 1999; Heng 2004; Trong 2013). By participating in sequentially linked activities which, as suggested by Iris Marion Young (2000), embrace a span of interests such as collective concerns regarding life and death ("private interests"), wider interests sustained by the volunteer work of dedicated members ("civic interests"), and the promotion of political ideas aiming at influencing political strategies ("political interests"), agents struggle to make an impact on political decisions and strategies (cf. Eto 2012; Howell 2007).

The fuzzy sphere of civil society provides an arena for the development of visions and strategies either in opposition to, or in favor of, the state in which organizations can engage in defining and redefining the boundaries

---

[7] On party name changes; see W. Turley (1980).
[8] These distinctions follow M. Eto (2012).
[9] See M. Carothers (1999/2000) and M. Kaldor (2003) for liberal and Marxist understandings of civil society and for discussion of how opposition to totalitarian states in Latin America and Eastern Europe during the 1970–1980s gave civil society new meaning as a space for global pro-democratic movements.

and division of power between the state and citizens (Eto 2012; London 2014; Vasavakul 2014). Given its coercive forces, as defined by constitutional conditions, the state holds a predominant position in the "war of position", while other agents (such as organizations) take part with varied degrees of "relative autonomy" to the state (Poulantzas 1982). In an attempt to make its interests universal, or hegemonic, the state attempts to institutionalize and mediate its force through bodies such as the media, education, and the family (Gramsci 1971).

Agents thus not only negotiate their proximity but also their autonomy in relation to the state. These negotiations, I would suggest, are carried out against a backdrop of what can be characterized as molar and molecular paradigms. Molar entities, according to Gilles Deleuze and Félix Guattari (2002), can be understood as units that are affiliated with the state apparatus. As more established bodies, they subscribe to a paradigm that aims at stability and continuity; as a formalized being which is extended over a prolonged period of time.[10] Molecular forms, on the other hand, refer to associations, agencies, organizations, or non-organized individuals, driven by desires and dreams and engaged in activities that appear ambiguous and contingent; in more informal processes of becoming. Yet, both molar and molecular activities can undergo transformations by integrating features of one another or by merging and thereby metamorphose into novel hybrid formations composed of both sets of characteristics (cf. Baum 2004; Parr 2010; Spivak 2009; Vasavakul 2014).

Mass Organized Feminism

Although two waves have been identified in Vietnamese feminism (e.g. Waibel and Benedikter 2013), I would rather refer to three phases.[11] As "the organized activism by women's groups for the improvement of

---

[10] Molar is a term borrowed from the chemical idiolect and represents geologically ground and telluric substance (Parr 2010: 175–177).

[11] Feminism understood as constructed and contextual (e.g. Butler 1990) rather than as a strategic essentialist notion and practice (e.g. Spivak 2009). In the words of W. Duong (2001: 194), "there is no word for 'feminism' or 'feminist' in the Vietnamese language". *Nu si* refers to the female literati and *nu anh hung* to heroine. The English word 'feminism', Vietnamese scholars refer to as a movement aiming at improving women's social position. 'Gender' (i.e. *gioi*) is a widely used term in Vietnamese, though.

women's status" (Roces 2010: 7), I approach women's movements as locally shaped and the feminism they practice as developed in dialogue with national, regional, and global politics. In Asia, for example, women's movements might be critical to the Western legacy of feminism and what has been disclaimed as a promotion of values that challenge indigenous traditions and even augment what is seen as Western imperialism (Hawkesworth 2013; Howell 2007; Roces 2010; Stivens 2010).

The first period of feminism in Vietnam, I would suggest, refers to women's fight for liberalization prior to 1975. This period includes the pre-revolutionary (i.e. 1945) struggle for emancipation from Confucian dictates,[12] the War of Liberation against French colonialism (1867–1954),[13] and the northern Vietnamese fight against the USA (1965–1975) (Bradley 2012; Rydström 2012; Tai 1996; WU 2015a, b). The second period covers the rebuilding of the nation after the war against the USA and the introduction of the *Doi Moi* policy (renovation) in 1986.[14] The third and current wave of feminism has its beginning in the early 1990s, when the American embargo was lifted and Vietnam became part of the global economy.[15] This wave is marked by a generational shift and shaped by a younger, internationally-oriented post-war generation, a generation inspired by globally traversing media images, narratives about economic prosperity and alternative lifestyles with gender relations, sexuality, education, and mobility as significant points of navigation (Appadurai 1996; Bræmer 2014; Hansen 2008; Hirsch et al. 2012; Ngoc 2013; Nguyen 2015).

The Union has undergone various phases of constellation. Just like women's movements elsewhere in the world, as highlighted by scholars such as Aili Mari Tripp and her co-authors (2010) in the context of Africa and Gabriele Griffin and Rosi Braidotti (2002) in the context of Europe,

---

[12] Confucianism suggests a patriarchal organization and was introduced into Vietnam by the Chinese conquest (BCE 111-CE 939) (Marr 1981: 191).

[13] In 1867, the southern part of Vietnam had been included into the Indo-Chinese Union. In 1883, French troops stormed the citadel of Hanoi and the Imperial Court in Hue recognized Annam and Tonkin as French protectorates (Marr 1981: 190–192).

[14] The *Doi Moi* program launched in 1986 caused huge societal transformations (Duiker 1995).

[15] See M. Bradley (2012) on the embargo against Vietnam inflicted by a majority of Western countries after Vietnam's invasion of Cambodia in 1978.

the women's movements in Vietnam been entangled with politics including nationalism, socialism, and conservatism (Chiricosta 2010; W. Duong 2001; Le 1989; Mai and Le 1978; Tai 1996). The first women's group in Vietnam was established in 1926, as the Association for the Study of Domestic Arts and focused on the improvement of women's education. During this period, large numbers of women in French-occupied Cochinchina (Vietnam, Laos, Cambodia) were engaged in reading and publication groups in which women's issues were addressed.[16] In 1930, when opposition to French colonialism was becoming increasingly well-organized, the Women's Union for Emancipation was founded to represent women in the fight for independence. In the War of Liberation, the Union joined forces with the Communist Party (established in 1930) and its leader Ho Chi Minh (Marr 1981; Tai 1996). Between 1930 and 1945, in the years leading to the August Revolution of 1945, the Union went through various name changes (some of which were coinciding) including Liberalization Women's Union (1936–1938), the Democratic Women's Union (1939–1940), the Anti-Imperialism Women's Union (1931–1945), and the Women League for National Salvation (1941–1950) (Taylor 1999; Turley 1972; WU 2015a, b).

At the First National Women's Congress held in May 1950, the Women League for National Salvation was renamed the Vietnam Women's Union. The Union already had three million members of which ten women were members of the National Assembly's First Tenure of the new Democratic Republic of Vietnam (WU 2015a, b). While the Union's predecessors had been associated with the National Liberation Front and embraced groups with differing political opinions unified in the fight against French dominance, the Women's Union was established as an agency of the Communist Party and defined as one of the mass organizations (Taylor 1999; Turley 1972; Vuong 1997).

Today the mass organizations include, besides the Women's Union, the Trade Union, Youth Union, Peasants' Union, Veteran's Union, and the Fatherland Front. Even though the mass organizations are not part of the Party, they refer to it at national, provincial, and communal level.

---

[16] Personal communication with Nguyen-vo, T-h.

Not unlike what has been described in regard to the Chinese setting by Jude Howell (2007), the mass organizations in Vietnam are run and sponsored mainly by the state. They therefore differ from other types of Vietnamese organizations such as professionals' organizations (such as the lawyers' organization) and issue-oriented NGOs (like iSEE). Those that are engaged in a mass organization are motivated by a wish to contribute to "the development of an equal, fair and just society" (Wischermann 2010: 19). Except for those who are active in the Women's Union, men are mostly engaged in mass organizations (Wischermann 2010).

The Women's Union is organized at the central, provincial, district, and commune levels and remains the largest of Vietnam's mass organizations with about 300 staff members and 13 million mainly female members who relate to about 10,500 local unions at commune level. Membership of a mass organization can come through employment in the public sector, for instance, or through registration.

As a member of the statutory National Council for the Advancement of Women, the Union is an established advocate for the improvement of the conditions for women and their families (Taylor et al. 2012; Thayer 2008; Wischermann 2010; WU 2013, 2015a, b). Together with Party cells throughout the neighborhood and the workplace, the broad network of the mass organizations provides a means for the state to remain in contact with the population. The representatives of the mass organizations are able to mediate various political objectives to their members and work to gain local support for the implementation of new state policies while at the same time communicating members' concerns and suggestions to the government (Heng 2004; London 2014; Kerkvliet 2001; Trong 2013; Vasavakul 2014).

Family Regime

The dual obligation to communicate the interests of the Party to women and the interests of women to the Party has fostered a narrative of hegemonic solidarity with women in heterosexual families. As a central agent in the promotion and implementation of equality politics in Vietnam, the Union is obliged to "educate and mobilize officials, employees and members as well as every citizen to build cultural families; provide counseling on marriage and family; reconcile family discords in time, protect the legitimate rights and interests of the family members" (Marriage and Family Law 2000, Art. 3.2). Defined as more than a naturalized and intimate site of procreation, pre-revolutionary families were pointed out by the government and the Union as a nest for the nurturing of 'backward' (*lac hau*), feudal, and Confucian values which allowed for men's domination over women and other dependents (Drummond and Rydström, 2004; Rydström 2003, 2010; Waibel and Gluck 2013; WU 2013, 2015a, b). This understanding is reflected in the first Law on Marriage and the Family of 1959, which aimed at destroying all "remnants of feudalism" in sex-related social roles and family structure, and to build "happy, democratic and egalitarian families" (Chin 1973; Mai and Le 1978). In the most recent Law on Marriage and Family of 2000, a socialist heterosexual family regime is put forward as the core of Vietnamese society, as "all citizens are responsible for building and consolidating a Vietnamese marriage and family regime" (Art. 1).

Women, in particular, are recognized for their important role in developing ideal families, as indicated by a recent slogan promoted by the Union in which it is emphasized that "women actively study, creatively work and nurture happy families" (WU 2015a, b). Over the years, the government and the Union have striven to shape families through nationwide campaigns such as the "Happy Family" (*gia dinh hanh phuc*) and the "Cultured Family" (*gia dinh van hoa*). These have, either directly through law regulation and local authorities, or more indirectly through mass media such as the Women's Newspaper *Bao Phu Nu*, reached a large majority of Vietnamese women to help them become less "backward" in their gender understandings and more "civilized", "modernized", and "developed" (Drummond 2004; cf. Hakkarainen 2015; Ngo 2004; Nguyen-vo 2008; Rydström 2003, 2010). Hence, "educational pamphlets, billboards, courses, and recreational activities [have] taught women how to handle family planning, manage households, and emotionally nurture husbands and children" (Leshkowich 2008: 13).

Even though the influential "Cultured Family" campaigns have, over the years, undergone various changes, the critical role of mothers in the construction of ideal families persists. When the movement was launched in 1962, it promoted a number of moral standards for citizens such as the significance of setting an example of executing Party policy and demonstrating good hygiene, the latter goal to be reached through mothers' day-to-day contact with their children. By the 1980s, family planning was the primary standard of a "Cultured Family" and women were directly targeted to reach the goal of building happy families consisting of only 1–2 children. In the 1990s, the standards of the "Cultured Family" were focused on "Happy and Harmonious Family Life" (*gia dinh hanh phuc hoa thuan*) (Drummond 2004; Leshkowich 2014). Such qualities were considered to be the core of Vietnamese society and women were acknowledged for their pivotal role in reaching these goals, for instance, by complying in order to maintain household harmony (Barbieri and Bélanger 2009; Ngo 2004; Rydström 2003, 2006, 2010).

The rhetoric of the campaigns of the 1990s has continued to circulate in Vietnamese society and discourse and is thus echoed in newspapers, television, social media, and daily talk.[17] As Ann-Marie Leshkowich (2008) has noted, on the one hand, women and their families have been under strong pressure to adjust to the family campaign goals. On the other, the campaigns resonate with a general concern in Vietnamese society about the ways in which the morality of the collective, family, and youth might be affected by Vietnam's inclusion in the global community and its fluctuating moral standards (Ngoc 2013; Nguyen-vo 2008; Rydström 2006, 2010). Not unlike what has been seen in other countries in the Southeast Asian region, such as Malaysia and Singapore (Hirsch et al. 2012; Stivens 2010), the moral impact of globalization causes anxieties in Vietnam, especially in regard to younger generations who grow up with social media, aspirations for social mobility, and desires for alternative lifestyles including free partner choice, sexual encounters before marriage, co-habitation prior to marriage, single parenthood, and same-sex partnership; activities which are thought to post a challenge to appreciated gender values, assumptions about womanhood, motherhood, and family life (cf. Bræmer 2014; Hansen 2008; Horton and Rydström 2011; Ngoc 2013).

---

[17] See e.g. *Giadinh Net.Vn* (Family Net Vietnam) and *Bao Xa Dinh va Xa Hoi* (Newspaper; Family and Society).

Womanhood/Motherhood

While we were sitting in a small Hanoi café, Nguyet, a representative of the national Women's Union explained to me how the Union holds "an important socialization role in society and for the progress of women [...]. It should help women in building economic prosperous families and educating their children to keep them away from 'social evils'". In this spirit, the feminism and womanhood advocated by the Union correspond with the ideals perpetuated in the family campaigns. Some of the central goals of the Union's most recent program aim at:[18]

1. Raising women's awareness, knowledge and capacity in order to meet the requirements of the new situation [that is, current economic growth and visions for industrialization]; cultivating healthy, knowledgeable, skillful, dynamic, innovative, cultured, and kind-hearted Vietnamese women.
2. Participating in the formulation, social counter-argument, and supervision of implementation of laws and policies on gender equality.
3. Assisting women in economic development, job creation, and income generation.
4. Assisting women in building prosperous, equal, progressive and happy families.
5. Building and developing a strong organizational structure for VWU.
6. Expanding international relations and cooperation for equality, development, and peace.

Traditionally, Vietnamese women were expected to confine themselves strictly within the familial circle. Orthodox Confucian texts fused with proverbs, dictums, and sayings provided various social tools for regulating women and girls' conduct. The Four Virtues (*Tu Duc*), for example, advised that women behave properly in regard to housework (*cong*), appearance (*dung*), speech (*ngon*), and conduct (*hanh*) (Marr 1981; Ngo 2004; Rydström 2010). As Ngo Thi Ngan Binh has described, "a woman's

---

[18] I.e. for the period 2007–2012.

place was by the hearth; her worth was largely measured by her skills at maintaining the warmth of that hearth, namely the well-being of her family" (2004: 50). Such Confucian female ideals were contested in the anti-colonial and anti-war contexts and a revolutionary image of womanhood was eventually crafted. After 1986, the femininity of the socialist "new woman in the national protection and construction", however, was replaced with more docile, yet Confucian-inspired, qualities such as "loyal, gentle, elegant, tactful, and resourceful".

The Union advocates the "equality of men and women", (*nam nu binh dang*) but all the while, women's capacities and duties as mothers are held out as pertinent features of womanhood. In this rhetoric, motherhood has been presented as a demand rather than an option and childrearing a responsibility of mothers primarily. Women in Vietnam are commonly appreciated for holding a "Heavenly Mandate" (*Thien Chuc*) thanks to their capacity to bear children (Drummond and Rydström 2004; Rydström 2010). This assumption is either subtly or overtly reiterated in connection with various family campaigns. Prominent Union members, for example, have pointed out that "women [...] have the function of becoming pregnant and giving birth" (Tran 1999: 16) because "the first function of the family is reproduction of human beings to ensure future generations" (Le 1999: 14; see also Blom et al. 2000; Waibel and Benedikter 2013).

Such ideas also are echoed in the Union's ongoing programs. Here, the heterosexual family and the good mother are at the fore of comprehensive interventions and assistance. The project "educating 5 million mothers on good parenting over the 2010–2015 period" is intended to support mothers with breeding exemplary families that do not suffer from "poverty, law violation, and social evils" because "building prosperous, equal, advanced, and happy families is the common goal of almost all the VWU's [i.e. Vietnam Women's Union] programs and activities" (WU 2013: 5). Girls and women are expected to identify themselves with future motherhood and the building of ideal families despite the ways in which such images might undermine the goal of "equality between men and women" toward which the Union strives. As a vehicle for governmental equality policies and strategies, the Union thus contributes to the improvement of the conditions for heterosexual women and their families (Hakkarainen 2015; Leshkowich 2008; Newton 2012; Rydström 2010).

Same-Sex Marriage

With the implementation of the *Doi Moi* policy, Vietnam opened its doors to a global world and foreign influence. Not unlike other governments in the region (such as Malaysia and Singapore) the Vietnamese government became concerned about the potential effects of what were deemed to be "social evils" (*te nan xa hoi*) (Rydström 2006, 2010; Stivens 2010). "Social evils" were believed to reflect bad foreign moral influence to Vietnam's "beautiful traditions and customs" (Nguyen-vo 2008: 45). In response to the perceived threat, in 1995, the Vietnamese government initiated a campaign to eliminate "social evils" and "poisonous culture" (*van hoa doc hai*). These labels have been applied by the government, in public discourse, and by citizens to categorize a wide range of social practices deemed damaging to Vietnamese society, morality, and tradition such as homosexuality, sexually transmitted diseases, domestic violence, sex work, and drug use (Khuat 1998; Horton and Rydström 2011; Vijeyarasa 2010).

While homosexuality was silenced in the Law on Marriage and Family of 1986 (cf. Khuat 1998), the Law from 2000 defines it as an oppositional negative to the heterosexual regime around which the law revolves. The 2000 version repeatedly puts forward that the matrimonial union consists of a man and a woman and thus stipulates that "marriage is forbidden [...] between people of the same sex" (Chap. 2, Art. 10.5). The 2000 Law thus prohibited same-sex couples from cohabiting without registration, or a marriage certificate (cf. Australian Government 2010; *tuoitrenews.vn*, 17 April 2013).[19] Even though Vietnamese law has on no occasion prohibited homosexuality, it has been stigmatized as an immoral practice against nature, and has even been associated with addiction (to drugs) and disease (HIV/AIDS) (Khuat 1998; Khuat et al. 2009; Khuat and Nguyen 2010; *tuoitrenews.vn*, 17 April 2013).

Homosexuality and same-sex partnership have been misrecognized by various governmental agencies as a family unit that falls outside the normalized regime. During the last decade, however, the dominant norm

---

[19] The newspaper *Tuoi Tre* (Youth) used to be mouthpiece of the Communist Youth Union but holds today a reputation as being pro-reform (Wells-Dang 2011).

for family life, as celebrated by various campaigns, has been contested in Vietnam, as it has been elsewhere (e.g. Halsaa et al. 2012: 3). In 1997, for example, two men arranged a wedding celebration in Ho Chi Minh City. The media reported that local residents protested the event which, nevertheless, gave rise to increased public attention to the rights of homosexuals. A year later, a lesbian couple went even further by attempting to register their marriage with the local authorities. The women were denied a marriage certificate and on instructions of the Ministry of Justice, a directive was issued to put an end to the marriage. As a result of this particular event, the National Assembly passed an amended marriage law which prohibited same-sex marriages, the Law of 2000 (Australian Government 2010; Khuat and Nguyen 2010; Newton 2012).

"War of Position"

Newly established smaller Vietnamese non-governmental organizations dedicated to working for the recognition and rights of homosexuals in Vietnam engage with varied degrees of relative autonomy in the blurred sphere of civil society in a "war of position" to gain influence over policies and strategies (Gray 1999; Heng 2004; London 2014; Taylor et al. 2012; Trong 2013). They collaborate with international aid agencies from which they not only obtain moral support but also funding to promote the rights of homosexuals by initiating various kinds of projects (Australian Government 2010).[20] Due to the efforts of these organizations, on 5 August 2012, Vietnam's first gay pride parade was permitted by the Vietnamese government to be held in Hanoi (*ABC News*, 5 August 2012). Since the 1998 wedding of the lesbian couple, the Ministry of Justice has taken a more progressive view on same-sex marriages and has, together with the Ministry of Health, supported revisions for increased legal and social recognition of homosexuals. In connection with the parade, the Minister of Justice thus explained that it might be time to legalize same-sex marriage in Vietnam (*Channels News Asia*, 6 August 2012; *The Diplomat*, 18 April 2014; *tuoitrenews.vn*, 10 March 2013).

---

[20] E.g. Csaga and iSEE.

Later the same year, the Ministry of Justice and the United Nations Development Program (UNDP) jointly organized a workshop "On Comparative Experiences in Protection of LGBT Rights in the Family and Marriage Relations". The chairman of the workshop stressed that "the Marriage and Family Law needs some fundamental changes to reflect the principle of respecting and protecting at the highest level the human rights and citizen rights that Vietnam has committed to" (isee.org.vn, 21 December 2012). As a first step in the process of possible legalization of same-sex marriages and revision of the Marriage and Family Law, on 24 September 2013 the government issued Decree 110/2013/ND-CP (with effect from November 2013) which removed the ban on same-sex marriage (*tuoitrenews.vn*, 10 March 2013; USAID and UNDP 2014).

On 19 June 2014, the National Assembly followed up on Decree 110/2013/ND-CP by passing the amended Law on Marriage and Family. The amended Law took effect in January 2015 and in line with the Decree, the ban on same-sex marriage was removed. However, the National Assembly did not go a step further and fully recognize same-sex marriage. Despite disappointment in the LGBT community, Vietnamese NGOs working for homosexual rights declared that the amendment with its lax legislation might be a wise first move made in working toward wider support in the population for full legalization of same-sex marriage (cf. *tuoitrenews.vn*, 27 April 2014; *tuoitrenews.vn*, 20 June 2014).

Molar and Molecular Agents

The Ministry of Justice and the Ministry of Health are both molar in character as solid agents of the state apparatus, yet they have demonstrated a certain willingness to take into consideration the arguments of the molecular forces, the NGOs fighting for the recognition and rights of homosexuals in Vietnam. In the 'war of position' concerning definitions of the family, these two ministries have reportedly communicated with the LGBT movement and negotiated with the National Assembly for legal revisions of the Law on Marriage and Family.

Other agencies of the state apparatus, on the other hand, have been hesitant to recognize homosexuality and the legal rights of same-sex couples.

Here, the Women's Union is conspicuous because it has not only been reluctant to accept same-sex marriages but is opposed to legalization. As observed by *The Diplomat* (18 April 2014), "the most vigorous opposition has come from the Vietnamese Women's Union, which perceives same-sex marriage as a threat to traditional family ideals". The Vietnamese newspaper *Tuoi Tre* (Youth) has similarly noted that "the Vietnam Women's Union and several other agencies believe the State should not recognize same-sex marriage, since it is against the nation's customs and habits" (*tuoitrenews.vn*, 10 March 2013). In regard to same-sex marriage, the Union thus perpetuates assumptions about a negative moral impact on Vietnamese society of what is seen as global (and promiscuous) norms (cf. Newton 2012; WU 2013, 2015a, b).

Regardless of a governmental willingness to debate the rights of homosexuals and ascribe the LGBT group legal rights similar to heterosexual couples in tandem with a growing, yet hesitating, public preparedness to recognize homosexual rights, the Union maintains its focus on women in heterosexual families. Grassroots experiences have been taken into account by the Union, for instance, by acknowledging that families could be fractured, or even broken, and the organization has devoted much of its work to providing support for women who have been subjected to partner violence,[21] who are single mothers,[22] or belong to particularly vulnerable groups (*GayAsiaNews*, 28 March 2014; Le 2008; Phinney 2005; Nguyen TBV; Waibel and Gluck 2013). Concerning questions of homosexuality, however, the Union has tilted to the molar side by positioning itself as one of the state apparatus' conservers of tradition and morality rather than as a molecular organization sensitive to visions and desires of all women regardless of sexuality (cf. L. Duong 2012; Newton 2012; Waibel and Benedikter 2013; WU 2013, 2015a, b).

Non-governmental Mass Organizations

The Union, nonetheless, has been eager to stress its molecular characteristics as a NGO voice of the grassroots. When the American embargo against Vietnam was terminated in 1994, international development

---

[21] See the the campaign *Keeping Silent is Dying* (GSO 2010).
[22] The 2011 exhibition on Single Mothers' Voices at the Vietnam Women's Museum in Hanoi indicated the Union's recognition of this group (*VietNam News* 8 March 2011).

organizations were allowed to set up office in the country. Constrained economic conditions in the post-war and isolation era urged Vietnamese agencies to constitute partnership with the incoming foreign donors. Like other mass organizations, the Union began to recast itself as a NGO and possible partner of collaboration. Assumed by the incoming aid organizations to be typical Western NGOs with a certain degree of detachment from the state and room for maneuver, the mass organizations became increasingly involved as partners in international development aid projects (Gray 1999; Heng 2004; Norlund 2007; Salemink 2006; Taylor et al. 2012; Vuong 1997).

In international aid work and Western scholarship, NGOs are generally appreciated as the heart of civil society, especially in countries undergoing sociopolitical and economic transition (such as eastern European countries and late-socialist societies). These organizations are widely celebrated for their molecular characteristics and as potential guarantors of progress, equality, and rights (Carothers 1999/2000). In this spirit, international organizations tend to see their work in Vietnam as a way of supporting what is recognized as the country's bourgeoning civil society (ADB 2011; London 2014; Thayer 2008). However, in countries that face rapid sociopolitical transition, NGOs, as understood in a typical Western optic, are not uncommonly dominated by elite-run associations which speak on behalf of particular groups of citizens to attract project funding (Carothers 1999/2000).

Integrating both molar and molecular paradigms, the Women's Union recognizes its collaborative work with international aid donors as a contribution to the implementation of development initiatives in support of state policy which aims at improving service to women in ideal families, fractured families, or families living under difficult circumstances (Thayer 2008; Salemink 2006; WU 2013, 2015a, b). Almost three decades after the introduction of the *Doi Moi* policy, Vietnam's fast societal transformation, including a booming private sector, has fostered socioeconomic inequalities (Ngoc 2013; Nguyen 2015).[23] Hence, a prospering urban middle-class and a growing group of *nouveau riche* live under much more privileged conditions than millions of poverty-ridden farmers (*BBC*, 15

---

[23] Vietnam's low-income status was improved into middle-income status by 2008 (ADB 2011).

May 2013; Le et al. 2005; Rydström 2011). Social protection has increasingly been promoted by the Vietnamese government as a family-based kin concern rather than a social policy matter. An increased level of privatization of common services means that women especially are expected to care for their elders and minors out of social obligation. Here, the Union intervenes by negotiating with the state over the implementation of aid initiatives to fulfill members' needs from which the government has gradually been retreating (Ngoc 2013; Tran and Norlund 2015; UNDP 2015; WU 2013, 2015a, b).

Conclusions

By simultaneously subscribing to molar and molecular characteristics, the Women's Union becomes kaleidoscopic in character. In maneuvering on the sociopolitical plateaus, the organization proficiently oscillates between its role as a Party-loyal mass organization, an NGO collaborating with international aid donors, and a sociopolitical grassroots movement. While obfuscating conventionally defined boundaries between the state, private, and civil society, the Union engages in a "war of position" to promote a range of interests of Vietnamese women and their families to the state and state strategies to its members. The Union's politics of representation when combined with the organization's opposition to the LGBT fight for recognition and its tendency to eschew same-sex issues facilitates the shaping of a story about hegemonic solidarity with heterosexual women and their families. This is a narrative which feeds into the Union's historical contribution to nation building, fighting for women's emancipation and equality, and struggling to improve women's living conditions. Owing to its dual representative role, as a link between the grassroots and the government, the Union—and its official representatives such as my two Union contact persons in Thinh Tri—do not necessarily see any hindrances in representing the sum of individual experiences and opinions of the majority of Vietnamese women by articulating a feminist narrative about hegemonic solidarity.

Acknowledgements Data was collected within two different research projects both of which have been generously funded by the Swedish Research Council (*Vetenskapsrådet*); i.e. (1) 'Challenged Feminism: The Women's Union in Late-Socialist Global Vietnam' which is part of a larger project on 'Imagining Change: Women and the Making of Civil Societies in the Arctic Region, Asia, Latin America, and Europe'. And (2) 'Recognition and Homosexuality: The Socio-Cultural Status of Same-Sex Relations in India and Vietnam'. James Scott, as well as Andrew Arato, provided helpful comments on a previous version of this text and so did Randi Gressgård and Nguyen-vo Thu-huong. At the Max Planck Institute for Social Anthropology in Germany to which I was invited by Kirsten Endres and Minh Nguyen, stimulating comments were offered on an earlier version of this chapter. Communication with Anindita Datta, Steffen Jensen, Naila Kabeer, Ravinder Kaur, Catarina Kinnvall, Don Kulick, Åsa Lundqvist, Diana Mulinari, Huong Thu Nguyen, Mina Roces, Oscar Salemink, and Gabi Waibel about civil society has been inspiring and so have the Civil Society workshops at *Vetenskapsrådet*. The volume editors, a referee, and the 'Ida Blom Conference on Gendered Citizenship, History, Politics, and Democracy' (University of Bergen, 2013) facilitated the work with this paper. I am very grateful to the persons and organizations in Vietnam who were willing to participate in this research.

References

ABC Net Australia. (2012). Vietnam holds first gay pride parade. *ABC Net Australia*, 5 August. Available from http://www.abc.net.au/news/2012-08-05/vietnam-holds-first-gay-pride-parade/4178626
ADB; Asian Development Bank. (2011). Civil society briefs Vietnam, ADB.
Appadurai, A. (1996). *Modernity at large*. Minneapolis, MN: University of Minnesota Press.
Australian Government. (2010). Country advice: Vietnam. 22 February 2010.
Baum, W. (2004). Molar and molecular views of choice. *Behavioural Processes, 66*(3), 349–359.
BBC. (2013). *News Asia: Vietnam profile*. BBC, 15 May. Available from http://www.bbc.co.uk/news/world-asia-pacific-16567315
Blom, I., Hagemann, K., & Hall, C. (Eds.). (2000). *Gendered Nations: The long eighteenth century*. Oxford: Berg Publishers.

Bradley, M. (2012). *Vietnam at war*. Oxford: Oxford University Press.
Bræmer, M. (2014). *Love matters: Dilemmas of desire in transcultural relationships in Hanoi*. Doctoral dissertation, Aarhus University.
Butler, J. (1990). *Gender trouble: Feminism and the subversion of identity*. London: Routledge.
Carothers, T. (1999/2000). Civil society. *Foreign policy*, Winter, 18–29.
Center for Studies and Applied Sciences in Gender, Family, Women, and Adolescents (CSAGA). Available from http://www.comminit.com/content/center-studies-and-applied-sciences-gender-family-women-and-adolescents-csaga
Channel News Asia. (2012). Vietname holds her first LGBT pride parade on Sunday, 5 August 12. *Channel News Asia*, 6 August. Available from https://www.youtube.com/watch?v=EdtFy2E0k5c
Chin, K. (1973). The marriage and family law of North Vietnam. *The International Lawyer*, 7(2), 440–450.
Chiricosta, A. (2010). Following the trail of the fairy-bird: The search for a uniquely Vietnamese Women's Movement. In M. Roces & L. Edwards (Eds.), *Women's movements in Asia: Feminism and transnational activism* (pp. 124–144). London: Routledge.
Decree 110/2013/ND-CP. (2013). Stipulation of acts of administrative violations. National Assembly of Vietnam, 24 September.
Deleuze, G., & Guattari, F. (2002). *A thousand plateaus: Capitalism and schizophrenia*. London: Continuum.
Drummond, L. (2004). The Modern Vietnamese Woman: Socialization and Women's Magazines. In L. Drummond & H. Rydström (Eds.), *Gender practices in contemporary Vietnam* (pp. 158–179). Singapore: Singapore University Press.
Drummond, L., & Rydström, H. (Eds.). (2004). Introduction. *Gender practices in contemporary Vietnam* (pp. 1–26). Singapore: Singapore University Press.
Duiker, W. (1995). *Vietnam: Revolution in transition*. Boulder, CO: Westview Press.
Duong, W. (2001). Gender equality and women's issues in Vietnam: The Vietnamese woman warrior and poet. *Pacific Rim Law & Policy Journal Association*, 10(2), 190–326.
Duong, L. (2012). *Treacherous subjects: Gender, culture, and trans-Vietnamese feminism*. Philadelphia: Temple University Press.
Endres, K. (1999). Images of womanhood in rural Vietnam and the role of the Vietnamese Women's Union. In B. Dahm & V. J. Houben (Eds.), *Vietnamese villages in transition* (pp. 155–174). Passau: Passau University.

Eto, M. (2012). Reframing civil society from gender perspectives. *Journal of Civil Society,* 8(2), 101–121.
Foucault, M. (2003). *Society must be defended, lectures at the Collège de France 1975–1976* (D. Macey, Trans.). New York: Picador.
GayAsiaNews. (2014). Most Vietnamese oppose gay marriages despite governmental approval. *GayAsiaNews,* 28 March. Available from http://gayasianews.com/2014/03/28/most-vietnamese-oppose-same-sex-marriage-despite-govts-approval/
General Statistics Office of Vietnam (GSO). (2010). *Keeping silent is dying: results from the national study on domestic violence against women in vietnam.*
GiadinhNet.Vn (Family Net Vietnam) and *Bao Xa Dinh* [i.e. gia dinh] *va Xa Hoi* (Newspaper: Family and Society). *Bo Y Te* (Ministry of Health). Available from http://giadinh.net.vn/gia-dinh/chuan-muc-van-hoa-gia-dinh-la-nentang-cua-hanh-phuc-20110111081841208.htm
Gramsci, A. (1971). *Selections from the Prison Notebooks.* London: Lawrence and Wishart.
Gray, M. (1999). Creating civil society? The emergence of NGOs in Vietnam. *Development and Change,* 30(4), 693–713.
Griffin, G., & Braidotti, R. (Eds.). (2002) *Thinking differently.* London: Zed Books.
Hakkarainen, M. (2015). Navigating between ideas of democracy and gendered local practices in Vietnam. Doctoral dissertation, University of Helsinki.
Halsaa, B., Roseneil, S., & Sümer, S. (2012). Remaking citizenship in multicultural Europe. In B. Halsaa, S. Roseneil, & S. Sümer (Eds.), *Remaking citizenship in multicultural Europe: Women's movements, gender and diversity* (pp. 1–20). London: Palgrave Macmillan.
Hansen, K. (Ed.). (2008). *Youth and the city in the global south.* Indianapolis: Indiana University Press.
Hawkesworth, M. (Ed.). (2013). *Feminist practices, signs on the syllabus.* Chicago: University of Chicago Press.
Heng, H.-K. R. (2004). Civil society effectiveness and the Vietnamese state: Despite or because of the lack of autonomy? In L. H. Guan (Ed.), *Civil society in Southeast Asia* (pp. 144–167). Copenhagen: NIAS Press.
Hirsch, J., Wardlow, H., & Phinney, H. (2012). 'No One Saw Us': Reputation as an Axis of Sexual Identity. In P. Aggleton et al. (Eds.), *Understanding global sexualities: New frontiers* (pp. 91–107). London: Routledge.
Horton, P., & Rydström, H. (2011). Heterosexual masculinity in contemporary Vietnam: Privileges, pleasures and protests. *Men and Masculinities,* 14(5), 542–564.

Howell, J. (2007). Gender and civil society: Time for cross-border dialogue. *Social Politics: International Studies in Gender, State, and Society, 14*(4), 415–436.
Institute for Studies of Society, Economics, and Environment (iSEE). Available from http://isee.org.vn/en
Kaldor, M. (2003). The idea of global civil society. *International Affairs, 79*(3), 583–593.
Kerkvliet, B. (2001). Introduction. In B. Kerkvliet, H.-K. R. Heng, & D. Koh (Eds.), *Getting organized in Vietnam: Moving in and around the socialist state* (pp. 1–24). Singapore: Institute of Southeast Asian Studies.
Khuat, T. H. (1998). *Study on sexuality in Vietnam: The known and unknown issues.* South and East Asia, Regional Working Papers, no. 11. Hanoi: Population Council.
Khuat, T. H., & Nguyen, N. H. (2010). *Understanding and reducing stigma related to men who have sex with men and HIV.* Hanoi: Women Publishing House.
Khuat, T. H., Le, B. D., & Nguyen, N. G. (2009). *Sexuality in contemporary Vietnam.* Hanoi: Women Publishing House.
Le, T. N. T. (1989). *Vietnamese women in the eighties* (pp. 23–33). VWU and Centre for Women Studies. Hanoi: Foreign Languages Publishing House.
Le, T. (1997). Vietnamese Women after 10 Years of "*Doi Moi*" (renewal) of the Country. In T. Le (Ed.), *Ten years of progress: Vietnamese women from 1985 to 1995* (pp. 23–54). Hanoi: Phunu Publishing House.
Le, T. (1999). *The role of the family in the formation of Vietnamese personality.* Hanoi: The Gioi Publishers.
Le, T. (2008). *Single women in Viet Nam.* Hanoi: The Gioi Publishers.
Le Bach Duong, Dang Nguyen Anh, Khuat Thu Hong, Le Hoai Trung, and Robert Bach (2005). Social protection for the most needy in Vietnam. Hanoi: The Gioi Publisher.
Leshkowich, A. M. (2008). Entrepreneurial families. *Education About Asia, 13*(1), 11–16.
Leshkowich, A. M. (2014). Standardized forms of Vietnamese selfhood. *American Ethnologist, 41*(1), 143–162.
London, J. (2014). Politics in contemporary Vietnam. In J. London (Ed.), *Politics in contemporary Vietnam: Party, state, and authority relations* (pp. 21–42). Basingtoke: Palgrave Macmillan.
Mai, T. T., & Le, T. N. T. (1978). *Women in Vietnam.* Hanoi: Foreign Languages Publishing House.
Marr, D. (1981). *Vietnamese tradition on trial 1920–45.* Berkeley: University of California Press.

Marriage and Family Law. 29 December 1986. Available at UNHCR's homepage at http://www.refworld.org/docid/3ae6b54dc.html
Marriage and Family Law. 22/2000/QH10, June 9, 2000. Official Gazette, no. 28. (31-7-2000). National Assembly of Vietnam.
VietNam News. (2011). Exhibit allows single mothers to speak out. *VietNam News*, 8 March.
Newton, N. (2012). *A queer political economy of 'community': Gender, space, and the transnational politics of community for Vietnamese Lesbians(les) in Saigon.* Doctoral dissertation, University of California, Irvine.
Ngo, T. N. B. (2004). The Confucian Four Feminine Virtues (*tu duc*). In L. Drummond & H. Rydström (Eds.), *Gender practices in contemporary Vietnam* (pp. 47–74). Singapore: Singapore University Press.
Ngoc, A. B. (2013). Words of a generation. *Research Insight*, 10 December. Available from http://www.edelman.com/post/words-of-a-generation-vietnam/
Nguyen, M. T. N. (2015). *Vietnam's socialist servants: Domesticity, class, gender, and identity*. London: Routledge.
Nguyen, T. B. V. (unpublished). Vietnamese women's museum activities targeting marginalized women groups for gender equality and development.
Nguyen-vo, T.-h. (2008). *The ironies of freedom: Sex, culture, and neoliberal governance in Vietnam*. Seattle: University of Washington Press.
Norlund, I. (2007). Civil society in Vietnam: Social organizations and approaches to new concepts. *Asien*, *105*, 68–90.
Parr, A. (2010). *The deleuze dictionary*. Edingburgh: Edingburgh University Press.
Phinney, H. (2005). Asking for a child: The refashioning of reproductive space in post-war northern Vietnam. *The Asia Pacific Journal of Anthropology*, *6*(3), 215–230.
Poulantzas, N. (1982). *Politisk magt og sociale klasser* (vol. 1 & 2). Copenhagen: Aurora.
Roces, M. (2010). Asian feminisms: Women's movements from the Asian perspective. In M. Roces & L. Edwards (Eds.), *Women's movements in Asia: Feminism and transnational activism* (pp. 1–20). London: Routledge.
Rydström, H. (2002). Sexed bodies gendered bodies. *Women's Studies International Forum*, *25*(3), 359–372.
Rydström, H. (2003). *Embodying morality: Growing up in rural northern Vietnam*. Honolulu: University of Hawai'i Press.
Rydström, H. (2006). Sexual desires and 'Social Evils': Young women in rural Vietnam. *Gender, Place and Culture*, *13*(3), 283–301.
Rydström, H. (2010). Compromised ideals: Family life and the recognition of women in Vietnam. In Rydström, Helle (ed) *Gendered Inequalities in Asia:*

Configuring, Contesting and Recognizing Women and Men. Copenhagen: NIAS Press.

Rydström, H. (2011). Studying rural families in *Doi Moi* Vietnam. In H. Rydstrom, D. L. Trinh, & W. Burghoorn (Eds.), *Rural families in late-Doi Moi Vietnam* (pp. 17–38). Hanoi: Social Sciences Publishing House.

Rydström, H. (2012). Gendered corporeality and bare lives: Local sacrifices and sufferings during the Vietnam War. *Signs, Journal of Women in Culture and Society, 37*(2), 275–301.

Salemink, O. (2006). Translating, interpreting, and practicing civil society in Vietnam: A tale of miscalculated misunderstandings. In D. Lewis & D. Mosse (Eds.), *Development brokers and translators* (pp. 101–126). Bloomfield, CT: Kumarian Press.

Spivak, G. C. (2009). *In other words*. Chichester: Wiley-Blackwell.

Stivens, M. (2010). Gendering Asia after modernity. Rydström, Helle (ed) *Gendered Inequalities in Asia: Configuring, Contesting and Recognizing Women and Men*. Copenhagen: NIAS Press.

Study Report. (2008). Forms of engagement: Between state agencies and civil society organizations in Vietnam. Dept. for International Development (UK) and Embassy of Finland.

Tai, H.-T. H. (1996). *Radicalism and the origins of the Vietnamese revolution*. Harvard: Harvard University Press.

Taylor, S. (1999). *Vietnamese women at war*. Kansas: University of Kansas Press.

Taylor, W., Nguyen, T. H., Pham, Q. T., & Huynh, T. N. T. (2012). *Civil society in Vietnam*. Hanoi: The Asia Foundation.

Thayer, C. (2008). One-party rule and the challenge of civil society in Vietnam. Available from http://www.viet-studies.info/kinhte/CivilSociety_Thayer.pdf

The Diplomat. (2014). Leading the way: Vietnam's push for gay rights. *The Diplomat* 18 April. Available from http://thediplomat.com/2014/04/leading-the-way-vietnams-push-for-gay-rights/

Tran, T. Q. (1999). *Gender basic concepts and gender issues in Vietnam*. Hanoi: Nha Xuat Ban Thong Ke.

Tran, A. N., & Norlund, I. (2015). Globalization, industrialization, and Labor Markets in Vietnam. *Journal of the Asia Pacific Economy, 20*(1), 143–163.

Tripp, A. M., Casimiro, I., Kwesiga, J., & Mungwa, A. (Eds.) (2010). *African Women's movements: Changing political landscapes*. Cambridge: Cambridge University Press.

Trong, P. L. (2013). Tracing the discourses on civil society in Vietnam. In G. Waibel, J. Ehlert, & H. N. Feuer (Eds.), *Southeast Asia and the civil society Gaze*. London: Routledge.

Tuoitrenews.vn. 10 March 2013a. Available from http://tuoitrenews.vn/society/13750/vietnam-to-remove-fines-on-samesex-marriage
Tuoitrenews.vn. 17 April 2013b. Available from http://tuoitrenews.vn/society/8841/a-legal-guide-for-samesex-couples-in-vietnam
Tuoitrenews.vn. 27 April 2014a. Available from http://tuoitrenews.vn/lifestyle/18641/50-protest-gay-marriage-legalization-in-vietnam-study
Tuoitrenews.vn. 20 June 2014b. Available from http://tuoitrenews.vn/society/20478/vietnam-removes-ban-on-same-sex-marriage
Turley, W. (1972). Women in the communist revolution in Vietnam. *Asian Survey, 12*(9), 793–805.
Turley, W. S. (Ed.). (1980). *Vietnamese communism in comparative perspective.* Boulder, CO: Westview Press.
UNDP. (2015). Poverty Reduction: Vietnam. Hanoi: UNDP.
USAID and UNDP. (2014). Being LGBT in Asia: Vietnam country report. Hanoi: USAID and UNDP.
Vasavakul, T. (2014). Authoritarianism reconfigured: Evolving accountability relations within Vietnam's one-party rule. In J. London (Ed.), *Politics in contemporary Vietnam: Party, state, and authority relations* (pp. 42–64). Palgrave Macmillan: Basingtoke.
Vijeyarasa, R. (2010). The state, the family and language of 'Social Evils'. *Culture, Health & Sexuality: An International Journal for Research, Intervention and Care, 12*(S1), 89–102.
Vuong, T. H. (1997). The activities of the women's unions for the equality and development of women. In T. Le (Ed.), *Ten years of progress: Vietnamese women from 1985 to 1995* (pp. 76–95). Hanoi: Phunu Publishing House.
Waibel, G., & Benedikter, S. (2013). Voluntary or state-driven? Community-based Organizations in the Mekong Delta, Vietnam. In G. Waibel, J. Ehlert, & H. N. Feuer (Eds.), *Southeast Asia and the Civil Society Gaze* (pp. 218–136). London: Routledge.
Waibel, G., & Gluck, S. (2013). More than 13 million: Mass mobilization and gender politics in the Vietnam Women's Union. *Gender and Development, 21*(2), 343–361.
Wells-Dang, A. (2011). *Informal pathbreakers: Civil society networks in China and Vietnam.* Doctoral dissertation, University of Birmingham.
Wischermann, J. (2010). Civil society action and governance in Vietnam: Selected findings from an empirical survey. *Journal of Current Southeast Asian Affairs, 2*, 30–40.

WU; Women's Union, Vietnam. (2013). Report on ensuring and promoting women's rights. Hanoi: Vietnam Women's Union.
WU; Women's Union, Vietnam. (2015a). Homepage. Available from http://hoilhpn.org.vn/newsdetail.asp?CatId=66&NewsId=819&lang=EN
WU; Women's Union, Vietnam. (2015b). Program 2007–2012. Available from http://www.hoilhpn.org.vn/newsdetail.asp?CatId=78&NewsId=10103&lang=EN
Young, I. M. (2000). *Inclusion and democracy*. Oxford: Oxford University Press.

Part IV

Can Exclusions Speak?

11

Can the Irregular Migrant Woman Speak?

Synnøve Bendixsen

Introduction

In *Who sings the nation state?* Judith Butler and Gayatri Spivak (2010) discuss the political significance of irregular migrants' singing the US national anthem—in Spanish—during street demonstrations in California. Examining this action, they consider its potential implications for politics, rights and belonging. This performance, Butler suggests, raises the question of "the plurality of the nation, of the 'we' and the 'our': to whom does this anthem belong?'" (Butler and Spivak 2010: 58). The singing becomes an assertion that makes claims on "modes of belonging, since who is included in this 'we'?" (Butler and Spivak 2010: 59). Likewise, it draws attention to how one can appeal for justice, or even be heard when the receiver is the nation-state. It also raises questions

---

S. Bendixsen (✉)
Department of Social Anthropology, University of Bergen,
Fosswinckelsgt. 6, 5007 Bergen, Norway

on the issue of representation: how are representations shaped by the nation-state context in which the voices are raised? What are the opportunities and limitations for representing ones' claims as a non-citizen woman, and for representing oneself as a particular political subject? It is to these questions this chapter responds.

In this chapter I draw on my anthropological fieldwork with Ethiopian irregular migrants who demonstrated in the public sphere against the Norwegian government's assessment of their asylum application and treatment as irregular migrants living in Norway. In February 2011, around 100 Ethiopian migrants entered the Oslo Cathedral and initiated a hunger strike. They subsequently set up a tent next to the Cathedral from which they sought to draw the attention of the Norwegian population, media, and politicians to their irregularized situation.[1] This chapter examines the dynamic interplay between Ethiopian irregular migrants' claim-making on the one hand and how this mobilization was framed in the media on the other. I am concerned with how the voices and frames of action of the migrants who demonstrated in the public sphere became shaped by gendered and socio-cultural perceptions of the "good citizen". A selection of moments and episodes reflecting the migrants' representation of themselves as political actors, how they were represented in the media, and how that in turn shaped their own representation, shed light on the ways in which irregular migrants' political engagements are mediated by existing gendered norms, expectations, and opportunities for agency in the nation-state in which they are situated. This chapter seeks to take a first step toward the analysis of political mobilization of irregular migrants shaped by gender differences, in terms of how the activities were constituted and responses given to migrants' political activism. It is precisely this perspective that allows us to access gendered differences in participation, representation, and speaking up in the public sphere. Are irregular women constructed in specific ways through the process of representation? Did this extraordinary space of demonstration also allow irregular women to re-define their subject position in Norway?

---

[1] Two other irregular migrant groups mobilized politically in the same period of time, an Iranian/Kurdish group and a Palestinian group. These groups remained ethnically distinct with little collaboration (see Bendixsen 2013).

This chapter points to how the public is a gendered socio-cultural space for irregularized women who struggle to have their voices heard. It draws attention to political acts and engagement as a dynamic process situated within power relations. This perspective is crucial to understanding how participation in public life is structured, how representation of migrants shapes participation in gendered ways, and the difficulties involved in contesting discourses that become, in that process, dominant. It also draws our attention to the various ways in which the conventional links between citizen, state, and nation are contested, reified or altered.

The chapter is divided into five parts. The first briefly situates the chapter within the existing research literature, while the second provides a background on irregular migrants in Norway. This is followed by an anthropological analysis of the Ethiopian migrants' political mobilization. The third examines the discourses about the protesters in the media. Fourth, I discuss how representations of the migrants' activities shaped their public intervention. Finally, I argue that the study of the migrants' mobilizations offer new perspectives on the potentiality of the non-citizen political subject position, as well as insights into how the public space is gendered and racialized. At the core of this argument is how struggles over representations become gendered.

Studying Irregular Migrants' Political Mobilization

In the last decade there has been a notable body of work on political mobilization of irregular migrants in Australia (i.e. McNevin 2011), the USA (i.e. Chavez 2008; McNevin 2011; Nicholls 2013), Canada (Ellermann 2010; Nyers 2010), France (i.e. Chimienti and Solomos 2011; Chimienti 2011), and Germany (Laubenthal 2013). The global increase of "no border" campaigns and articulations of "no one is illegal" in various cities such as Paris, Montreal, and New York are sites from which we can investigate "acts of citizenship" (Isin 2002) or acts "contesting citizenship" (McNevin 2011), and enhance our understanding of political community, political action, and political subjectivity (McNevin 2011; Nyers 2010).

In France, Balibar (2000, 2002) has discussed how the *sans papier* movement in the 1990s contributed to a "recreation" of citizenship through increasing visibility, insisting on speaking out, and contesting existing stereotypes, thus providing a transnational dimension to political activity needed in an era of globalization. Peter Nyers (2010: 141) has argued that the political agency of irregular migrants, both at the state and city levels of governance, interrupts and transforms the political: "They are not merely the citizen's Other, but also other claims-making and rights-taking political beings". In the USA, the focus has been both on the construction of a "Latino threat" through which Latinos, particularly Mexicans, are represented as an "invading force" in the media (Chavez 2008), and also on young irregular migrants in the DREAMers movement who transformed the debate on migrant rights (Nicholls 2013). The latter movement refers to youth who in 2010 initially mobilized to pressure the Senate to support the Development, Relief and Education for Alien Minors Act (DREAM Act), which would provide youths the legal rights to stay in the USA. These scholars demonstrate the importance of irregular migrants as agents of change, and suggest that the migrants produce new notions of political belonging and citizenship. Simultaneously, Chimienti and Solomos (2011) have called for a refocus on the voice of the migrants (and not that of their supporters) when considering the claims that underpin the mobilization of irregular migrants. They stress that researchers should study "the importance of their everyday struggle for existence rather than for citizenship and human rights" (2011: 343). The recent work by Boehm (2012) deals with this gap in that her ethnography of "illegality" examines how the personal and intimate lives of migrant families must be considered within, although cannot be extracted from, the context of state power.

This chapter seeks to contribute to the dearth of analyses of the nation-state's responses toward migrants' mobilization, and its impact on migrants' voices. One of the few studies here is Ellermann (2010), who argues that liberal states are constrained in their dealing with irregular migrants by the international legal order and their constitutions, which limit the use of coercion against the individual. She suggests that "state power disappears when the state can no longer offer that which the individual desires or requires. Ironically, then, in disempowered spaces, individual acts of desperation often succeed in thwarting social control. Despite the vast scope of state power, the liberal state's hands are tied by its own Constitution" (2010: 425). Thus, she argues that those individuals with the weakest claims against the liberal state can resist the state's use of its sovereignty the most.

However, as this chapter will show, this manner of understanding the power relation between the state and the irregular migrant ignores the broader nation-state's capacity for coercion in shaping the public space; of who can be listened to and who can be silenced. As Butler and Athanasiou (2013: 78) importantly draw attention to: while a "conventional perspective on the politics of recognition tends to conceive of subjects as pre-existent human agents who ask for recognition", this obscures the power relations that "condition in advance who will count or matter as a recognizable, viable human subject and who will not". It remains important to examine the conditions of recognition for irregular migrants and how these are shaped by the power of the nation-state, which is the aim of this chapter.

Becoming Visible: Irregular Migrants' Initial Representation

While more of a guestimate, a recent report suggests that there are between 18,100 and 56,000 persons "without legal residence" in Norway, the lowest denominator being the most plausible (Mohn et al. 2014). The irregular migrants with whom I conducted fieldwork had all applied for asylum but were irregularized as a consequence of the final rejection of their application, and then overstayed the date of exit. Classified or publicly discussed as bogus asylum seekers, illegal, or economic migrants, they are assumed by government officials, and sometimes by the media, to be in no need of protection, and to be undesirable (Agier 2011) and deportable (de Genova 2010).

In Norway, irregular migration was a topic of little public concern until 2010, when the debate about it flared, partly initiated by the release of an autobiography by a young woman, Maria Amelie (pseudonym), who wrote about her life in the country as an irregular migrant. The same period was characterized by increasing public anxiety over the so-called lack of nation-state border controls, relative to other European countries or the USA (Nicholls 2013). Ideas of securitization, an "influx" of Eastern European migrant workers, and refugees from the "third world" have intensified the stigmatization of irregular migrants as a threat to the Norwegian nation-state. State responses to this threat include denying irregular migrants basic rights, such as rights to healthcare beyond "emergency" care, in order to induce their return to their country of origin and prevent more from coming.

I interviewed and pursued fieldwork with approximately 25 Ethiopian individuals who in Spring 2011 were living in a tent set up in front of the Oslo Cathedral.[2] Research has noted that irregular migrants' mobilizations take place not directly as a response to the general restrictiveness of life, but primarily when a shift from (relative) tolerance to restrictiveness occurs, making the situation appear unfair both to the people it targets and to the general population (Laubenthal 2007; Chimienti 2011). The Ethiopian mobilization was initiated when they lost their opportunity to work and when this was experienced as a collective injustice.[3] The reason why Ethiopian migrants could no longer work was that the Norwegian tax department had discovered its flawed practice of annually sending tax-cards to migrants without working-permission, and subsequently did not resubmit tax-cards to the same in 2011 (Bendixsen 2013).

In an effort to reconstitute themselves as equal subjects of justice they wrote letters to the Prime Minister, participated in public meetings arranged at the House of Literature, talked actively with the media, established Facebook groups and internet portals, participated in the May Day Parade, and hung slogans in front of the Cathedral. Avoiding

---

[2] Within the last 10 years there have been 2928 applicants from Ethiopia (UDI, October 2011). Forty-one percent of those who received an answer to their application have been granted a permit. In 2010, there were 505 Ethiopian applicants (the fifth largest group, after Eritrea, Somalia, Afghanistan and Russia). There are 242 Ethiopians in Norwegian asylum centers with numbers declining. In 2010, a total of 29 persons returned voluntarily to Ethiopia. In the last seven years, a total of 67 persons have returned voluntarily to Ethiopia. http://www.udi.no/en/statistics-and-analysis/statistics/ (accessed 10 August 2014).

[3] Importantly, in early 2012, Norway finalized an agreement with Ethiopia that made it possible for the Norwegian government to return irregularized migrants to Ethiopia. More or less simultaneously, the Norwegian government offered a program of voluntary return to Ethiopian migrants (Bendixsen 2013).

invisibility by setting up their tent next to the Cathedral was a conscious choice: strategically situated in the middle of the city, they expected to easily approach the Norwegian population. Furthermore, since they were on church grounds they had reason to believe that the police would not remove them. I was informed that they had mobilized in order to raise awareness and empathy about their situation. One woman said "We are not criminals, all we need is protection", another woman said: "We refuse to be silenced". A few stressed that this was not a demonstration: "We are not demonstrating really, but actually asking for our human rights".

The irregular migrants insisted on their legitimate need for asylum, notwithstanding their rejected asylum applications, due to Ethiopia's lack of democratic values and consistent use of torture and unlawful detention of political dissidents and journalists. They also argued that their asylum applications had been evaluated collectively.[4] Yet the main focus of their public representation was on their efforts to integrate themselves in Norway, by being diligent workers and paying taxes. The slogans included "We were tax payers but are now on the street", "We are on the same planet", and "Where are our rights?" In their discussions with media and with myself, several of the migrants stressed that they had been working in Norway for several years when that possibility, as mentioned, was suddenly taken away. As one 25-year-old Ethiopian man told me: "Actually, we are an asset to society. We have been working in the Norwegian society—in the health system. Actually, we have been productive, working and helping, contributing to society positively. We are not criminals; we are not cold souls doing illegal things and everything. We have been contributing, working and paying taxes. But they reject what we do. They do not want to admit this. They are giving their own impressions that we are criminals, we are illegal. So asking your rights make you illegal, I don't know…"

Their emphasis on work could, perhaps, be understood as part of an effort to represent themselves as human beings in a more substantial manner, rather than as noncitizen versus citizen. Hanna Arendt (1973)

---

[4] In their letter to the Prime Minister, the migrants argue that "Application for political asylum of Ethiopians is treated unjustly unfairly and collectively, rather than treating [sic] on an individual basis, i.e. on a case by case basis"—a claim which the Norwegian Directorate of Immigration later rejected.

has pointed to the fact that labor, work, and action are together the fundamental activities of human life and form the *vita activa* (active life). Referencing themselves as good (Christian)[5] tax payers became part of a representational struggle for the migrants. By representing themselves as already "integrated" in society through work and paying taxes, they sought to be viewed as potential "good citizens". This representation was in sharp contrast to the existing public discourse, which suggests the "flow" of refugee and asylum seekers will undermine the welfare system, and that refugees are potential "welfare cheats", "criminals" or "illegal". Thus, emphasizing their contributions to the labor market (and thus the tax base) can be viewed as part of an effort to disassociate their group from the perceptions of stigmatized minority bodies associated with expensive welfare—and instead position themselves as contributing to the welfare state (Bendixsen 2013). Indeed, liberal ideology has a tendency to assess citizens as human capital, where those who can manage on their own are weighted against those who are economically dependent (Ong 2003). Within this dynamic, minority groups may feel pressured to perform economically, increasing stigmatization of those who rely on the welfare state (Ong 2003). By stressing their integration into the labor market, the protesters challenge and circumvent the efforts of Western nation-states to *not* integrate asylum seekers until they receive the refugee status that will decide whether they be allowed to stay or be sent "home" (Diken and Laustsen 2005). As such, they circumvent the prescribed subject position as asylum seekers who should be limited to asylum centers.

In sum, their self-representation expressed a particular mode of belonging and invoked, notwithstanding their irregular status, a community of citizens and political subjects. It expressed that, despite not being formally recognized, they were economically integrated into the Norwegian community, legitimizing their claim for existential rights. One may ask whether they were in this process also promoting ideas of citizenship based on labor (transnational labor citizenship) rather than national borders (national citizenship).

---

[5] While some of the Ethiopian migrants were Muslims, this identity was silenced during the demonstrations, while those who were Christian emphasized their religious identity.

Being Represented: Public Representations of the Irregular Migrants

What were the government's responses to the migrants' practices and utterances? The government declared that they had offered these irregular migrants a place to stay—namely reception centers. Consequently, the government stressed, there was no reason for the migrants "to live in tents". The tent camp was portrayed as the migrants' refusal to accept that the government could not fit all Ethiopian migrants in the same reception centre, due to the size of the group and administrative difficulties that would imply. The government presented itself as humanitarian and fair, concerned with the migrants' current living situation. Frustrated, several Ethiopian migrants told me: "That is not our focus of demonstration! They have not understood what we are saying". Additionally, rejecting the contention that all the migrants' asylum application decisions had been group-based, the government presented the asylum application system as methodical, insisting that they were assessed individually.

As weeks went by, several migrants complained to me about the lack of media attention and misunderstandings regarding their actions and concerns. A majority believed that the government, as well as the media, focused primarily on the children included in the hunger strike. Whether or not the perception of Ethiopian migrants toward the media coverage was well-founded, statistically speaking, is beyond the scope of this chapter. A database search revealed 70 media hits under "Ethiopian asylum seekers" (February 2011). Several newspapers discussed the distress of the Ethiopian migrants and their reasons for protesting.[6] However,

---

[6] A search on the database Retriever (at the University of Bergen) shows that while there were only 9 matches for "Ethiopian Asylum seekers" in 2009, and 13 in 2010, there were 126 hits in the media about Ethiopian asylum seekers in 2011. Of these, 70 were published in February 2011, which is the period of time Ethiopians entered the church in Oslo. Another 23 were published in April 2011. In 2012 there were a total of 177 results, while in 2013 it went down again to 36 results. While the newspaper articles in 2011 mainly centered around the demonstrations of irregular migrants in Oslo, in 2012 it mainly concerned the return agreement between Norway and Ethiopia, Ethiopian migrants' fear of deportation, the nationally well-known irregular migrant child Nathan from Bergen, and arguments for and against returning Ethiopian migrants. Of the 177 results in 2012, 83 were in March 2012, same period when the treaty between Norway and Ethiopia facilitating return was signed.

the situation of their children was highlighted with headlines (both local and national) such as "Small children among the activists".[7] Interestingly, however, the numbers fluctuated between three and six children in the various newspapers. One media commentator who was particularly active was the neoliberal right-wing populist Progress Party Deputy Chair, Sandberg, then in government opposition, known for taking a restrictive strand on migration issues.[8] In the past, he favored the forced return of migrants and wanted deportation centers (similar to medium security prisons), to also house families, including children. However, about the Ethiopian protest, he said: "This is an abuse of the children who are forced to stay in the church. Here the government must intervene. (…) To make use of such forms of actions, which I compare to blackmailing, will not advance anything in a democratic country such as Norway. (…) They must leave the church room out of consideration of the women and children".[9]

In this address, Sandberg represents the migrants as uninformed about democracy, de-politicizing, and criminalizing their actions (such as by comparing them to blackmailers). The migrants' efforts to represent themselves as future good citizens are rejected and delegitimized in this speech. Additionally, while women were as active in the mobilization as men, they are constructed here as passive and, together with the children, abused by the protest. Casting the migrant men as not concerned with the wellbeing of "their women and children" fuels an idea of Ethiopian men as child abusers, as uncaring, uncivilized and as treating women badly. At the same time, Sandberg promotes himself as a protector of these women and children.

---

[7] *Bergens Avisen*. http://www.ba.no/nyheter/irix/article5482514.ece (accessed 10 January 2014).

[8] In 2013 the Progress Party (Fremskrittspartiet) entered for the first time into the government—in a minority government coalition together with the largest party, the Conservative party (Høyre). I am here not viewing Sandberg's statements as representing the political specter in Norway. Rather, his voice became particularly relevant in this case because several newspapers quoted Sandberg's comments, his utterances were discussed by the irregular migrants and it shaped their representation in the public.

[9] http://www.ba.no/nyheter/irix/article5483304.ece (accessed 10 January 2014) and http://www.dagbladet.no/2011/02/08/nyheter/innenriks/papirlose/15357742/ (accessed 8 March 2015).

Notably, the media did give space to the migrants to speak. In the same article that references Sandberg, one irregular migrant was interviewed during the hunger strike:

> "We have been without rights for several years, and we cannot live like that anymore. We have lost our work permits and tax cards, and have no income. That is why we are here now", says Bizualem Beza, spokesperson for the Ethiopian asylum association in Norway. (…) Six small children will spend the night in the Cathedral Monday night. Opse Dihnsa is among the mothers that are protesting. "We hope this will make the government open their eyes and look at us. We are not animals, we are humans, and we need protection", says Dihnsa, with six-month-old Christian in her arms. "Now I have children, but I am not receiving any child benefits or public assistance, so how can I live? My child is illegal; he has only received a personal number, no residence permit. I don't eat, but he does", says Dihnsa. She has a package of diapers and a package of baby formula, in case the lack of food should make her incapable of breast feeding. Hauge [the church's provost] says that they are in close contact with the child protection authorities. "We have said that we cannot provide children of that age a satisfactory stay, and have asked them to leave [the church]. We have asked them not to let the children suffer even if they want to protest, and we feel that we are being heard", says Hauge.[10]

While Sandberg stressed that the children were "forced" to stay in the church, and the provost suggested they were suffering, Dihsna emphasized that their living conditions and actions were a consequence of how the migrants, including their children, were treated in Norway. According to her and Beza, their protest was not a choice—it was the only option possible considering their lack of rights as rejected asylum seekers living in Norway. Yet, while stressing that the government's policies and practices contributed to making their lives extremely difficult, the provost also stated that staying in the church was ill-advised for the children (in this case for a six-month-old baby who stayed with her mother). In the provost's media-speech, the children's suffering became a consequence of the parents' *wish* to demonstrate, while the children's living conditions

---

[10] http://www.ba.no/nyheter/irix/article5482514.ece (accessed 10 January 2014).

before and after the public protest was tacitly unexpressed. Although the voices of the migrants were given a space, they became partly delegitimized by the media's presentation of the provost's and politician's focus on the migrants' ill-advised treatment of their children during the course of the protest. Instead of discussing how asylum claims are processed, or the migrants' inability to legally work and sustain themselves (an important condition for parenting) the focus of the media was on how migrants treated their children while protesting. The migrants became relegated to the category of uncivilized subaltern parents who are unqualified to care for their own children.

The Force of Representation: Transforming Migrant's Voices

What effect did this framing of the migrants' actions have on the available space for contestation against Norwegian policies? How did these representations affect irregular migrants' political engagement or self-presentation? The scrutiny of the children's living conditions during the protest became a matter of concern among the Ethiopian migrants, as evident in their public discussions. One public event which focused on Norway's "paperless" migrants highlights their concerns. This was held at the House of Literature in the center of Oslo, and organized by the Anti-Racist Center. During this event, Ethiopian migrants were invited to talk about their situation and protest with approximately 80 Norwegian citizens and other irregular migrants in the audience. One woman, Astar, from the Ethiopian group was invited onstage where she was interviewed by a female priest from the Oslo Cathedral. In a calm and quiet voice the priest asked Astar: "Why as a mother, why choose hunger?" to which Astar answered: "Every minimum right was lost. Even my baby lost her right to stay when she was 10 months old. (…) We are fighting for our right. For our right to stay. I have no family here, so I could not leave the child outside the church".

While this event represented a space for the migrants to defend their decision to include children in the demonstrations, it also testified to the power of representation in the media. Rather than referencing their contributions to Norwegian society through working and paying taxes (which had been their initial slogan and focus) at this moment, parenthood became the focus. This emphasis on Astar's position as a mother on the one hand allures to a gendered citizenship position where her motherhood became of particular significance. Her subject position as a mother was foregrounded and made to be the most relevant identity. Yet, on the other hand, this position became a double-bind: in order to be a political actor she had to present herself as a good mother—however to Astar the inter-relationship between being a political actor and a good mother was differently constituted than their connotations in the Norwegian media. In this process, Astar's actions as an activist, political, and critiquing subject became partly ignored, suppressed and deemed of second importance—after her position as a mother. For her voice to be heard as a political actor or her actions to be viewed as representative of citizenship, it seemed she needed to first present herself as a good mother, which meant not including her child in the church demonstrations. This implies that voice is always articulated from "a distinctive embodied position" (Couldry 2010: 8), and calls attention to how citizenship is a gendered embodied subject position.

After the talk, I approached Astar, explaining my research to her, and she was very anxious to explain why she had decided to enter the church and join the hunger strike despite being a mother. Because of this decision, she felt many Norwegians saw her as a bad mother, and it clearly upset her. Depicted as not up to the task of motherhood, she seemed to feel accused and misunderstood.

The stigma of "bad mother" had a double negation for her being-in-the-world: she was neither represented as a political subject nor as a "good mother". These two subject positions were linked both by her and in media representations. For Astar, her protest against the Norwegian government was an act of being a good mother since her political claims concerned her child's future. The construction of her as a "bad mother" both repudiates Astar's acts as those of a political subject, and dismissed the fact that her political mobilization was also about being a "good mother". For many women, going through dangerous roads to reach a country in which they can apply for asylum, and their struggle to be accepted as "real" asylum seekers deserving of rights, is an act of good parenting, trying to create a better, safer and prosperous future for their children. Protesting in Norway was in many ways a continuation of the struggle of arriving, of being accepted in Norway, and being allowed to stay. To some extent, demonstrating with their children in the church, a protest relatively safe and under control (there were constant check-ups from medical personnel) can be seen as a continuation of the more dangerous activities that these women had already pursued, namely their frequently hazardous travel to Norway, sometimes with children, which no government, politician or authority had recognized.

Yet it became clear to Astar that in order for her activities to be understood by the white majority as those performed by a political subject, she had to be represented as a "good mother" as defined within a sociocultural coded space, although viewed as a universally defined premise. Through the media's framing and her response toward this framing, being a mother became the only authentic subject position. As this takes place in a church, one could argue that in this process, the church is yet again transformed from being a political space belonging to the migrants to that of a symbolic realm where women as subjects are interpellated and hailed by others—it becomes a space "in which the performative enactment of gender occurs" (Lloyd 1999: 197).

Importantly, there was a gendered difference among the Ethiopian migrants in their response to the public focus on the children. The women I spoke to were concerned with the stained representation of their role as mothers. The men, however, suggested that the media and politicians did not care for the children, but were staging a performance to undermine the recognition of irregular migrants as political actors with a voice. One Ethiopian man, for example, told me about the accusation that they had "hijacked", "kidnapped", or were "using" the children. Yet afterwards, he argued, when they had left the church, no one from the government had talked to the children or followed up. He rhetorically asked: "Does anybody care about those children? (…) They just want to make us look bad". Similarly, in another interview, the issue of the children was also brought up by another irregular male migrant. Abel tells me:

When we were on the street they came first and asked if any children are here [in the tents]. We said to them "we are not stupid. We are not bringing children to sleep on the floor". So they go, no one come back. No one. [Before], in the church, every day they came and they intimidate us. Even they said to us, you know, "we are going to take your children away". They said (…) "child welfare is going to come and they are going to collect your children because they are not here by their own will". "Their will", they said. So we were so upset at that time, of course.

Abel's mocking of the Norwegian authorities' use of the concept "lack of will" among the children suggests that his and his co-demonstrators' actions were in fact a result of the felt lack of any other opportunity—of having no other choice but to protest. Indeed, many Ethiopian migrants emphasized that the hunger strike and protest were the only options left considering the Norwegian government's treatment of them. Rather than feeling targeted as a father, Abel understood the heightened public attention paid to the children was an indication of the important place of children in Norwegian society. Simultaneously, Abel experienced a differentiation toward how children are treated and cared for in Norway. Abel's understanding of the government's sudden public concern toward irregular migrants' children suggests that he views the government as projecting a Goffmanian front stage in the media (concerned with the children when they are visible in public) and a backstage in their interaction with them at the reception centers (neglecting the children when they are not visible in public).[11] It fur-

---

[11] A search on Retriever (UiB) for 'paperless children' indicates that the concern in the media increased more than 100 % in 2011, relative to 2008. In 2008 there were 45 matches, in 2009 there were 56, in 2010 there were 104, in 2011 there were 541, in 2012 there were 434 and in 2013 it fell down to 136. Looking at the year 2011, there were 210 results in January, 88 in February, 30 in March, 24 in April and 17 in May. In June there were 8 and in July there were 3. Importantly, in January, Marie Amelie (originally from Russia) who became an icon of "paperless" children in Norway was given prominence in the media. There are some difficulties related to such searches because there are several terms being used for the same group of people, including "illegal", "asylum seekers", and "irregular" (which is less frequently used). Breaking it down to "Ethiopian children" the result shows: 38 results in 2000, 33 in 2005, 63 in 2008, 70 in 2009, 62 in 2010, 133 in 2011, 243 in 2012, and 95 in 2013. Looking at the year 2011, there are only 5 results in January (before the Ethiopian migrants entered the church), and 51 results in February, in March there is 6, in April the result is 7, in May the result is 3, in June the result is 7, and in July the result is 6. Ethiopian children were thus decreasingly mentioned as the public demonstrations by the Ethiopian irregular migrants came to a halt.

ther alerts us to a growing sub-class of people living in Norway, namely children born in Norway to irregular migrant parents. He indirectly draws attention to the importance of becoming visible to provoke some kind of responsibility or reaction from the government or the public. Neither Abel, nor any of the other men, felt their fatherhood being threatened in any way. However, the men also recognized the importance of being considered "good" parents for their situation to be heard, acknowledged and respected by the Norwegian public.

While there were gender differences in representational power, there were no gender differences regarding the role of children in subsequent protests. Some months after the church demonstration in Oslo, other irregular migrants who had mobilized, namely groups of Iranian and Kurdish activists, came together with the Ethiopian migrants to plan future public events and activities. At one moment during the organizational planning, the group of around 20 people had a long discussion on whether to include children in the three-week-long asylum march they planned, emphasizing that there would be opportunities for the children to rest. The Ethiopian representatives, both men and women alike, argued vehemently against including the children. They contended that during their protest in the church, the media had been very negative toward the inclusion of children. Although several Iranian irregular migrants of both genders, some of them parents, maintained that "the children are also part of this situation which we are demonstrating against", in the end they decided against involving them. This leaves open the question of what happens to the voices of children and their spaces to be heard.

It also reveals how the Ethiopian political mobilization, as a process, was a form of social and political education into the socio-cultural expectation of the Norwegian nation-state discourse on the qualities and ideals of a "good citizen". Exploring the complex interaction between irregular migrants and their native co-organizers in the DREAMers, Nicholls (2013: 101) examined how the irregular migrants improved their representational skills through campaigns, community outreach activities, and media interviews. Through such activities, in which the migrants developed cultural and symbolic skills, they could think about what worked and what did not, and modify their language, symbols and tone to improve the power of their public arguments.[12] In Norway, however, the irregular migrants did not only become more effective communicators, as Nicholls argues—in this process they also transformed their communication and representation.

(Un)available Spaces for Enacting Citizenship

The mobilization by non-citizens can be viewed as an "act of citizenship" or a political action from below. Isin (2002) has drawn attention to the naturalization of citizenship as a consequence of how its current form is represented as a historically continuous identity—an ideal type. The shifts in the Constitution of political membership—the history of citizenship—from including only Greek men of high-ranking birth to the extension over centuries to former slaves, colonial subjects, women and indigenous people brought along new specific forms of exclusion. Citizens and the insider alien without citizenship (the Other) are mutually constitutive: an insider identity is made possible by a parallel marking of the outsider (Isin 2002; see also Agamben 1998). Isin draws attention to the insider/outsider dynamics of citizenship as a continuous feature of all political communities, one that is modified in time and space as the form and character of the polity changes. Acts of citizenship then bring into being new modes of subject recognition, and rupture existing models of status and institutions. The concept of "acts of citizenship" brings a focus to the performative aspect of citizenship and includes in its analysis acts of those who do not have formal legal status. Further, acts of citizenship are about contesting, rupturing and transforming ideas about the same. Acts of citizenship are thus more than seeking formal citizenship status—they are also about the struggle to define what it means to be a citizen in a particular space and time (cf. McNevin 2011).[13]

---

[12] Although Nicholls neglects the gendered aspects of these processes, he pinpoints that university training received by activists transmits "middle-class" cultural attributes to those otherwise raised in working-class families and neighborhoods.

[13] McNevin (2011) makes use of the concept "contestation of citizenship" rather than "acts of citizenship".

Looking closely at how the Ethiopian migrant mobilization-process unfolds, changes and transforms, we can see how the public space is highly structured and that symbolic power obfuscates being political (as a process of rupturing). Despite focusing on their contributions to the work force, and the government's assessment of their asylum claims, the irregular migrants saw that their message was not heard. Instead, the representation of irregular migrants as "bad parents" contributed to delegitimizing the migrants as social and political agents engaged in the process of political mobilization and claim-making around issues of legal residency and work. The construction of irregular migrants as "bad parents" concerns not only migrants who are mobilizing in the public sphere. Migrant parents who remain in Norway after their asylum applications have been rejected are also sometimes labeled as bad parents who expose their children to a life without legal residency and the threat of deportation. This draws parallels to the debate in the USA where "anchor babies", children born in the country to irregular migrant parents, are represented in the media as those conceived to improve their parents' chances of attaining citizenship (Chavez 2004). This politics of representation has a direct outcome for issues of political and civic participation, inclusion, and ethnic group mobilization.

The public concern with the migrants' children comes to signify a situation in which white men and women are rescuing brown children from their brown parents (cf. Spivak 1988: 296). Such a discursive set-up of the situation in which white men are seen as saviors and brown men and women scapegoated as oppressors serves to legitimate a specific treatment or intervention toward brown parents. It suggests that othering can be constructed in various ways, contributing to delegitimizing the voices and political engagement of noncitizens. A sense of moral superiority in Western societies has long been related to how the Other, often the (male) migrant, treats their women, and thus the scale of reference for their equal worth and potential as citizen is shaped by an evaluation, both subtle and blatant, of how equal they treat women. In this instance, notions that irregular women were badly treated were not frequently mentioned in the media (after all, the women, many of them single, were highly active during the demonstration). Instead, the image of irregular migrants as ill-using their children contributed to this othering process.

This perception of the Other shapes opportunities and spaces available to those so constructed for speaking up, and for representing themselves as future citizens. In their struggle to be recognized as political subjects, the irregular migrants were continuously situated, and situated their own representation and political mobilization, in a public space sutured by power relations which normatively regulate what is viewed as viable political subjectivities. In this process, the conditions for recognition become interlinked with normative ideas and ideals of the subject (as political actor, as father or mother), universally framed.

The existence of such power structures that are by no means legally defined points to the more subtle ones outside of being "illegal" that migrants face and must negotiate in their acts of citizenship. Mobilizing from the standpoint of an irregular migrant woman presents different opportunities and challenges than that of an irregular migrant man— or a citizen (male or female). It suggests that irregular migrant women with children cannot speak unless they adapt the hegemonic language and position of a white middle-class parent. As Spivak (1988) famously argued, the subaltern "cannot speak", because her speech does not become fully authorized, *political* speech. Her message is not heard, socially and politically, because too much gets in the way. Indeed, Spivak clearly did not mean that the subaltern does not cry out in various ways, but that speaking is a transaction between speaker and listener. This transaction is impeded by the representational process through which the migrants must conform to those social norms that "define which category of subjects is more or less valued as citizens of the nation" (Ong 2003: 9) and perform according to normative citizen subjectivities and ideals.

Yet, arguing that they cannot speak deals only partially with the relationship that was constituted between the irregular migrants and Norwegian citizens. In refusing to be "underground", the migrants challenged established public conflations of irregular with illegitimate. In the longer run, their protests may destabilize state authorities' ability to use arguments of legality and illegality to control migration and access to social welfare benefits (Bendixsen 2013). Their protest becomes a radical symbolic speech act asserting the right to work and live in Norway, which they are denied. To some extent, the irregular migrants were making the ironic act of having the right to protest, but no other rights, visible in the public sphere (cf. Ben-Asher 2009). Simultaneously, one might argue that by making themselves visible, the irregular migrant's mobilization is in itself a radical political act, and that "giving an account of oneself" in public is a possible starting point for being recognized as a political subject (Couldry 2010: 109). Their acts represent a moment of being political by "overturning various strategies and technologies of citizenship in which they were implicated and thereby constituted themselves differently from the dominant images given to them" (Isin 2002: 33). Even if the migrant as "illegalized" is excluded from the nation-state imagined community, noncitizens' acts ruptured the prescribed citizenship definition of who can be included and excluded as a political actor. This potentiality for rupturing was only partial, as the power of the nation-state is reconstituted through the importance of being represented as a potential ideal citizen as a precondition to being heard.

Conclusion

This chapter has discussed the issue of representation of non-citizens and their space for action and voice in the nation-state of Norway. Examining the stages of the public struggle by Ethiopian irregular migrants has drawn attention to the ways in which the migrants initially drew on their economic contributions to the welfare state, and their willingness to become "good" productive citizens. In this process, however, the involvement of children in the migrants' protests became a preoccupation in the framing of the migrants' action in the media. The representation of migrants as "bad parents" had gendered implications for the migrants' subject positions. Many of the women felt that their ways of mothering were unjustly devalued and that it depoliticized their subject position. Many of the male migrants boomeranged the critique back to the government and the governments' treatment of them and their children. In subsequent actions, however, women and men alike were conscious about excluding children in public protest activities. Their acts of citizenship became in this process less about rupturing the content of who can be included as a citizen in Norway. Instead, irregular migrants responded to the implicit and explicit cultural and gendered discursive expectations existing in the nation-state in which they mobilized. This illustrates that the space for migrant voice and political action is shaped by socio-cultural perceptions and representations of gender and subject positions, and propelled by the need to somehow respond in culturally and socially acceptable or expected ways. Indeed, in their public struggle it became imperative to address how they were represented in the media, as well as engage the unstated norms from which "being Norwegian" emerges, norms that were simultaneously manifested and became visible in those very moments of their citizenship acts. The discourse around their political actions exemplifies how the public sphere, regardless of legal status, continues to be shaped by gender, class, race and/or ethnicity.

Contributing to the scarce research that examines the process through which irregular migrants become political agents, this chapter has demonstrated how migrants' political agency is constituted by the interrelated process of the socio-historical definition of who should belong in the nation-state and the responses that follows from their public voices. This chapter has shown how the nation-state sovereignty—by means of governing the public discourse on who makes a potentially good citizen—shapes the lives, self-representation and subjectivation of irregular migrants. This demonstrates how the use of coercion by nation-states is possible through symbolic and governmental power, even against people who are denied legal membership. Thus, this modifies Ellermann (2010: 425), who claims that because the state cannot offer the migrants any meaningful incentives it becomes powerless in eliciting voluntary compliance from those who are denied legal membership.

As this chapter has shown, the nation-state has other meaningful incentives that can powerfully elicit the direction of strategies of resistance, namely the offer of the good of membership which for irregular migrants always remains a potentiality. The nation-state affects migrants' space of action and can provide meaningful incentives because it fundamentally sets the conditions of recognition. Simultaneously, the Ethiopian migrants are a part of a genealogy of citizenship in which certain moments rupture and transform, to some extent, the content of the political community and indeed its conditions of recognition. These moments take place at uneven intervals, such as when those defined as aliens denaturalize the content of insider and outsider.

References

Agamben, G. (1998). *Homo sacer: Sovereign power and bare life*. Stanford, CA: Stanford University Press.
Agier, M. (2011). *Managing the undesirables*. Cambridge: Polity.
Arendt, H. (1973). *The origins of totalitarianism*. Orlando, FL: Harvest Book.
Balibar, E. (2000). What we owe to the Sans-papiers. In L. Guenther & C. Heesters (Eds.), *Social insecurity* (pp. 42–43). Toronto: Anansi.
Balibar, E. (2002). *Droit de cité*. Paris: Quadrige/P.U.F.
Ben-Asher, N. (2009). Who says "I Do"? In *Pace Law Faculty Publications*. Paper 611. Accessed January 10, 2014, from http://digitalcommons.pace.edu/lawfaculty/611
Bendixsen, S. (2013). Becoming members in the community of value: Ethiopian irregular migrants enacting citizenship in Norway. In A. Edelstein & M. Dugan (Eds.), *Migration matters* (pp. 3–22). Oxfordshire: Inter-Disciplinary Press.
Boehm, D. (2012). *Intimate migrations. Gender, family and illegality among transnational Mexicans*. New York: New York University Press.
Butler, J., & Athanasiou, A. (2013). *Dispossession: The performative in the political*. Boston, MA: Polity.
Butler, J., & Spivak, G. C. (2010). *Who sings the nation-state? Language, politics, belonging*. London: Seagull Books.
Chavez, L. R. (2004). A glass half empty: Latina reproduction and public discourse. *Human Organization, 63*(2), 173–189.
Chavez, L. R. (2008). *The Latino threat. Constructing immigrants, citizens, and the nation*. Stanford, CA: Stanford University Press.
Chimienti, M. (2011). Social movements of irregular migrants: A comparative analysis in Western Europe. *Ethnic and Racial Studies, 34*(8), 1338–1356.
Chimienti, M., & Solomos, J. (2011). Social movements of irregular migrants, recognition, and citizenship. *Globalizations, 8*(3), 343–360.
Couldry, N. (2010). *Why voice matters. Culture and politics after neoliberalism*. London: Sage.
De Genova, N. (2010). The deportation regime: Sovereignty, space and the freedom of movement. In N. De Genova & N. Peutz (Eds.), *The deportation regime: Sovereignty, space and freedom of movement* (pp. 33–65). Durham: Duke University Press.
Diken, B., & Laustsen, C. (2005). *Culture of exception: Sociology facing the camp*. New York: Routledge.

Ellermann, A. (2010). Undocumented migrants and resistance in the liberal state. *Politics and Society, 38*(3), 408–429.

Isin, E. F. (2002). *Being political. Genealogies of citizenship.* Minneapolis, MN: University of Minnesota Press.

Laubenthal, B. (2013). The negotiation of irregular migrants' right to education in Germany: A challenge to the nation-state. In A. Bloch & M. Chimienti (Eds.), *Irregular Migrants: Policy, politics, motives and everyday lives* (pp. 86–102). New York: Routledge.

Lloyd, M. (1999). Performativity, parody, politics. *Theory Culture Society, 16*, 195–213.

McNevin, A. (2011). *Contesting citizenship. Irregular migrants and new frontiers of the political.* New York: Colombia University Press.

Mohn, S. B., Sigmund Book Mohn, Dag Ellingsen, Øyvind Bugge Solheim, & Kristine Torgersen (2014). *Et marginalt problem? Asylsøkere, ulovlig opphold og kriminalitet.* Kristiansand: Oxford Research.

Nicholls, W. J. (2013). *The DREAMers. How the undocumented youth movement transformed the immigrant rights debate.* Stanford, CA: Stanford University Press.

Nyers, P. (2010). No one is illegal between city and nation. *Studies in Social Justice, 4*(2), 127–143.

Ong, A. (2003). *Budda is hiding: Refugees, citizenship, the New America.* Berkley, CA: University of California Press.

Spivak, G. C. (1988). Can the subaltern speak? In C. Nelson & L. Grossberg (Eds.), *Marxism and the interpretation of culture* (pp. 271–313). Urbana, IL: University of Illinois Press.

12

Pin Ups and Political Passions: Citizenship Address in Post-War Men's Magazines

Laura Saarenmaa

While the overall aim of this volume is to recognize the gendered nature of representational practices of citizenship, this chapter aims to recognize self-evidently gendered spaces of representation as potential ones for political citizenship address. The notion of address opens a media-specific perspective to representation by bringing forward the practice of representation in a journalistic context. The notion of address captures how representation works in the textual context of journalism by representing public voices—views, arguments and opinions—in the written, published pieces.

Men have typically been represented, but perhaps not so often explicitly addressed, as "men" in the public sphere. The few exceptions have been men's magazines that combine entertainment, erotic and lifestyle

---

L. Saarenmaa (✉)
Tampere Research Centre for Journalism, Media and Communication (COMET), University of Tampere, Kalevantie 4, Main Building, 33014 Tampere, Finland

© The Author(s) 2016
H. Danielsen et al. (eds.), *Gendered Citizenship and the Politics of Representation*, DOI 10.1057/978-1-137-51765-4_12

content—for men. The academic research conducted on men's magazines has primarily included analyses in terms of male sexuality and heteronormative, masculine identity.[1] However, the post-war Finnish men's magazines of the late 1940s and 1950s presented a political agenda. The men's magazines *Adam* [Aatami] 1944–1954, *Between Men* [Miesten kesken] 1949–1951 and *Kalle* [Kalle] 1950–1956, participated in ongoing political debates and addressed their (implied) male readers as political citizens. Moreover, they challenged the dominant, negative representations of Finnish men as violent drunks by outlining the idea of "common gentleman". Men's magazines thus provided forums for the contemplation of sexual and moral issues concerning male behaviour. Although men as political citizens dominated the public sphere, men as sexual and moral beings did not have other arenas for "deliberation among themselves" about their "identities, interests and needs" (Fraser 1990: 67).

In this chapter it is argued that situating post-war men's magazines in the theoretical frameworks of citizenship, the public sphere and the recent theorizations of counterpublics diversifies the understanding of gendered citizenship in a popular media context. This approach is inspired by the work of Dutch media scholar Joke Hermes (2005, 2006). She has studied the way popular cultural practices work as resources for an engaging public sphere and how outlets of the same address members as citizens. As an audience researcher, Hermes has been interested in the representation of ordinary people in the media and the ways in which they have engaged in public debates. By traditional definition, citizenship refers to a person's rights and responsibilities within a given state. American media scholar Toby Miller (2007: 35) defined three partially overlapping but distinct zones of citizenship: (1) political citizenship refers to the right to

---

[1] Before the beginning of 2000, men's magazines as a media have been an almost non-existing field of study internationally. During the early years of 2000s, several textbooks (Jackson 2001; Osgerby 2001; Benwell 2003; Crewe 2003) and journal articles (Ticknell et al. 2003; Attwood 2005; Benwell 2007) on men's magazines where released. The focus in these studies was strictly on the rise of new British lad magazines and the development of laddism in British culture; the kinds of discourses, figures and subjects that are constructed in the rise of British men's lifestyle magazines such as Loaded, FHM and GQ. Men's magazines and their sexual imageries have also been referred to in a general manner in studies of pornography (Kipnis 1996; Dworkin 1989; Kappeler 1986) and studies of social and cultural construction of masculinities (e.g. Edwards 2006; Kimmel et al. 2005; Connell 1995; Seidler 1994; Kimmel 1987; Ehrenreich 1984).

reside and vote; (2) economic citizenship is the right to work and prosper; and (3) cultural citizenship is the right to know and speak. In Miller's analysis, cultural citizenship refers to a sense of belonging within the nation-state—the question of inclusion and exclusion of certain groups or individuals representing minorities of race, ethnicity, gender, religion or language. Miller points to the role of the media in these practices of inclusion and exclusion in contemporary American culture. In this chapter, the question of cultural citizenship is presented in a historical context; in the post-war public debates about the redefinition of ideal manliness.

Feminist citizenship theories have played a crucial role in the critique of classical models of citizenship by demonstrating how gendered the process usually is (Halsaa et al. 2012; Plummer 2003: 60). For David Evans, "The history of citizenship is a history of fundamental formal heterosexist patriarchal principles and practices" (1993: 9). However, rather than ideologically charged generalizations, we need detailed analysis of the rootedness of these "heterosexist patriarchal principles and practices" in the historical development of the public sphere. Post-war men's magazines provide an appropriate empirical case to explore this development.

Recent gender-sensitive studies of cultural citizenship have emphasized the importance of television drama and the hidden debates embedded in this programming (Hermes 2006; van Zoonen 2005; McGuigan 2005). Popular magazines, including men's magazines, cannot be neatly categorized in terms of current issues, entertainment, fact or fiction. These media include content that engages the readership through entertainment as well as political and civic address, thus challenging both theories of cultural citizenship and the public sphere. British media scholar Jim McGuigan (2005) has used the concept of cultural public sphere to examine the role of the popular media within the same. According to McGuigan, the cultural public sphere refers to the articulation of politics as a contested terrain through affective modes of communication. An example of this, he states, would be "watching soap operas, identifying with the characters and their problems and arguing with friends and relatives about what they should or should not do" (McGuigan 2005: 435). The concept of cultural public sphere, like cultural citizenship, is thus firmly situated in the genre of television drama and intrinsically bound to questions of identity, celebrity and scandal and the emotions and actions they evoke. This chapter aims to argue for popular media as a platform for the material directly addressed in the political public sphere. The next section will introduce the research material of the chapter (that is, the three men's magazines published in post-war Finland between the mid-1940s and early 1950s).

Forums for Countercultural Reform

There is a long tradition of men's magazine publishing in the Nordic countries. In Sweden, there have been popular magazines with distinctive masculine emphases since the 1890s (*Förgät Mig Ej* from 1895–1926; *Hvar 8 Dagar* from 1899–1923; *Lektyr* since 1923; and *Levande livet* since 1930) (Hafstrand 2009: 95–96). After the Second World War, from the mid-40s to early 50s, several short-lived men's magazines began publication in Finland. In Norway, there has been a magazine for men (*Vi Menn*) since 1951, combining articles about adventure, war, travel, hunting, sports, cars and women[2]. Compared to Swedish and Norwegian examples, the post-war Finnish men's magazines *Adam* [Aatami] (1944–1954), *Between Men* [Miesten Kesken] (1949–1951), and *Kalle* [Kalle] (1950–1956) have been historically exceptional in including references to domestic politics and current issues.

Each of these magazines had a distinctive voice and profile but consisted of similar content: features and articles covering politics and current issues, editorials, columns, culture, style and fashion, entertainment and erotic-themed short stories. Pin-up pictures and artistic nude pictures, most of international origin, were a common feature, as well. The magazines published substantial amounts of material in the aftermath of the Second World War, the horrors of the Holocaust and the brutality of the SS officers during the Nazi regime in Germany. This is partially explained by the magazines' interdependence on the international

---

[2] There is very little information to be found on the histories of Danish men's magazines before the 1970s. Sören Anker Madsen (2010) has written about the successful 1970s *Ugens Rapport* porn magazine.

press syndicates for the distribution of appropriate textual and pictorial material. The international content was mostly of American and British origin, analysing wartime Europe from the Anglo-American perspective.

After the lost wars against the Soviet Union (1939–1940 and 1941–1944), the political and cultural climate in Finland was tense, and its citizens were restless. Street violence, illegal abortion, prostitution, alcohol and drug addiction and a growing divorce rate were all problems related to the demobilization and reconstruction process. Men's magazines became a forum for countercultural reform, where individual writers could express concerns about the societal circumstances and debate issues in a seemingly non-political context.

In the Finnish press history, men's magazines have been mostly ignored, and when they are mentioned, it is concerning sex, erotic images and narratives for male readers (Malmberg 1991: 133, 149, 343). However, the political content of the magazines served a different function. For instance, *Adam*, first published in December 1944, featured a large amount of political content. At first, *Adam* addressed its readers as "fellow soldiers". In Finland, one of the original functions of men's magazines was the stabilization of post-war conditions, including figuring out how to settle after long years lost on the front. The tone of the editorial of *Adam*'s first issue was decorous:

> We are now out of the war, we have accomplished peace—the price was hard, and so are the compensatory obligations. Now we have to start to build our life all over again, from the ashes and remains. We are still strong, even stronger because of all the suffering. Without sense of hopelessness, we start to work and build ourselves a new future. From fighting to the labour of peace has Finnish man devolved (*Adam* 1, 1944).[3]

There were traits of similar address in the post-war American macho pulps, which targeted blue-collar workers and ex-servicemen. However, the tone of the American magazines was more cheerful and triumphant. The hard-boiled American macho pulp titles of the late '40s and early '50s, such as *Male, Stag, Man to Man, Man's Magazine* and *Man's Life*,

---

[3] English translations L.S.

combined true tales of wartime heroics with a range of fiction and feature articles about crime, fighting, hunting and other so-called manly pursuits. According to Bill Osgerby (2001), the post-war American macho pulps contested the ideal of the domesticated breadwinner and fought desperately to put women back in the role of mother and homemaker (Osgerby 2001: 79–80).

Post-war American masculinity was formed around leisure activities and consumption, while the ex-servicemen in poor, agricultural Finland struggled to survive within the demobilization process. The resettlements of the evacuees, war indemnities and the truce agreement necessitating the change of the political order were heavy burdens for the poor nation. Many ex-soldiers returning from the front had to resort to poor relief. In addition to the austerities of poverty, the period was characterized by street violence, rudeness, alcohol abuse, disconnected families, increased venereal disease, prostitution and illegal abortion.

Points of convergence in Finnish post-war men's magazines with political satire magazines holding longer traditions of national and international examples can be seen. *Adam*, *Between Men* and *Kalle* all circulated similar material, including political causeries, caricatures, jokes and anecdotes. However, Finnish men's magazines separated themselves from political satire magazines with the distinctive erotic—and eventually pornographic—emphasis. While focusing on the political and societal content of men's magazines, their low cultural status and particular erotic functions must be considered. Although the magazines addressed the political public sphere, they were certainly not considered part of it. On the contrary, these magazines were often met with disgust and rejection. At least in the Finnish popular remembrance, reading men's magazines has been marked by shame and secrecy (Saarenmaa 2010). This dynamic of attraction and rejection, excitement and exclusion, is the key element in understanding the countercultural status of men's magazines during the post-war decades. The concept of counterpublics is applied in exploring this complexity. The next sections examine the three magazines following the two definitions of counterpublics in the critical readings of Nancy Fraser's (1990) influential definition of the same by Michael Warner (2002) and Robert Asen (2000).

Redefining Counterpublics: In Conflict with the Dominant

Approaching men's magazines from the perspective of counterpublics is far from self-evident. However, this chapter argues that the concept of counterpublics is relevant to the understanding of the post-war Finnish men's magazines in their historical context. Moreover, the concept of counterpublics is relevant in rethinking the representation of citizenship by drawing attention to the journalistic spaces and the set of practices where the representations are formulated. Men's magazines offer an appropriate case for the rethinking and development of the concept of counterpublics. But why "counterpublics"? Why not frame men's magazines as one of the various, parallel sub-publics, consisting of audiences interested in the particular material the magazines circulated (Warner 2002: 84–85)?

Various traits separated post-war Finnish men's magazines from the dominant publics and sub-publics gathered around specialized media content. Most importantly, the magazines were in *conflictual relation* with what was a more dominant public. In her influential article, Nancy Fraser (1990: 67) has characterized counterpublics as parallel discursive arenas, where "members of subordinated social groups invent and circulate counter-discourses to formulate oppositional interpretations of their identities, interests and needs". In his discussion of Fraser's definition, American literature scholar Michael Warner (2002: 84–85) underlined the importance of conflict with the dominant public in distinguishing counterpublics from various subaltern publics.

Finnish post-war men's magazines were in conflict with the dominant public in multiple ways. Although their erotic content was far from the pornographies of today, in the 40s and 50s, the erotic imagery presented was not tolerated in the general public. For many, reading men's magazines would have meant exposing themselves to social stigma. As Warner (2002: 86) formulates: "Addressees are socially marked by their participation in this kind of discourse; ordinary people are presumed to not want to be mistaken for this kind of person who would participate in this kind of talk or be present in this kind of scene".

Low cultural tolerance was apparent in the legal measures taken in an attempt to control men's magazines, including paper rationing between 1943 and 1949, and sales taxation in the 1950s. Throughout the late 40s and 50s there were publicly expressed concerns about the low quality of pastime reading. In 1946, the parliament had already debated a tax for low-quality reading. The purchase taxation law was given on 22 December 1950.[4] The men's magazine *Kalle* was one of the three magazines considered subject to additional taxation.

Men's magazines were also in conflict with the dominant public due to their distinctively male address. This distinctiveness can be traced back to the wartime brothers-in-arms relationships and collective experiences of soldiers. During the long periods of stabilized war, sharing pictures and details about women and joking about sex were socially binding activities for troops in the dugouts (Kivimäki 2013: 224–225). After the war, men's magazines continued this war-borne tradition by addressing their readers as fellow soldiers, circulating sexually explicit pictures and stories and commentary on politics and current affairs from the perspective of war-experienced veterans. *Adam* appealed to the brothers-in-arms spirit to control the street violence and stabilize the restless conditions of the country: "It is a national shame, if we cannot control a bunch of slackers after being able to defend ourselves for years from the greatest military power in the world" (*Adam* 1, 1945).

The magazines were also conflictual in their rhetoric and argumentation concerning various societal issues. In one of the early editorials of *Kalle*, the writer revealed that the publication considered certain societal problems its duty to address, because, according to him, no one else would: "Our aim is to become publication for manly men—and also women—that draw into light issues that *somebody must talk* about" [italics original]. [...] (*Kalle* 10, 1950) The mainstream media formed by public service radio, national daily newspapers and news magazines

---

[4] At this point, the Parliament set a committee to consider which papers and magazines would be liable to taxation. The opponents appealed to freedom of the press, protected by constitutional law. In the final report of the committee, only three magazines were seen liable to taxation. *Cocktail* consisted of erotic short stories and *Outsider's Magazine* stories on crime and violence. The third convicted magazine, *Kalle*, combined erotic fiction and a broad range of current issue topics (Malmberg 1991: 133).

avoided many subjects and allocated little space to topics such as alcohol and drug addiction, growing divorce rates, street violence, prostitution and illegal abortion. In men's magazines, these issues were openly discussed in an effort to redefine the "decent man" and demonstrate how to live morally as a man in a post-war society. Men's magazines thus provided forums for the contemplation of sexual and moral issues concerning male behaviour. Although men as political citizens dominated the public sphere, men as sexual and moral beings did not have other arenas for "deliberation among themselves about their needs, objectives and strategies", or where they could "circulate counter-discourses to formulate oppositional interpretations of their identities, interests and needs" (Fraser 1990: 67).

This does not mean that the views presented in the magazines would have been progressive or liberal in the present sense. Countercultural forums are not necessarily free to everyone (Fraser 1990: 69). For instance, homosexuality was not accepted, but it was covered and discussed as an existing phenomenon. In *Kalle* magazine, the phenomenon was daringly covered in 1951 in a series of articles titled, "The Third Sex". In the magazine's editorial, homosexuality was referred to as a controversial topic. In Sweden and Denmark, homosexuals had established associations. However, gays in Finland were forced to hide their lifestyle because it was condemned by legislation.

> Homosexuals themselves claim that they have the same rights to live as normal people. They claim that their tendency is birth given quality. They are not abnormal; they are normal representatives of the third sex. But the law defines them as sick, and isolates them from the society. We do not seek sensations [with the article series], but to just try to show what is hidden in homosexuality (*Kalle* 7, 1951).

The first article in the series included an illustration depicting two men dancing together. In the article, there was a list of professions with homosexual members, and the writer made special note of the fact that homosexuals could be found in every field. Altho ugh the magazine certainly did not campaign for gay rights in the present sense, homosexuality as a phenomenon was recognized and covered pertinently. Relationships between two women were also mentioned. However, for this chapter, a more topical conclusion is that sexuality in its different forms was covered altogether. In addition to titillating stories and pictures, sex was covered in an educational spirit, with the help of medical professionals. Masturbation, impotence, frigidity, infertility and other issues of marital life and the wellbeing of spouses were discussed. In *Adam* (10, 1946), one editorial even suggested that national broadcast company (YLE) should include sexual education in their programming to advance citizens' knowledge of sexual matters.

In the summer and autumn of 1945, *Adam* generated a debate around the growing rate of illegal abortion. The magazine introduced the opinions of key experts and drew attention to men's responsibility in unwanted pregnancies. The article also discussed alternative solutions to the problem. Additionally, the magazine published pen named letters to the editor, allowing comments from a female point of view.

In the numerous applications following Fraser (1990), social position of counterpublics is associated with subordinated social categories such as "women, workers, people of colour, and gays and lesbians". Here, rather than assuming that counterpublics are limited to social categories marked by race, class, gender, sexuality or other historically oppressed social categories, the critical approach of American communication scholar Robert Asen (2000) is followed. Asen asserts that that counterpublics can emerge in any social field (see also Hess 2011). According to Asen, the way in which counterpublics set themselves against the wider public may be most productively explored by attending to the recognition and articulation of exclusion through alternative discourse (Asen 2000: 427). In other words, rather than fixing on particular persons, places or topics as necessary markers of counter status, Asen draws attention to the *collectives that emerge* in the recognition of various exclusions from the wider public, and the resolve that builds to overcome this exclusion (Asen 2000: 441). The next section discusses the alcohol debate as presented in Finnish post-war men's magazines, applying the definition of articulation of exclusion by emergent collectives as another redefinition of counterpublics.

Emergent Male Collectives

The Finnish men's magazines launched after the Second World War referred to the lack of high-quality magazines for women and the lack of magazines able to represent men. In December of 1944, *Adam* was launched with the purpose to "fill the gap there was in the field of magazines". Until then, there had not been, in the precise sense, a magazine for men that served to represent "men's cause[s]" (*Adam* 1, 1944). In a similar spirit, 1949 saw the launch of *Between Men* [Miesten kesken], which defined itself as the "interpreter of manly thinking".

> Without a political program, *Between Men* aims to influence in the political life by advancing manly thinking, free from hypocrisy and sentimental idealism. In addition, the magazine aims to have an influence on social conditions by representing decent, manly attitude and by seeking for the characteristics of a Finnish gentleman (*Between Men* 1, 1949).

When he used the words "hypocrisy" and "sentimental idealism", the writer was referring to the progenitors of alcohol legislation. Alcohol prohibition was one of the issues where politics, legislation and cultural norms and expectations concerning male behaviour clashed.

Wartime led many Finnish men (and women) to the habit of heavy drinking. Towards the end of the war, particularly after the German troops began to retreat from their positions on the Eastern Front, civil morality began to erode. After the war, heavy drinking became common among university students, which generated great concern in the older population. The Moral Movement [Ryhtiliike] was established with the support of the Alcohol State Monopoly Company [Alko] and included a 1945 campaign to sober-up students and establish better manners in society (Peltonen 2002: 12–13, 35–38).

Campaigns against drunkenness existed during the war, but, at that time, the Morale Movement struggled to root out poor habits and redefine what they believed to be the standards of moral life in Finland. The first national campaign, The Moral Week [Ryhtiviikko] of 1948 was targeted to turn public opinion against drunkenness. The newspapers covered the campaign extensively (Peltonen 2002: 39), and the launching of *Between Men* the next year served as a reaction to the campaign. The magazine's first editorial directly attacks the Morale Movement by defining it as a "mental waste" of the bygone prohibition mentality.

> As a young nation, we have many adolescence flaws. There are deluded idealism, sentimental views, and all sorts of baggage from the days we were under the power of others. But why talk with metaphors. Just remember the children's disease that three young nations, The United States, Norway and Finland resorted: the prohibition law (*Between Men* 1, 1949).

The prohibitionary law mentality is deeply rooted in Finland. In the early 1900s, the country was one of the driest in Europe. Alcohol laws were tight, and the temperance movement was strongly supported in all social classes. Early twentieth-century Finland was a model country in terms of the temperance movement's sobriety ideals (Peltonen 1996: 63). In the revolutionary year 1917, the senate accepted the prohibitionary alcohol law. Leaders justified the tight legislation based on a genetic susceptibility to alcohol intolerance in many Finnish people, which made them vulnerable to alcohol abuse. The prohibitionary law was declared null in 1932, but alcohol regulations were still tight after the Second World War. At the end of the war, the Alcohol State Monopoly Company [Alko] launched a regulation system that tied each customer to one of the company's member stores. Customers were forced to get a purchase card, on which all purchases were recorded. The card system was a failure and was dismantled by 1957. Men's magazines were one of the vociferous arenas where this failure was articulated. *Between Men* took a vocal position against prohibition, claiming that regulation systems, high taxation and poor alcohol quality encouraged misbehaviour and social problems.

The magazine arguably specialized in questioning alcohol regulation. Its editorials commented broadly on current alcohol politics, including the monopoly system of alcohol distribution, continuous price increases, beer diluting and the "patronizing", "pretentious" and "cocky" standpoint of the Morale Movement. The magazine envisioned an alcohol culture that drew on the urban lifestyle of European metropolises. One editorial marvelled at the outstanding service in London, claiming a wide selection of brands and merchants who were polite and helpful, even providing home delivery, "Quite unlike in Finland, where the customer who wishes to buy alcohol is treated like a half-criminal" (*Between Men* 5, 1951). In a similar vein, the magazine wrote about Copenhagen:

> In Copenhagen, there are no drunken people in the streets. And still one can buy alcohol almost any store. [The Danes] can enjoy their Carlsberg's and Tuborg's anywhere, but they do not even want to get drunk. And is there anything nicer than sit over beer or coffee in some of the cafes of Copenhagen. But here, try to sit in the grass in a park and you have the guards coming after you (*Between Men* 6, 1951).

In addition to magazine editorials, alcohol culture was promoted in articles created to educate readers about choosing the right drinks in the right situations: spirits kill the taste, so no spirits and cocktails right before dining, dry sherry will do better (*Between Men* 7, 1951). There were articles about choosing the right shape of glass for the most pleasurable drinking experience. One writer said, "Sobriety of citizens is best advanced through the idea that drinking is a pleasure and not a gloomy slog. Since they are drinking anyway" (*Between Men* 7, 1951).

Alcohol culture promoted by *Between Men* intertwined with a comprehensive male style that included proper social behaviour, dress and leisure activities, including films, literature, theatre, music, magazines and a satisfying sexual life. The Finnish gentleman ennobled in the men's magazines was based more on the American perception of the modern man than the peasant, brisk teetotaller envisioned by the Morale Movement. He embodied manly hopes and dreams of freedom: a modern, international life, free from control and limitations. However, distinct to the American hedonist male consumer promoted by *Esquire*, *True* and eventually *Playboy* in 1953, in poor and peasant Finland the opportunities for acting out this lifestyle were limited, not the least because of the degrading alcohol regulation policies. Alcohol politics were thus used as a tool to promote a better future from the male point of view.

Well-known names were behind the magazines. These included established journalists and writers and members of the cultural male elite. They were patriotic, political conservatives, some famously against postwar Leftism and modernism. They also had strong opinions about the alcohol problem and how it should have been managed.[5] In his critical response to Nancy Fraser's (1990) definition of counterpublics, Robert Asen (2000) discusses how *emergent groups* and *emergent collectives*, rather than subordinate groups, are the primus motors of counterpublics. He claims that emergent collectives are not necessarily composed of persons excluded from wider public spheres. Thus, the definition of counterpublics does not draw on exclusion but rather the *recognition of exclusion* and the resolve to overcome it. In other words, emergent collectives refer to people who may participate in multiple and potentially conflicting publics and counterpublics (Asen 2000: 439).

The established male journalists and writers on the editorial board of *Between Men* magazine can hardly be described as a subordinate group, yet they perfectly fit the mould of the emergent group or collective. Furthermore, they can be seen as critical players in the emergence of *gender awareness of men* and the rising intent to address the *male collective* to make a difference in society. For *Between Men* magazine, the contribution was specific through the influence on alcohol politics and the redefinition of the ideal male citizen. Launching a men's magazine was one instrument in this debate.

To define counterpublics in terms of the contributions of emergent collectives highlights the communicative qualities of the same. Furthermore, it reflects "counter" as a constructed relationship (Asen 2000: 427). From the perspective of emergent collectives, counterpublics did not necessarily mean representing an argument that was entirely against public opinion. In the alcohol debate, men's magazines expressed an attitude towards alcohol that was supported elsewhere in the public, particularly in the manuals and guidebooks of manners that were written free from the influence of alcohol authorities (Peltonen 2002: 100–104). In the post-war years of the late 40s and early 50s, there was a wide consensus

---

[5] The editorial board of *Between Men*: Olavi järvi, Ensio Rislakki, Kai Kivijärvi and Yrjö Kivimies. Kivimies was a well-known author. Ensio Rislakki was a sub-editor of the influential *Suomen kuvalehti*. Moreover Rislakki was one of the original writers of the *Guide of Proper Behavior* [Hyvän käytöksen opas], launched in the Olympic year 1952 in order to prepare the Finnish people for the arrival of international guests. Peltonen (2002: 90, 110–111) refers to disagreements in the editing process of the *Guide* and the definition of the Finnish gentleman. *Between Men* magazine reflects this disagreement by promoting the idea of international gentleman instead of the rooty, common gentleman that was outlined by the other parties of the debate.

about the need for a new male ideal, but disagreement on the constituents of this ideal (Peltonen 2002: 96, 111, 116).

The conflict was not constructed between counterpublics and public opinion, but counterpublics and authorities representing the dominant political and governmental culture. In *Kalle* magazine, the alcohol authorities and legislators were addressed directly: "Does the senate know? Does the alcohol monopoly company [Alko] know?"

> Are the members of the parliament aware that scalping of alcohol is executed in the streets on a regular basis, and that citizens get alcohol for the scalpers with their purchase cards, and that thousands of speakeasies, brothels and gambling dens flourish everywhere? Do they know that public toilets are used as drinking places (because there are no bars), and that tens of thousands of people poison themselves with homemade alcohol? So, honourably members of the parliament, it would be time to do something about this. I wait the public response of social politicians in this matter (*Kalle* 8, 1950).

Kalle magazine also contributed to the debate with coverage of the favoured drinking places in the centre of Helsinki. The report was sarcastically titled, "The Central Railway Station, the Most Popular Bar in Helsinki" (*Kalle* 9, 1951). In another report, the magazine depicted a group of male alcoholics drinking and loitering in the streets of Helsinki. "What says the society? This group of men has changed the normal life into slacking and boozing. Because of their addiction for booze, they have lost their dignity and honor" (*Kalle* 9, 1951). At the same time the men's magazines outlined the new male ideal, they outlined the characteristics of unappreciated male behaviour.

In accordance with Toby Miller's (2007) definition of cultural citizenship, the magazines established countercultural forums for their publishers, writers and readers to speak out, share information and be addressed as male citizens. They provided a forum for questioning the dominant public address and redefining the ideal male citizen in a historical context. In the '50s and '60s, the political tone in men's magazines began to fade in the interest of more daringly erotic and, eventually, pornographic content. In the politically turbulent post-war years, the presentation of political address in the same context as pin-up pictures and erotically exciting stories highlights the controversial nature of the political views presented in the magazines. However, the counterpublic function of men's magazines should not be generalized as a generic quality. As Asen (2000) puts it, it is important to pay respect to the historical temporality and the dialectical movement of the public sphere in its theorization: the counterpublic gains of some particular publication or genre are not permanent (Asen 2000: 441). The cultural meanings and function of media formats change over time.

The post-war years were a breaking point in Finnish society. At that time, there was a great need for public controversy but limited arenas for it. The launch of men's magazines for the purpose of promoting individual political views is one of the many ways emergent, male collectives benefitted from the dynamic relations between publics and counterpublics. The perspective of emergent collectives thus nuances understanding of gendered counterpublics, recognizing simultaneity, overlap, diverse affiliation, partiality and contestation among publics and between publics and counterpublics.

Conclusion

In this chapter, it is argued that post-war Finnish men's magazines addressed their male readers as citizens and functioned as gendered counterpublics for their male producers, writers and readers. The definition of counterpublics applied here draws on two theoretical standpoints: firstly, of Michael Warner's redefinition of Nancy Fraser's conception, and secondly, Robert Asen's critical redefinition of Fraser's concept. Rather than assuming that counterpublics are limited to race, class, gender or sexuality as a historically dominated or oppressed social category, Asen suggests that counterpublics can emerge in any social context. Saying this does not imply that men's magazines necessarily function as counterpublics in every historical time and place. Different media genres and formats and their status in the public sphere are particular, as is the status of men's magazines in the public sphere. This chapter has argued for the counterpublic functions of men's magazines in a specific temporal context, post-war Finland.

After the lost war, the political and cultural climate in the country was tense. Street violence, illegal abortion, prostitution, alcohol and drug addiction and a growing divorce rate were all problems related to the demobilization and reconstruction process. The mainstream avoided many subjects and allocated little space to their discussion. As it has been presented in this chapter, in men's magazines, these issues were openly discussed. Men's magazines provided forums for the contemplation of sexual and moral issues concerning male behaviour. Moreover, men's magazines were vociferous arenas articulating failures in alcohol policies and redefining the ideal male citizen. As shown here, launching a men's magazine was one instrument in this debate.

Returning to the concept of cultural citizenship defined in terms of right to know and speak and in terms of inclusion and exclusion of certain groups or individuals, what can be learned from the historical and quite particular case study of post-war Finnish men's magazines? In the research on representing men in popular media, the focus has been on illustrations, images and visual representations of male bodies and audience identifications with the portrayed ideals. Turning attention from visual to textual spaces of gendered representation, the self-evidently gendered popular media can be recognized as a potential space of political representation.

In discussing new avenues for research on gendered citizenship in the context of media representations, it is worthwhile to reconsider the theories and concepts of the public sphere. For example, the redefinitions of counterpublics brought up here are not limited to social categories marked by subordination. Thus, these redefinitions might be helpful in studying various forums and spheres of publicity that were not known beforehand as spaces for political interaction. In the modern digitalized society, public discussions around the issues of citizenship are not limited to certain forums, spheres or frames of reference. Again, there are gendered media formats that cannot be neatly categorized in terms of current issues, entertainment, fact or fiction that might be more political than they seem. And there are people who may participate simultaneously in multiple and potentially conflicting publics and counterpublics.

Capturing the conclusions of this chapter in two methodological principles in studying gendered representations, one should, first, beware the simplistic divisions of subjugated women and empowered men. As emphasized here, there are many kinds of men and many kinds of struggles within the male-dominated spaces of representation to be considered other than excluding women. Second, one should beware the taken-for-granted notions of popular media genres as their ways and functions might change over time—in other words, not to judge a magazine by its cover.

References

Asen, R. (2000). Seeking the "counter" in counterpublics. *Communication Theory, 10*(4), 424–446.
Attwood, F. (2005). 'Tits and Ass and Porn and Fighting'. Male heterosexuality in magazines for men. *International Journal of Cultural Studies, 8*(1), 83–100.
Benwell, B. (Ed.). (2003). *Masculinity and men's lifestyle magazines*. Oxford: Blackwell.
Benwell, B. (2007). New sexism? *Journalism Studies, 8*(4), 539–549.
Connell, R. W. (1995). *Masculinities*. Cambridge: Polity.
Crewe, B. (2003). *Representing men: Cultural production and the producers in the men's magazine market*. Oxford: Berg.
Dworkin A (1989/1979) *Pornography: Men possessing women*. New York: E.P. Dutton.
Edwards, T. (2006). *Cultures of masculinity*. London: Routledge.
Ehrenreich, B. (1984). *The hearts of men. American dreams and the flight from commitment*. New York: Anchor Press.
Evans, D. (1993). *Sexual citizenship. The material construction of sexualities*. London: Routledge.
Fraser, N. (1990). Rethinking the public sphere: A contribution to the critique of actually existing democracy. *Social Text, 25/26*(1990), 56–80.
Hafstrand, H. (2009). *Herrtidningsmode förr och nu. Den Svenska pressens historia 7, Konkurrens och förnyelse*. Nordicom: Göteborgs Universitetet 95–XX.
Halsaa, B., Roseneil, S., & Sümer, S. (Eds.). (2012). *Remaking citizenship in multicultural Europe. Women's movements, gender and diversity*. Basingstoke: Palgrave Macmillan.
Hermes, J. (2005). *Re-reading popular culture*. Cambridge: Blackwell.
Hermes, J. (2006). Hidden Debates: Rethinking the relationship between popular culture and the public sphere. *Javnost-the Public, 13*(4), 27–44.

Hess, D. (2011). To tell the truth. On scientific counterpublics'. *Public Understanding of Science*, August 2011.
Kappeler, S. (1986). *The pornography of representation*. Cambridge: Polity.
Kimmel, M. S. (1987). *Changing men. New directions in research on men and masculinity*. Thousand Oaks, CA: Sage.
Kimmel, M. S., Hearn, J., & Connell, R. W. (2005). *Handbook on studies of men & masculinities*. Thousand Oaks, CA: Sage.
Kipnis, L. (1996). *Bound and gagged. Pornography and the politics of fantasy in America*. New York: Grove Press.
Kivimäki, V. (2013). *Murtuneet mielet. Taistelu suomalaissotilaiden hermoista 1939–1945*. Helsinki: WSOY.
Madsen, S. A. (2010). *Historien om Ugens Rapport*. Köpenhagen: Gads Förlag.
Malmberg, R. (1991). Yleislehtien kuohuvat vuodet 1934–1980. In T. Päiviö (Ed.), *Suomen lehdistön historia 8, Yleisaikakauslehdet* (pp. 107–188). Kuopio: Kustannuskiila.
McGuigan, J. (2005). The cultural public sphere. *European Journal of Cultural Studies, 8*(4), 427–443.
Miller, T. (2007). *Cultural citizenship. Cosmopolitanism, consumerism and television in neoliberal age*. Philadelphia, PA: Temple University Press.
Osgerby, B. (2001). *Playboys in paradise. Masculinity, youth and leisure-style in modern America*. Oxford: Berg.
Peltonen, M. (1996). *Rillumarei ja valistus. Kulttuurikahakoita 1950-luvun Suomessa*. Helsinki: SKS.
Peltonen, M. (2002). *Remua ja ryhtiä. Alkoholiolot ja kasvatus 1950-luvun Suomessa*. Helsinki: Gaudeamus.
Plummer, K. (2003). *Intimate citizenship. Private decisions and public dialogues*. Seattle: University of Washington Press.
Saarenmaa, L. (2010). *Intiimin äänet. Julkisuuskulttuurin muutos suomalaisissa ajanvietelehdissä 1961–1975*. Tampere: Tampere University Press.
Seidler, V. J. (1994). *Unreasonable men. Masculinity and social theory*. London: Routledge.
Ticknell, E., Chambers, D., Van Loon, J., & Hudson, N. (2003). Begging for it: "New Femininities", social agency, and moral discourse in contemporary teenage and men's magazines. *Feminist Media Studies, 3*(1), 47–63.
Van Zoonen, L. (2005). *Entertaining the Citizen. When politics and popular culture converge*. Lanham: Rowman & Littlefield.
Warner, M. (2002). *Publics and counterpublics*. New York: Zone Books.

13

"The Venus Hottentot Is Unavailable for Comment": Questioning the Politics of Representation Through Aesthetic Practices

Jorunn Gjerden, Kari Jegerstedt, and Željka Švrljuga

Over the last years, there has been a proliferation of political, cultural, and academic/scientific refigurations of Sara Baartman alias the Hottentot Venus. The interest in her life story attests to a significant discursive shift: from being a symbol of the so-called lower races, Baartman has become a symbol of the critique of the very construction of race, as well as a signifier of the struggle for freedom and rights along racial and sexual/gen-

---

J. Gjerden (✉)
Department of Foreign Languages, University of Bergen, Sydnesplassen 7, 5020 Bergen, Norway

K. Jegerstedt (✉)
Centre for Women and Gender Research, University of Bergen, 5020 Bergen, Norway

Ž. Švrljuga (✉)
Department of Foreign Languages, University of Bergen, Sydnesplassen 7, 5007 Bergen, Norway

dered lines. Associated with monstrosity, Baartman came to be known for her performances in "freak shows" in London and Paris in the early 1800s. George Cuvier's anatomical scrutiny and dissection secured her an "afterlife" in the Musée de l'homme in Paris, where her genitalia, skeleton, and body cast were on display until the early 1970s. Subsequently, Baartman has become a key figure in attempts to restore the abjected, racialized female body in feminist, anti-racist and postcolonial terms. When her remains were finally repatriated to South Africa in 2002, she had already become a symbol of the suffering of the African people both abroad and at home, and of the need to restore dignity for new collectivities to prosper.

Baartman's emblematic role in recent discourses can be understood as an affirmation of the need to rework colonial constructions of "racialized woman" in order to generate more inclusive and egalitarian notions of citizenship and democracy in the postcolonial world. As South African author Zoë Wicomb notes, her case epitomizes central postmodern concerns: "the inscription of power in scopic relations; the construction of woman as racialized and sexualized other; the colonization and violation of the body; the role of scientific discourse in bolstering both the modernist and colonial projects" (Wicomb 1998: 93). But how can contemporary practices revise the nineteenth-century objectifying gaze on the Hottentot Venus without simply repeating it? Can attempts to grant her voice and perspective result in anything but new reductive representations? And does not the attempt to do her justice re-appropriate her iconic status in new ideological discourses?

Gayatri Chakravorty Spivak's assertion that "the figure of woman is pervasively instrumental in the shifting of the function of discursive systems" (Spivak 2003: 74) neatly encapsulates the dilemmas involved in refiguring Baartman. Offered by Spivak as an allegory that signals an "unimaginable future 'to come'" (Spivak 2003: 32), the assertion aims to "restore social agency to the dreamer" (Spivak 2003: 75). In this sense, it may be seen to advance a feminist practice: that the (reading of the) re-figuration of woman may in fact result in the shifting of discursive systems. At the same time, however, the sentence functions as a warning to feminist practices: Insofar as the re-figuring of "woman" is always already part of the shifting of the function of discursive systems, how can we know whether feminist re-figurations do not, unwittingly, take part in a more general shift which serves to uphold power relations instead of providing radical breaks?

The dilemmas involved in feminist attempts to refigure derogatory conceptions and images are closely related to the problem of representation insofar as representation always implies the double meaning of "'speaking for,' as in politics and… 're-presentation' ['speaking about'], as in art or philosophy" (Spivak 1988: 275). Unable to escape the question of who speaks for whom and in whose (and what) interest, representation does not only constitute the very mechanisms of inclusion and exclusion, or even radical alterity, but also subordinates the subject to the laws of discursive power and hegemony. The figure of Baartman is exemplary in this respect: entangled with questions of representation from the beginning, it has always been steeped in power relations. The derogatory alias under which Baartman performed combines the Dutch colonizer's perception of the Khoisan vernacular (Hottentot) and the image of the Roman goddess of love (Venus) as the epitome of beauty, femininity, and sexuality; her exploitation by different "managers" made her into economic, cultural, and sexual currency both in life and posthumously. The issue of representation and power has thus been vital to the critical debates on Baartman: from discussions of nineteenth-century medical and artistic constructions of black female sexuality (Gilman 1985) to the materialist concerns and class struggle involved in constructions of race—including the degree of re-commodification entrenched in the very establishing of Baartman as an object of research (Magubane 2001; Qureshi 2004). As a result, the debate has moved on to representational alternatives and the ethics of representation, exploring the possibilities of re-presentation without representation (Gquola 2010; Baderoon 2011). The question that arises from these debates is whether art (and philosophy) may in fact supplement, rather than merely complement, politics.

The following pages examine three recent generic re-visions of the Hottentot Venus story that adopt various aesthetic practices that address the problems of representation in its double meaning: *Venus* by the American playwright Suzan-Lori Parks (1997), *David's Story* by the South African novelist Zoë Wicomb (2001), and *Vénus noire* by the French-Tunisian filmmaker Abellatif Kechiche (2010). They not only share the desire to ascribe different significance to the figure of Baartman by reworking archival material and contemporary discourses, but also the critical awareness of taking part in what has come to be known as the "Baartman industry", wary of the risk of yet another recommodification. Situating themselves aesthetically within this double bind—the need to rework and the danger of co-optation—they both highlight and seek to subvert the diverse contexts in which Baartman has acquired symbolic status. Notably, they do so through the aesthetics of dismemberment/dissemination and emptiness/absence, thus recalling the narrative mechanisms of earlier colonial representations of her. Of special interests here is Cuvier's detailed autopsy report in which the description of Baartman's features is either rendered poetically or is compared "scientifically" to those of other races and species (Cuvier 1817). The ensuing result is a fragmented narrative which teems with an excess of information that distorts the woman the document seeks to describe. Another example is the French vaudeville *La Vénus Hottentote ou Haine aux Françaises* (Théaulon, Dartois and Brasier 1814), contrived to profit from Baartman's success in Paris and to jettison its competition, which literally reduces the Hottentot Venus to masquerade and caricature, signifying her presence through absence by dramatizing the absent core. In their engagement with colonial power structures, contemporary political issues and parodic modes of rewriting, Kechiche, Parks and Wicomb redeploy these colonial representational modes—dismemberment and absence—in an attempt to make Baartman signify otherwise. To what extent might this "otherwise" open for what is radically different and new?

In order to explore the issue, the differences between these three texts need to be taken into consideration. They do not only refer to historical and geopolitical contexts (French, American, and African) and genres (film, drama, novel), but also relate to the specific aesthetic strategies through which dismemberment and absence are played out. In what follows, Kechiche's attempts to interrupt Western meaning production as a neutral approach to the understanding of others will be analysed as a manifestation of opacity. Park's rewriting of historical documents and its own dramatic utterance will be examined as the embodiment of recycling aesthetics. In turn, Wicomb's more radical gesture of withdrawing the figure of Baartman from dominant discourses will be analysed according to Alain Badiou's concept of subtraction.[1] Ultimately we suggest that the aesthetic dimensions of these works have the potential to initiate a deliberation beyond the hegemonic discourse of representational politics, not because the texts avoid the double bind of rejecting/reproducing stereotypes, but precisely because they confront it.

Covers and Silence: *Vénus Noire*

In comparison with Parks's play and Wicomb's novel, Kechiche's *Vénus noire* is a fairly traditional narrative that doesn't seem to undertake much in order to represent Baartman otherwise. But the film's subdued tone may in fact be considered its very opposition to instrumentality, which may be argued with reference to Martinican Édouard Glissant's term "opacity". Inspired by the linguistic and cultural diversity of the Caribbean archipelago, opacity implies both resistance to the Western colonial image of the world as transparent and available for conquest, and possibilities of new conceptions of community. The following will focus on how the impassable and the silence of *Vénus noire* may lead in similar directions.

From the very start, *Vénus noire* associates the representation of Sara Baartman with the dilemmas of covering and uncovering. The film's first footage enigmatically dwells on a cloth covering a full-size plaster cast of her body, which is eventually unveiled in the Royal Academy of Medicine where Cuvier, two years after her death, presents his meticulously illustrated analysis of her body as an example of the lowest specimen of the human race. At first sight, then, Kechiche appears to ruthlessly render and leave uncontested the nineteenth-century's objectifying gaze on the Hottentot Venus; the scene even insists on the eagerness to uncover, expose, and dismember that characterizes colonial knowledge produc-

---

[1] Badiou argues that subtraction, defined as "the affirmative aspects of negation" (Badiou 2007), is an integral part of all revolutionary change and suggests that today we need a preliminary or "originary" subtraction: a withdrawing of oneself from under the dominant laws of the political reality (of a situation) to create an autonomous space in which revolutionary possibilities can be thought anew.

tion. While such a strategy might be efficient in order to provoke the spectator's resentment and disgust when faced with the exploitation of Baartman, it also constitutes an ethically problematic enunciative position. As Aylin Basaran notes: "*Black Venus* is a balancing act, which poses itself on the thin line between displaying a (historical) social reality and—by trying to depict this—reproducing its gaze, especially with the medium film which has the tendency to facilitate some kind of voyeurism" (Basaran 2010).

At the same time, since the establishment of Baartman as an iconic victim of gendered colonial oppression risks becoming equally instrumental, the film enacts Spivak's double bind through a set of narrative strategies that undermine its own reproduction of the nineteenth-century's gaze, but without annulling it. Interestingly and provocatively, Kechiche seems to achieve this by adopting and imperceptibly reworking the mode of figuration of the 1814 vaudeville mentioned in the introduction. Constructed as a simple comedy of errors, *La Vénus Hottentote ou Haine aux Françaises* ("The Hottentot Venus or the Hatred of Frenchwomen") represents the Hottentot Venus solely by means of a disguised female French character posing as her. She thus appears as nothing but an absent and shadowy figure deprived of speech, situated out of reach behind the veils that mask or indeed replace her. However, when the opening scene of *Vénus noire* poignantly echoes this covered archival representation, staging it as a clear contrast to Cuvier's uncovering, it has the effect of announcing and installing a supplementary representational mode that hampers and works against the stereotyped colonial gaze through a subtle re-vision.

A crucial component of such supplementing re-vision in the film is reflexivity. A series of discursive, pictorial and plastic representations of the Hottentot Venus appearing throughout the narrative (statuettes, drawings, a popular song, a critical article, her own performance), serve on the one hand to emphasize the image of Baartman as objectified victim of Western typecasting. This is very evident in a scene where Caezar, the South African "managing" her London exhibition, is shown modelling one of the clay statuettes, letting his fingers slide along her represented body, powerfully materializing how he literally moulds Baartman into the Hottentot Venus, as if the other could be grasped and manipulated

13 Questioning Representation through Aesthetic Practices   287

like any matter or object at one's disposal. A suggestive parallel to this gesture reappears in the closing dissection scene, where Baartman's body is smeared in grease before plaster is poured onto it to make the cast that will solidify her figure for posterity. These scenes thus critically associate the nineteenth-century staging of the Hottentot Venus, whether gendered/sexual or scientific, with the connected (male) Western projects of making sense of the world and appropriating it (Spivak 1988: 76–86). But simultaneously, they also reflexively accentuate the movie itself as a fabricated, provisional figuration in need of subsequent correction. After all, even the unveiling of the cast in the opening scene only reveals an empty shell. Moreover, the unveiling sequence is part of a circular composition, as we return to the scenario at the end of the film, where Cuvier's assistant, silent and expressionless, *covers* the cast with the cloth prior to the professor's speech, suggesting that we know nothing more about Baartman at this point than we did at the beginning of the film. The film's circular and reflexive composition thus plays the double bind of retaining and subverting previous representations by setting up opposite positions which are granted equal weight while at the same time mutually problematizing one another.

In a similar manner, Kechiche's subtle combination of style and narration establishes a formal structure that both gives and does not give voice to Sara Baartman by relating the story from her own perspective, but only in a limited and unclear way.

As far as narrative perspective is concerned, what we learn is largely limited to what Baartman herself perceives and knows at any time (except for the essential scenes taking place after her death). Some point-of-view shots allow us to share her perceptions (like a frontal glimpse of the audience from inside the bars of the cage she is kept in on stage), and shot/reverse shot technique is used in some dialogues in a conventional manner, but in others carefully avoided, for instance during the scientific examination in the Jardin des Plantes, where Baartman is only ever looked *at*. Even if we thus partly share her subjective experiences, the narration does stay mainly external, and we sometimes get crucial information concerning the main character that she does not herself have access to (for instance, during scenes where she is heavily drunk, or is being spied on).

In addition, Baartman's understanding of what goes on around her, and the spectator's insight into it, are limited by language problems. While she does participate in dialogue, and actually sporadically protests against details concerning her exhibition as well as the scientists' examination of her, as a rule her utterances are few, short, and often ambiguous. Not only has she trouble understanding what others say, and communicating her views, but some of her statements also contradict previous ones, like her testimony given during the trial against Caezar, where she insists that she is not a slave but an actress who gets half the show's income. The words are rendered in her voice, but to what extent may the assertions be attributed to her? The film doesn't take sides, or elaborate on the matter.

Finally, the main reason for the Baartman character's both restricted and paradoxically poignant impact on the narrative is an unusual combination of framing, that is, frequent facial close-ups, and impassive acting style. Extreme close-ups of the faces of the show's audience, of Caezar and the judges during the trial are crosscut with parallel close-ups of Baartman's face. The effect of this procedure is striking: although we get so close that we see pores in the character's skin and emerging drops of sweat, we actually find ourselves miles away, since Baartman's face (and often those of other characters) remains almost completely motionless. The combined emphasis on physical closeness and inaccessibility to inner life thus powerfully triggers strong emotional involvement, but without granting the spectator the secure conventional positions of either psychologically identifying with the main character as subject or objectifying her through othering victimization.

As already indicated, this may be interpreted as an ethically motivated narrative choice which paradoxically seeks to represent Baartman by insisting on her *opacity*, in a way that recalls Glissant's use of this term.[2] According to Glissant, opacity is whatever interrupts the working of the Western ideal of transparency that considers itself a neutral approach to the understanding of others. Opacity "distracts me from absolute truths whose guardian I might believe myself to be" and makes me "sensitive to the limits of every method" (Glissant 2000: 192). If we are to be able

---

[2] Dominque Widemann employs the same term in a similar way to analyze Kechiche's close-ups, but without relating it explicitly to Glissant (Widemann 2010).

to envision a humanity where "[e]very Other is a citizen and no longer a barbarian" (Glissant 2000: 190), this change requires a radical "right to opacity that is not enclosure within an impenetrable autarchy but subsistence within an irreducible singularity" (Glissant 2000: 190). To Glissant, linguistic, cultural and geographical opacity which separates individuals and groups at the same time is the very condition permitting them to get close to each other: in order for connections to actually be connections—and for representation to actually re-present—they must avoid dissolving into appropriation and assimilation.

In Glissant's thinking, opacity thus becomes a key condition for the possibility of achieving agency and participation without instrumentalizing subordination, and for the forming of more inclusive communities in a globalized world. *Vénus noire* cinematographically articulates and acts out a similar non-binary logic in a scene where racialized typecasting is interrupted by the unexpected, and by a following onset of a new kind of affective and embodied response and involvement that allow singularity and togetherness to equally amplify one another.

One of the numbers of the Hottentot Venus's stage performances in London consists of singing while playing an African instrument. On one occasion, she decides to alter this act: rather than produce barbaric noises out of tune, in accordance with the audience's expectations, she starts to sing a real song. All of a sudden, as if she remembers something from the past, she straightens her back and starts performing the song very softly, apparently forgetting completely about both her role and her audience. The song is a lullaby, characterized by a trance-inducing, repetitive rhythm. It is the only example in the film of Baartman expressing herself in her own Khoe language. Interestingly, from the middle of the sequence, in a point-of-view shot attributed to Baartman, close-ups focus on *her* perception of the audience's responses: confusion, astonishment, slightly opened mouths, bodies swaying gently to the rhythm of the music, even eyes filling up with tears. Some spectators start singing along, adopting the incomprehensible words of the foreign lyrics offered to them.

This brief episode seems crucial for the film's questioning of representational modes in the sense that through specific narrative choices, it brings into play dynamics of inclusion and exclusion constituted not by a conquering establishment of sameness, nor by a construction of gendered and/or racialized otherness as the dialectical negation of the self, but by an experience of the drawing near of alterity through which both previous positions are unsettled. As such, the collective yet unshared experience of the lullaby performatively changes performer and audience alike, if only for a moment, and so appears as an opening towards new textured forms of relationship which may enable the founding of non-instrumental representation and non-assimilative communities—through the tangible closeness of impenetrability.

Re-membering the Hottentot Venus: *Venus*

As an example of a larger diasporic paradigm, Baartman has lent her name to the figure of Black Venus in the Atlantic world of chattel slavery which has enabled a double exploitation of black female bodies—the alleged embodiments of concupiscence and otherness, pleasure and repulsion. As a symbol of sexual and racial oppression, Baartman has struck a chord in the USA, judging by the creative and critical output.

Parks's *Venus* signals with its title a restorative agenda by leaving out the pejorative moniker from Baartman's stage name. Its aim—to inspire humanity and dignity in the subject of history—follows the playwright's understanding of theatre as "the perfect place to 'make' history", "to create 'new' historical events" (Parks 2013b: 4–5). This new event is a postmodern project that contrives representation by way of recovering practices that work with repetition with a difference: re-cycling, re-membering, and re-vision. A somewhat daring concept in name—re-cycling—is adopted as a creative means of reworking historical material into a new plot and alternative representation which jazz aesthetics of "forming, reforming, and informing" boosts (Drukman et al. 1995: 57). Predicated on reformulation, the deployed aesthetic strategies work towards provisional solutions at the level of the political as well.

By configuring the title figure as the goddess of love, the play switches the focus from the particular (bodily markers) to the general (potential to love and be loved) through naming. Registered with her full name only in the *dramatis personae*, the title character appears under generic designations: The Girl or The Venus (as *subject* of utterance and desire) and as The Venus Hottentot (as the *object* of the gaze, desire, and the statements of others). Parks adopts a generic politics of naming for the entire cast, intimating, as it were, generality and particularity which the definite article grants (Larson 2012: 27), allowing the general to signify on many Black Venus figures and their exploiters in the Black Atlantic. When, in turn, the eponymous character speaks of herself as The Venus Hottentot, it is always by way of detachment and dissociation: "I am called The Venus Hottentot", and "The Venus Hottentot is unavailable for comment" (Parks 1997: 74). Hence, what the Hottentot Venus qua myth "states", the "woman" cannot since she is both outside of the myth and cannot identify with it. Accordingly, the second line signals Parks' politics of representation that resists speaking for her title figure in political terms.

Representation in *Venus* and of The Venus is predicated on the figure of circle (or cycle) that is associated with the circulation of images, language, myth, money, and a cyclical understanding of time. The figure of the cycle is also embedded in the play's re-cycling aesthetics: official historical documents (newspaper clippings, dictionary entries, glossaries, and Cuvier's autopsy report) and the popular culture material of the day (advertisements, cartoons, the broadside ballad, and the vaudeville) are adopted and adapted as "evidence" of the colonial archive against which the title figure is cast. As footnotes, asides, and parabases, in other words Brechtian *Verfremdungseffekte* that disrupt and punctuate the narrative, these textual fragments testify to the limits of knowledge about the historical figure that can only provisionally be fashioned by way of imaginative making. The play's double bind has somehow been underplayed and Parks' representation critiqued for its "re-objectification" and "re-commodification" (Young 1997). Even if there is a danger in critiquing the colonial politics of hostility by staging it, despite the fact that representation is done by inversion and narrative and rhetorical mechanisms that provide ironic distance and ludic, linguistic turns, Parks's play gestures towards what Spivak, following Derrida, calls "a politics of friendship to come" (Spivak 2003: 13). The politics of presenting "otherwise" underlies the production of meaning and the impossibility of knowing the other. A cut-and-paste technique that the playwright adopts as a way of cutting up the historical evidence appears to mime the anatomists' dissection procedure in reverse, whereby pieces of historical fabric are disseminated throughout the *Venus* body. The re-cycled historical scraps in one way or another relate to the image of the Hottentot Venus, to which the playwright's "Rep and Rev" (short for "Repetition and Revision") aesthetics gives life (Parks 2013a: 8–9).

As a result, re-cycling and "Rep and Rev" provide an alternative reading of historical material that sheds light on the play's politics of representation. The play within the play, *For the Love of the Venus*—a riff on the earlier mentioned French vaudeville—expands the love agenda with a critique of power relations through parody: inspired by the colonial plot, the white man commissions "something called 'The Hottentot Venus'" (Parks 1997: 49) to be brought to him,[3] which compels his fiancé to impersonate the Hottentot Venus, eventually winning him back. An allegory on Cuvier's access to Baartman's corpse, which an excerpt from the autopsy report in the penultimate scene punctuates, the inserted plot demonstrates how the great chain theory is the white man's need for self-confirmation and justification of his superiority, with the white woman as his accomplice in exploiting the Khosian body for self-interest. By a series of displacements, from the advertisement (which announces the Hottentot Venus show), to the fiancé in disguise (that replaces and erases her), and lastly to The Venus as audience in the final scene of the inserted play, Parks unmasks the colonial parody as *méconnaissance*, thus a result of white ideological convictions. Displaced in the fiancé's body and babble which is construed as what the white man wants to hear, the Hottentot Venus is presence qua absence in the white imaginary; she is a commodity to be put to whatever ideological use the white plot needs, whereby The Venus is both a means and a witness to her commodification.

By putting the "thingified" woman—"something wild" (Parks 1997: 48)—on a par with available exotic imports, the play puts its finger on the commodification of the racialized female body as part of a larger, desire-driven colonial enterprise. The established nexus between the Hottentot Venus and chocolate as sexual and pleasure stimulants respectively is used as a critical tool to ponder the colonial mindset. Like her body, choco-

---

[3] Parks differentiates between "The Venus Hottentot" and "The Hottentot Venus" designations, of which the latter is historical thus negatively charged and only appears in the inserted play.

lates are associated with sexuality and race in their shape, design, and colour: "Capezzoli di Venere" (annotated as chocolates in the shape of the nipples of Venus in the provided Glossary) and lozenges with imprinted images of an African child and a Pharaoh link up consumerism and Africa that the Hottentot Venus personifies. For The Venus, chocolates are treats and antidepressants; according to the appended "Brief History of Chocolates", they are also "a great source of fat" (Parks 1997: 156), thus a general condition with which the play hints at the historically racist reading of the Khoisan body geography as racial anomaly, judging by detailed measurements of subcutaneous fat of her thighs and steatopygia that the autopsy report details.

The carnivalesque conjoining of top-down/bottom-up snippets of history—in principle all related to The Venus's body configuration—places her anatomy centre stage, either as object of the voyeuristic, consumerist gaze of the general audience or of the anatomical scrutiny and scalpel of the men of science. Both, however, disregard the woman behind her body parts. Hence, as the play reveals with a signature of mourning that a disjunctive "but" grants—"But No One Ever Noticed/Her Face Was Streamed with Tears" (Parks 1997: 42, 47)—all attention is awarded her genitalia and buttocks, which a few newspaper clippings and sympathetic testimonies confirm. Although sporadic, the loathing attitude to the general audience's characteristic cheer that accompanies The Venus' showing extorts a single lament by the title figure—"Oh, God: Unloved" (Parks 1997: 36)—that bemoans the verbal and sexual abuse that she suffers. A rare case of grievance that vents the protagonist's point of view in contrast to an array of external representations, the moan is one of the signs of resignation that the character, who has been schooled in coercion and submission, utters in an imaginary transfer of agency that the play allows. But agency is literally a matter of question that she asks—"Do I have a choice?" (Parks 1997: 17, 87)—which is a clever rhetorical stunt that gets and does not get an answer and remains a rhetorical question at the level of the plot.

Though choice is limited, desire and dreams are limitless, which is how Parks installs imaginary social agency into her dreamer, albeit cautioning that a dream cuts both ways: from dreams of marriage, home, and love to dreams of social ascent and abuse of servants that is fashioned on the experience of the colonial enterprise. Hence, an imaginary conversation with Napoleon over "the Negro issue" and questions of slavery reads as a farce (Parks 1997: 135). No dream of a common language that would work towards gender and class equality but a dream of dominance that would uphold the system that has kept her down underlies the reverie and serves as warning against the contagious effects of power relations.

Parks' love plot between The Venus and The Docteur is only a provisional solution. This imaginary, reparative act gestures "a to comeness" (Spivak 2003: 6), which will not question the possibility of the proposed relationship. Motivated by traces of uncanny tenderness towards Baartman that Cuvier's autopsy report divulges (Cuvier 1817: 263, 266), the love plot appears to be out of accord with the document's focus on her shape and simian looks. Placed in the very centre of the play, the report qua conference talk titled "The Dis(-re)memberment of the Venus Hottentot" is literally displaced because it is delivered during the Intermission. Thus the play's double message that calls for a break yet undercuts it with the talk reveals a politics of representation that critically stages its taxonomic, anatomical contents for The Chorus of the 8 Anatomists. Unless the audience follows The Docteur's unremitting encouragement to take a break and leave the "Anatomical Theater", it joins the Anatomists as witnesses to and accomplices in the horrendous dissection report. Its anatomical vocabulary fuels estrangement that "A Glossary of Medical Terms" provided at the end of the play enhances, which in part justifies why Parks's plays have been characterized as "dense, i.e. unreadable, impenetrable" (Diamond in Drukman et al. 1995: 63; Oddenino 2011: 121). In a series of displacements that the *Verfremdungeffekt* produces, The Venus Hottentot is dismembered and disremembered in a *pars pro toto* ruse. Concurrently, the report's fragments are disseminated throughout the play signifying, as it were, on the Venus' mutilated body. In a similar gesture, the play displaces the Cuvier study's centrepiece—the discussion of the enigmatic Hottentot apron, or the labia minora—to its end, as if trying to hide the title figure's intimate parts with which Cuvier's study is obsessed.

The masculine/feminine nexus that rests on the profit/love and intellect/sensory dichotomy is not unambiguous and neither is The Venus figure's representation. When words are lacking, or a scene demands reflection, the Rest and Spell stratagems as breaks of different length are deployed to carve space for the protagonist both on paper and on stage. Instead of an exchange of words, the play stages a quiet exchange of looks, allowing brief moments of silence to "speak" by simply listing the names of "interlocutors" on the page. As open signifiers, Rest and Spell detain action and mediate representation by the very presence in space that the figures occupy, at the same time as they prefigure one of the textually proposed causes of the Venus figure's death—the gaze.

By inserting her title character in the midst of different collectivities that the play's four choruses stand for—the Spectators, the Human Wonders, the Court, and the Anatomists—Parks seems to suggest that agenda-driven communities act in self-interest and deploy the sexual, racial, and/or ethnic other for their own political purposes. By proposing love as a means of overcoming binary thinking, opening to the other, and accepting difference, the playwright opens for an egalitarian politics in an unimaginable future.

Signifying Through Subtraction: *David's Story*

Wicomb's *David's Story* portrays the anti-apartheid freedom fighter David's attempts to recreate his family history, thus constructing for himself an identity as a "coloured" comrade within the ANC. It is the only text in our material that does not explicitly retell Baartman's story; nor does Baartman figure in the title. Nonetheless, the novel opens by positioning her as the very nucleus of (historical) narration. As the female scrivener (to whom David relates his story) states in her "preface":

> [David] was adamant about including a piece on Saartje Baartman, the Hottentot Venus placed on display in Europe. One cannot write nowadays, he said, without a little monograph on Baartman; it would be like excluding *history itself* (Wicomb 2001: 1; our emphasis).

Yet, although David seems to have written a small treatise on Baartman, and although the female scrivener seemingly agrees to include it in the book, this monograph—history itself—is nowhere to be found. It is only alluded to, in the preface and in a couple of references to David's work with it—references which, in fact, cast doubt on whether he wrote it at all. As such the piece on Baartman is inscribed negatively, as a "broken promise". Instead, the novel presents us with a mockery of David's whole project—to construct a "pure colored identity" along bloodlines—which is not only historically (and biologically) dubious (there is no such thing) but which also repeats the apartheid logic David ideally opposes.

David's Story may be read as a fictional elaboration of Wicomb's earlier quoted essay "Shame and Identity" (Wicomb 1998). Here she proclaims Baartman as her icon because "of the nasty, unspoken question of concupiscence that haunts coloured identity, the issue of nation-building implicit in the matter of her return, her contested ethnicity (Black, Khoi or 'coloured') and the vexed question of representation" (Wicomb 1998: 93), yet embarks on a critique of "coloured" identity politics without mentioning Baartman again. In both instances, the naming and withdrawal of Baartman can be said to constitute a "politics of subtraction" that makes visible a negativity through which Baartman is refigured apart from the hegemonic rhetoric of rights and nation-building in which she is steeped. The subtraction also questions how the female body can be described within systems of representation, whereby the body is already marked and defined in specific gendered and racialized terms. Rather than re-present Baartman, this gesture serves to cast her in a more radical critique of representation as such.

Like Wicomb's essay, *David's Story* constitutes a critique of the role and logics of identity politics in post-apartheid South Africa. The efforts to create a multicultural nation state along neo-liberal lines demands that a long history of racial and sexual exploitation be "smoothed out", as it were, yet, at the same time, that race, sexual difference, and "women's rights" be recognized and accounted for, as a founding gesture of the very multiplicity of the new state. Baartman's burial played a pivotal role in these efforts; at her funeral former president Thabo Mbeki even claimed that her story is "the story of the African people" (Mbeki 2002). Yet, as Wicomb points out, as long as the economic, social and epistemological structures of apartheid are left intact, to cover Baartman's body with native soil does not obliterate, nor solve, the remainders of her fate.

Subversively mimicking the burial, Wicomb's initial naming and subsequent withdrawal of Baartman as an icon and/or nucleus of narration inscribes her in the discourses of nation-building yet withdraws her from under them at the same time, letting her play along in covert ways. Indeed, words and images that are associated with her are scattered around in the novel, attached to different female characters (historical and present, the scrivener included) and serving different functions. The constantly recurring *steatopygia* (protruding buttocks) is for instance used to carry water and hide secret documents, as well as to signify obesity, sexual desirability, visibility and invisibility; David's wife bears different versions of her first name (Saartjie, Sarah, Sara, Sally). Ironically the novel also traces David's lineage back to George Cuvier, from whom David purportedly has inherited the green eyes that not only mark him as "hybrid", but also aligns his words with the male colonial gaze. Thus Baartman's story is figured as a series of displacements that destabilize David's own narrative. Most importantly, the novel's very "un-telling" of Baartman's story is duplicated in its struggle to give form to Dulcie, David's female "coloured" comrade (and possibly love object) in the freedom struggle. Having been tortured, or being tortured, though it is not known for what reasons or by whom—possibly even by David himself—Dulcie only appears as glimpses of a mutilated body, hints of betrayal and unfulfilled love. David's most elaborate attempt to tell her story, secured on a piece of paper that the scrivener claims to have gotten from him, conveys only abstract geometrical forms, resembling Cuvier's autopsy report:

> There are the dismembered shapes of a body: an asexual torso, like a dressmaker's dummy; arms bent the wrong way at the elbows; legs; swollen feet; hands like claws./There is a head, an upside-down smiling head, which admittedly does not resemble her, except for the outline of bushy hair./(…) it is Dulcie who lies mutilated on the page (Wicomb 2001: 205).

By aligning Baartman with Dulcie through displacement, the novel inscribes Dulcie in a longer history of sexual and racial injustice, dramatizing how the figure/figuration of woman continues to haunt South African politics. This re-figuring of Baartman points to the continuity between the colonial and the postcolonial (old and new South Africa), rather than to a break. But the continuity is not left intact; it is broken up. As with Baartman, all that remains of Dulcie—in the text, the written word—is a series of body parts, scattered around. In the last instance this dissemination also makes up the text as such, tying back to Cuvier's narrative strategies once more. As the scrivener repeatedly notes, her words similarly "slither [...] hither and dither" on the page (Wicomb 2001: 34–35).

David's Story is most commonly read as a typically postmodern novel, questioning the notion of one, knowable truth. Rather, truth is multiple and diverse and cannot be pinned down anywhere (Driver 2001: 216; Samuelson 2007; Marais 2005; Harrow 2006). Indeed, the very first sentence in the novel: "This is, and is not, David's story" (Wicomb 2001: 1) serves to postulate an ambiguity or uncertainty that will come to structure the text as a whole, where several voices interact and intersect: What is "fact"? What is "fiction"? Who speaks? When and why? Is it, or is it not, David's story? On the level of the plot, David is not only recording (or making up?) a family past; he is also caught up in a series of present betrayals forming an impenetrable mystery. Yet, as Kenneth Harrow has pointed out, although the novel constantly demands that the reader asks questions as to what is actually happening, it does not provide any answers (Harrow 2006: 65). Instead, "truth" is displayed on the surface of the text—and quite literally so—through the recurrent Caaps dialect "misspelling" of the very word: TRURT, TRURT, TRURT, TRURT (Wicomb 2001: 136), forming a palindrome which leads us in circles, back and forth in the text, back and forth on the page.

At the root of this dispersion, however, is a suppressed truth—the truth of the female body—that cannot be named, cannot be signified but even so, or precisely therefore, structures the whole field of differences. Following the initial subtraction, we can give it a name: Sara Baartman. She is drawn away from under the story, yet at the same time this is precisely how she figures in it. Thus *David's Story* is also Baartman's story; or more precisely, recalling the first sentence of the novel: "This is, and is not, David's story", it both "is" and "is not" Baartman's story. This "is" and "is not" is an effect of a formal subtraction. This subtraction is moreover a primary gesture, making it clear that *David's Story* cannot simply be read as a postmodern multiplication of diverse (and absent) truths.

But the subtraction also exists prior to its naming it "is" and "is not" Sara Baartman, unknown to both David and the scrivener. This primary subtraction is, however, represented in the novel, but only negatively, forming, as it were, a missing, or absent, *mise en abyme*.

When David tells the scrivener about his trip to Scotland, a trip somehow connected to his entanglement in treachery and betrayal, he also conveys that he has visited Glasgow museum where he saw the portrait of John Glasford and family, painted by Archibald McLauchlan in 1767. The painting intrigues him and propels him into an almost uncanny moment, drawing his eyes upwards where he clearly sees a black servant amongst the family, staring directly back at him. At a closer look, the figure is gone. It is not in the picture; everybody there is white. Only upon reading the inscription on the plaque does David learn that the painting originally "included a black slave on the left hand, which has since been painted over" (Wicomb 2001: 193). The moment is completely bewildering to David; he swears he didn't read the description beforehand: "There was nothing to make him think of a black man, not in the People's Palace, where he did not expect to find the effacement of slavery to be betrayed in representation, as an actual absence" (Wicomb 2001: 193). The scrivener, who doesn't know the painting and thinks it sounds awful, dismisses David's story as nonsense.

Nonetheless, the term "actual absence" reads as a comment on the very theme of the novel. It encapsulates the return of the repressed, the whole colonial history David strives to come to terms with and thus unwittingly repeats. But he misconstrues the image. Or rather, he sees only one specific aspect of it. And this misconstruction is gendered. The black man is namely not the only face that has been painted over; the story of the actual painting tells us that it also hides a female face. This face David does not see—nor is it mentioned on the plaque, nor in the novel. Unlike the missing black figure, she is not an "actual absence" but an "'absent' absence". This "invisible" subtraction of a nameless woman forms an absent *mise en abyme*, only negatively present through the reference to the painting, mirroring the "visible" subtraction of Baartman, displaced to the "absence" of Dulcie, displaced to the "absence" of all the stories that cannot be told, yet exist as disconnected body parts, disconnected words, disseminated on the surface of the text. To the extent that the painted over faces in McLauchlan's painting also recall the barely visible silhouette of Jeanne Duval, Baudelaire's Black Venus, in Gustave Courbet's *L'Atelier du peintre* (1855)—painted over at Baudelaire's own request—all these untellable yet (un-)erasable stories uncannily point back to the figure of the Hottentot Venus.

Thus the formal gestures of subtraction enacted in this novel not only redeploys the image of Baartman in a critique of the sexism inherent in the South African fight for freedom (without appropriating Baartman's story for itself), it also raises the question of how the female body *can be* described within a system of representation that has already marked and defined it in very specific terms. In *David's Story* this body only speaks through its absence, through what is left of it after its representation has already taken place—as that which cannot be decided, named or represented, but nonetheless functions as the basis for representation as such.

Conclusion, No Closure…

The figure of the Hottentot Venus, which this chapter has singled out as embodiment of the politics of representation by way of aesthetic practices, testifies to a larger cultural and gender/sexual-political agenda that still haunts the multicultural society of today, almost two hundred years after Baartman's death and three decades after the initial historical and critical scholarship brought the ill-fated figure to the attention of the general public (Gould 1985; Gilman 1985). Its many returns in different cultural environments—France, the USA, and South Africa—that in different ways struggle with a politics of inclusion—be it ethnic, cultural, "racial", gender/sexual, class, or other—attest to a need for focusing on the culturally repressed or oppressed that the recent, turbulent events in the three countries have brought to the fore. While unable to undo history or allow bygones to be bygones, the aesthetic projects that we have plumbed do not skirt politics but still avoid the pitfalls of representation in crude political terms to the benefit of re-presentation that will keep the memory of the horrific history alive. It is in the politics of re-presentation, in a never-ending need for a renewal that a "representing otherwise" is born.

The many returns that the figure of the Hottentot Venus has "suffered" testify to her symbolic status at the same time that they signal a danger of re-objectification or re-commodification that potentially lie at the heart of "the Baartman industry". Unless a politically-inspired art fronts a politics of *aesthetics* by seeking alternative modes of re-presentation, it risks repeating what it tries to challenge or critique. The three texts that this chapter examines debunk in different ways traditional ways of seeing/re-presentation by way of metonymic displacement (dismemberment and absence) and/or defamiliarization (making the familiar unfamiliar), drawing on a common cultural memory yet searching for alternative ways to signify the familiar—with a difference. Paradoxically, this entails that our analysis and conclusions concerning the double bind of revision/repetition cannot avoid falling prey to the very mechanisms to which we draw critical attention. For, by returning to the figure of the Hottentot Venus, our project, too, inevitably participates in the said Baartman industry from a critical-aesthetic perspective as a (white) cultural "intruder", which should relativize and put into perspective our assertions. As a consequence, the very formulation of this conclusion ultimately becomes problematic. The "representing otherwise" implies that neither art nor critical discourse, including this one, can ever come to an end because they always rest on an ongoing re-negotiation of the past/present and the political/aesthetic dichotomies.

References

Baderoon, G. (2011). Baartman and the private: How can we look at a figure that has been looked at too much? In N. Gordon-Chipembere (Ed.), *Representation and black womanhood: The legacy of Sarah Baartman* (pp. 65–83). Basingstoke: Palgrave Macmillan.

Badiou, A. (2007). Destruction, negation, subtraction. On Pier Paolo Pasolini. Accessed January 30, 2014, from http://www.lacan.com/badpas.htm

Basaran, A. (2010). Representation and the Dominant Gaze. Accessed September 10, 2013, from http://www.jgcinema.com/single.php?sl=dominant-gaze-colonialism-representation

Cuvier, G. (1817). Extrait d'observations faites sur le cadavre d'une femme connue à Paris et à Londres sous le nom de Vénus Hottentote. *Mémoires d'Histoire naturelle* 3. Paris: G Doufour, 259–274.

Driver, D. (2001). Afterword. Wicomb Z *David's Story*. New York: The Feminist Press.
Drukman, S., Diamond, L., & Parks, S.-L. (1995). Doo-a-Diddly-Dit-Dit: An interview. *The Drama Review, 39*(3), 56–75.
Gilman, S. (1985). Black bodies, white bodies: Toward an iconography of female sexuality in late nineteenth-century art, medicine, and literature. *Critical Inquiry, 12*(1), 204–242.
Glissant, É. (2000). *Poetics of relation*. Ann Arbor: University of Michigan Press.
Gould, S. J. (1985). *The Flamingo's smile. Reflections in natural history*. New York: Norton.
Gquola, P. D. (2010). (Not)representing Sara Baartman. In *What is slavery to me? Postcolonial memory and the post-apartheid imagination*. Johannesburg: Wits University Press.
Harrow, K. (2006). The marks left on the surface in Zoë Wicomb's *David's Story*. In F. N. Emenyonu (Ed.), *New directions in African literature*. Oxford: James Curry Africa World Press.
Kechiche, A. (2010). *Vénus noire. Un film d'Abdellatif Kechiche*. Paris: MK2.
Larson, J. (2012). *Understanding Suzan-Lori Parks*. Columbia: University of South Carolina Press.
Magubane, Z. (2001). Which bodies matter? Feminism, poststructuralism, race and the curious theoretical Odyssey of the "Hottentot Venus". *Gender and Society, 15*(6), 816–834.
Marais, M. (2005). Bastards and Bodies in Zöe Wicomb's *David's Story*. *Journal of Commonwealth Literature, 40*(3), 21–36.
Mbeki, T. (2002). Speech at the funeral of Sarah Bartmann, 9 August 2002. Accessed August 20, 2014, from http://www.dfa.gov.za/docs/speeches/2002/mbek0809.htm
Oddenino, I. (2011). "I Wanna Love Something Wild": A reading of Suzan-Lori Parks's *Venus*. In N. Gordon-Chipembere (Ed.), *Representation and black womanhood: The legacy of Sarah Baartman* (pp. 121–135). New York: Palgrave Macmillan.
Parks, S.-L. (1990/1997). *Venus*. New York: Theatre Communications Group.
Parks, S.-L. (1995/2013a). Elements of style. *The American play and other works* (pp. 6–18). New York: Theatre Communications Group.
Parks, S.-L. (1995/2013b). Possession. *The American play and other works* (pp. 3–5). New York: Theatre Communications Group.
Qureshi, S. (2004). Displaying Sara Baartman, the "Hottentot Venus". *History of Science, 42*(2), 233–257.

Samuelson, M. (2007). *Remembering the nation, dismembering women?* Scottsville: University of KwaZulu-Natal Press.

Spivak, G. C. (1988). Can the Subaltern speak? In C. Nelson & R. Grossberg (Eds.), *Marxism and the interpretation of culture* (pp. 271–313). Chicago: University of Illinois Press.

Spivak, G. C. (2003). *Death of a discipline.* New York: Columbia University Press.

Théaulon, Dartois and Brasier. (1814). *La Vénus Hottentote ou Haine aux Françaises.* Accessed May 9, 2013, from http://gallica.bnf.fr/ark:/12148/bpt6k57721188

Wicomb, Z. (1998). Shame and identity: The case of the coloured in South Africa. In D. Attridge & R. Jolly (Eds.), *Writing South Africa.* Cambridge: Cambridge University Press.

Wicomb, Z. (2001). *David's Story.* New York: Feminist Press.

Widemann, D. (2010). Cinéma. Vénus noire, d'Abdellatif Kechiche. Accessed September 10, 2013, from http://www.humanite.fr/26_10_2010-cin%C3%A9ma-v%C3%A9nus-noire-dabdellatif-kechiche-456487

Young, J. (1997). The re-objectification and re-commodification of Saartjie Baartman in Suzan-Lori Parks's *Venus. African American Review, 31*(4), 699–708.

Index

A

abortion, 265–6, 269–70, 277
Ackerman, B., 18
aesthetics, 12, 281, 283–5, 290–2, 300–1
affect, 186–8, 194, 199, 203–4, 263, 289
Arab Spring, 138, 142, 146–8, 155
Arendt, H., 243
Asen, R., 270, 274, 276
Athanasiou, A., 241
authoritarian regime, 147, 152

B

Badiou, A., 285
Balibar, E., 240
Banaji, S., 187, 188, 197
Barro, R.J., 25

Basaran, A., 286
Bengtsson, M., 46
Bennett, T.W., 123
Ben Salem, L., 147
Bernstein, B., 194
bio-politics, 20, 23, 25
Bingham, A., 168, 174
Blom, I., 17, 22, 34–5
Boehm, D., 240
Brown, W., 63, 75, 77–8, 81
Buckingham, D., 187
Butler, J., 3, 78, 237, 241

C

Centre for Applied Legal Studies (CALS), 122–3
Chakrabarty, D., 189
Chatterjee, P., 189, 191

children, 23–5, 29, 33, 40, 49, 116, 118, 122, 125, 130, 141, 144, 147, 169–76, 179, 196, 217–20, 245–56, 272, *see also* other people's children
Chimienti, M., 240
citizenship, 2–4, 6, 8, 10–11, 18, 30, 33, 41, 64, 73, 97, 116, 137–43, 145–7, 151, 154–5, 162, 164, 166, 173, 175, 180, 185–90, 203–4, 239–40, 244, 249, 253–7, 261–3, 277, 282
   act of, 253–6
   cultural, 4, 11, 263, 277
   economic, 41–2, 99, 263
   familial, 189–90
   gendered, 1–2, 4, 8, 11, 33, 37, 39, 115, 138–9, 141–2, 154–5, 180, 185, 249, 262, 277
   political, 10, 40, 42–3, 54, 261–2
citizen-subject, 9, 61, 63–4
civic engagement, 185–8, 197, 202–3
civil society, 31, 89, 95–7, 113, 122–30, 146–55, 186–90, 212, 222, 225–7
class, 3, 6, 9, 18, 21–3, 29–30, 33, 43–4, 52, 65, 88, 92, 96, 143, 169, 257, 270, 276, 282, 294, 300
   middle-class 11, 33, 38–44, 52, 75, 185–204, 225, 253, 255
   working-class 18, 20, 40–2, 52, 70, 87, 170, 198, 253
Code of Personal Status (CPS), 138, 142–6, 150, 153–4
Collins, K., 23

colonialism, 25, 214–15
colonial state, 22, 143
communication facilitation, 94, 98–106
community, 6, 18, 92, 124–6, 137, 139, 173, 188–9, 192, 223, 239, 244, 252, 256–7, 285
Connell, R., 38
constitution, 10, 39, 53, 97, 111, 121–4, 126, 137–8, 142, 146–55, 240–1
content analysis, 165, 177–8
counterpublics, 262, 266–77
Crenshaw, K., 95–6
culture, 6–7, 11–12, 25, 29, 34, 78–9, 112, 115, 122, 175, 197, 200, 221, 263–4, 272–3, 275, 291

D

Dahlerup, D., 5
Davidoff, L., 38
de facto legitimacy argument, 98–101
Deleuze, G., 213
democracy, 2, 4, 8–9, 22–3, 30–4, 43, 48, 76, 87, 91, 102–6, 117, 121, 246, 282
   deliberative, 188
   feminist, 89
   liberal, 62–6, 77, 189
   representative, 4, 11, 64–6
   social, 96–100
democratization, 41, 51, 56, 91, 95–7, 100–2, 106, 138–9
depoliticization processes, 77–9
Derrida, J., 31, 291

Development, Relief and Education for Alien Minors Act (DREAM Act), 240
Dighe, A., 192
discourse, 2–3, 7, 10, 12, 20, 63–4, 67–70, 74–9, 114, 129, 137–54, 162, 167–70, 185–203, 218, 221, 239, 244, 252, 257, 267–70, 282, 284–5, 297, 301
Doi Moi policy, 214, 221, 225
domestic politics, 171–3
Domestic Relations Bill, 125–6, 128
domestic violence laws, 116, 125–30
Doordarshan, 191, 193
Du Bois, W.E.B., 30

E

education, 8, 9, 20, 23–9, 37, 40–2, 44–7, 51, 54–6, 61, 63, 74, 96, 147–8, 174, 176, 179, 213, 214, 217, 252, 270
election, 18, 29, 32, 65, 69, 118, 121, 123, 148, 161, 164–80, 188
Ellermann, A., 240, 257
emergent collectives, 270–6
equality, 2, 9, 21, 30, 61–8, 78, 91, 102–6, 138–51, 216, 225–6, 294, *see also* gender equality
essentialism, 91–2, 97, 99, 106
ethnographic fieldwork, 186
Evans, D., 263
exclusion, 2–4, 11–12, 67, 77, 138–9, 164, 180, 189, 253, 263, 266, 270, 274, 277, 283, 289

F

family, 11, 38, 40–56, 144–50, 163, 168–70, 174, 185–204, 210–13, 217–26, 248, 295, 298, 299
as heterosexual regime, 209, 211, 216–17, 221
patriarchal, 189, 193, 202–3
family law, 10, 111–32, 141–6, 223
femininity, 7, 38–9, 45, 47, 50–2, 191, 193, 220, 283
difference, 9, 39–40, 47–9, 54, 56–7
equal rights, 9, 53–4
feminism, 3, 4, 7, 35, 49, 61, 65, 67, 70–2, 89–90, 121, 213–14, 219, 227
equal rights, 54, 78, 81
intersectional, 71, 105
standpoint, 64, 66, 68
state, 9, 87, 89–91, 95–104
feminist claims/demands, 75, 113–17, 121, 131
movement, 9, 61–2, 64, 141, 146
politics, 9, 62, 68, 73
scholarship, 2, 139, 141, 168, 187, 190
Feministisk Initiativ (Fi), 9, 63, 69, 71, 73–4, 77
party platform, 73–4
Ferree, M.M., 114
film, 20, 192, 273, 285–9
fitness to vote, 8, 18–19, 26
framing, 10–14, 119–20, 126–8, 131, 248, 250, 256, 288
Fraser, N., 266–7, 270, 274, 276
French feminists, 7
Frykman, J., 46

G

gender, 20–2, 38, 41, 47, 52, 62, 65, 70–4, 88, 92, 95–6, 121, 124, 130, 137–42, 146, 155, 185, 186, 191–3, 201–4, 217–18, 250, 252, 257, 263, 270, 294, 300
  equality, 4, 63, 74–9, 89, 95–6, 113, 116, 119, 121–2, 128, 140, 148–55, 219–20, 294
  gaps, 102
  identity, 9, 37–44, 47, 49–50, 52, 54–5, 57, 73
  inequality, 102, 111, 142
gender-neutral citizen, 140, 146, 155
Glissant, É., 285, 288–9
Global Media Monitoring Project, 163
Gramsci, A., 21–3, 212
Gross National Income (GNI), 27
Guattari, F., 213

H

Hall, C., 38
Hall, S., 7
hegemonic solidarity, 11, 209, 211
hegemony, 2, 23, 186, 203, 283
  discursive, 115, 129
Hermes, J., 198, 262
Hernes, H., 50, 88–9, 91, 95–7, 100
Hindess, B., 3
homosexuality, 221, 223–4, 227
Hottentot Venus, 12, 281–4, 86–93, 300–1
Howell, J., 188, 216
Human Development Index (HDI), 8, 25–8

human rights, 23, 67, 72–4, 77–8, 118, 150, 152, 154, 223, 243

I

identity, 2–3, 9, 42, 50, 53, 56, 66, 68–9, 72, 74, 77–9, 81–2, 92, 115, 193, 197, 249, 253, 262, 264, 295–6, *see also* gender identity
identity politics, 12, 66, 68, 70–5, 77–9, 296
imaginative activism, 19, 26, 33
imagined community, 189
imperialism, 214
imperialistic processes, 3
inclusion, 2–4, 9, 12, 61–2, 68–70, 77–80, 138–9, 164, 218, 252, 254, 263, 277, 283, 289, 300
intersectionality, 91, 95, 101–2, 106
irregular migrants, 11, 237–43, 245, 247–57
Isin, E.F., 253
Islamic law, 116

J

Jasmine Revolution, 138, 147
journalism, 261

K

Kant, I., 18–19, 21, 34
Kechiche, A., 284–7
  Vénus noire, 283, 285–9
Kessler-Harris, A., 41
Kimmel, M., 38

Kiros, J., 71
Krishnan, P., 192

L

Labidi-Maïza, M., 152–3
Lacan, J., 35
Landes, J.B., 164, 167
language, 2, 7–9, 18, 20, 23–4, 31, 153, 162, 252, 255, 263, 288–9, 294
law reform, 111–17, 120–21, 124, 126–32
Lee, J.-W., 25
LGBT rights, 223
liberalism, 9, 63, 66, 72, 80–1, 140
Lister, R., 140–1, 146, 164, 169
literature, 19, 20, 24, 273

M

magazines, 197–8, 263–4, 266, 271, 273, *see also* men's magazines
Mansbridge, J., 88
Marks, M., 149
Marshall, T.H., 4, 41, 139, 158
masculinity, 9, 38–9, 45, 47, 50, 266
  fearful 48–9
  hegemonic, 44, 47, 49–50
  superiority of, 45–48, 52, 54, 56–7
Mbeki, T., 296
McGuigan, J., 263
media, 6–7, 10–11, 63, 70, 72, 75, 151, 161–4, 171, 175, 179, 185–7, 191, 193, 213–14, 217–18, 222, 238–43, 245–52, 254, 256–7, 261–4, 267–8, 276–8

melodrama, 186, 197
men's magazines, 12, 161–77
migration, 241, 246, 255
Miller, T., 262–3, 275
Moberg, E., 76
Moghadam, V., 142
Monteiro, A., 198
Moral Movement, 271–3
motherhood, 174–5, 218–20, 249
Mouffe, C., 63, 79, 81

N

National Constituent Assembly (NCA), 148, 151–2
National Health Service (NHS), 177–8
National Plan of Action for Integrating Women in Development (PANIFD), 118–19
National Resistance Movement (NRM), 124–7
National Women's Congress, 215
nation-state, 80, 139, 143–4, 236, 238, 241–2, 252, 256–7, 263
Niyamraja, 33
New Public Management (NPM), 62, 75
Non-governmental Organizations (NGOs), 23, 211–12, 216, 223–6
non-instrumental argument, 95, 98, 100–2, 194
Norwegian Housewives Association, 50, 56

Norwegian Women's Rights Association, 44
Nyers, P., 240

O
Osgerby, B., 266
other people's children, 23–4, 30

P
Parks, S.-L., 283–5, 290–5
  Venus, 283, 290–5
Pateman, C., 190, 200
pedagogy, 185, 197
  invisible, 11, 197
Pitkin, H., 5
Phillips, A., 5
pluralism, 87, 91, 102, 123
political ties argument, 92
political mobilization, 238–9, 249, 252, 254–5
politicians, 5–6, 10, 65, 70, 89, 119, 162, 164, 169–70, 172, 174, 176, 178–9, 238, 250, 275
postcolonial state, 18, 138, 142, 154
post-liberalization period, 186
poststructuralist critique, 69, 75
post-war period, 172, 174, 176, 214
Probyn, E., 193
private sphere, 46, 115, 121, 171, 175, 178–80, 190
prohibitionary law, 272
proxy argument, 93
public sphere, 12, 40, 48–9, 140–1, 163–4, 169, 172–3, 178, 180, 238, 254, 256–7, 261–4, 266, 269, 276, 277

Q
queer, 21, 69–71
quotas, 6, 87–8, 91, 93–5, 101–2, 104, 106, 189

R
race, 6, 23, 41, 61, 65, 70, 74, 88, 257, 263, 270, 276, 281, 283–5, 293, 296
racism, 74, 77
Radway, J., 215
Rajan, S., 191
religion, 65, 115–16, 120, 122, 131, 191, 200, 263
representation, 2–3, 8–10, 40, 61–6, 68–72, 75, 77–8, 88, 92–3, 101, 105, 112, 138, 147, 154, 161–5, 179–80, 185, 191–3, 201, 203–4, 238–9, 241, 243–5, 240–50, 253–7, 261–2, 267, 277–8, 283–7, 289–91, 293, 295–6, 299, 300
  as standing in/acting for, 5–6
  as re-presentation, 2–3, 5–7, 300–1
  descriptive, 5–6, 9, 87–95, 97–102, 104–6, 117
  gendered, 7, 9, 155, 277
  politics of, 1, 63, 209, 211, 226, 281, 291, 294, 300
  substantive, 5–6, 89, 92–5, 100, 111–12, 114, 119, 131
  symbolic, 5

rights, 2, 4, 9–10, 37–44, 48–56, 62–4, 67–8, 70, 72–3, 75, 78–81, 111–12, 115–16, 120–3, 125, 126, 130–1, 137–40, 142, 145–6, 148–55, 167, 192, 217, 222–5, 237, 240, 242–4, 247, 250, 255, 262, 269, 281, 296, *see also* human rights and LGBT-rights
Roseneil, S., 4, 8

S

same-sex marriage, 11, 211, 221–4
Sarkar, S., 189
Scott, J., 67, 75
secure gender identity, 39–40, 43, 47, 49, 52, 54–5
Seekh, 194–6
Sen, A., 67, 75
sexism, 71, 300
sexuality, 61, 70, 73–4, 96, 214, 224, 262, 270, 283, 293
Siltanen, J., 163
social evils, 219–21
Solomos, J., 240
South African Law Commission (SALC), 122–4, 128, 131
Spivak, G.C., 3, 7–8, 20, 23–4, 79, 189, 190, 237, 255, 282–3, 286, 291, 294
Stanworth, M., 163
stereotypes, 94–5, 100, 106, 240, 286
subject, the, 3, 7–9, 43, 62, 64–8, 75, 78–80, 82, 163–4, 191, 193, 197, 199, 203, 238–9, 241–2, 244, 249–50, 253,

255–7, 282, 288, 290, *see also* citizen-subject
subaltern, 7, 9, 20–3, 31–4, 202, 248, 255, 267
suffrage, 2, 9, 18–19, 39–40, 43–4, 46, 51–6, 140
symbolic annihilation, 163

T

tabloid news, 177
target groups argument, 93
television drama, 281
transition, 121, 143, 155, 225
Tuchman, G., 163

U

Uberoi, P., 190–1

V

Vietnam Women's Union (VWU), 11, 209, 215, 220, 224, 237
vote, the, 40, 44, 47–8, 51, 55, 103, 165–6, 170, 172
vote, to, 8, 17–18, 22, 31, 52, 55, 65, 151, 162, 164–9, 174, 176, *see also* fitness to vote right to, 56, 80, 146, 169, 173, 262–3
voters, 10, 31, 51–2, 65, 80, 93, 105, 161–2, 164–80

W

Walby, S., 139–40
Warner, M., 276

Wicomb, Z., 282–5, 295–6, 299
  David's Story, 283, 295–300
Wollstonecraft, M., 19

Y
Yassine, N., 119
Young, I.M., 212
Yuval-Davis, N., 139, 190